THE
INCA
SMILED

Richard Poole is Field Director of the
Andean Programme for International
Voluntary Services Inc., a Washington DC aid
agency, and lives in Quito, Ecuador. He has worked
in the field of development aid for twenty-five years,
serving in East and West Africa and the Caribbean
as well as Latin America. This is his first book.

Campesino woman spinning sheep's wool – Chimborazo Province
(Photo: R.G. Torske)

THE
INCA
SMILED

The Growing
Pains of
an Aid Worker
in Ecuador

RICHARD POOLE

ONEWORLD

OXFORD

The Inca Smiled

Oneworld Publications
(Sales and Editorial)
185 Banbury Road
Oxford OX2 7AR
England

Oneworld Publications
(U.S. Sales Office)
County Route 9, P.O. Box 357
Chatham, N.Y. 12037
USA

ISBN 1-85168-078-0

Printed and bound by
Werner Söderström Osakeyhtiö, Finland

Hernando Pizarro warmed to his subject. He told Atahualpa that the Governor loved him dearly. If he had any enemy he should tell the Governor and he would send to conquer that person. Atahualpa said that four days' march away there were some very savage Indians with whom he could do nothing: the Christians should go there to help his men. Then Pizarro told him that the Governor would send ten horsemen, which was enough for the entire land. His Indians would be needed only to search for those who hid. Atahualpa smiled, as someone who did not think much of us.

—John Hemming, *The Conquest of the Incas*

Dedication

With great love and admiration for American Indians.

May their trials, Lord, soon be over.

Contents

Acknowledgements

A number of people have been important to the Latin American dream and I would like to express my deep appreciation and affection for them here: Tim and Gloria Baker, Ruth Pedder, Bob Yeates, Ric Luxton, David and Pat Small, Jerry Hildebrand, Alicia Ritchie; the families of Don Serafín Pulgar, Don Jaime Velasco Cellerí and Don Gualberto Congo Méndez; Juan García, Miguel Puwainchir, Rosa Cujilema, Roberto Torske, Joel Mullen, Mr G.H. Calvert who arrived just in time; my parents, grandfather, and brother Steve who gave me encouragement, and my wife, Catherine, who has the patience of a saint. And a special word of thanks to Voluntary Service Overseas and International Voluntary Services Inc. of Washington DC, both fine organizations.

PART
I

THE
PROMISED
LAND

CHAPTER ONE

ARRIVAL

THE BOAC FLIGHT – my first ever – terminated in Lima, Peru and I spent the night in the new airport lounge, twisting and turning in a plastic seat as I tried vainly to get some sleep. And then, just about daybreak, we took off and headed north for Quito, tracking the snowcaps all the way. The day's platinum light exposed awesome Andean wastes as we flew, and sharpened the profiles of peaks stretching out ragged and white against an empty, frozen sky.

There are occasions in life when things go so wrong that one could be forgiven for thinking that the whole of creation is conspiring to cause havoc; and now and again there are times that provide the balance – when, for no reason at all, fate seems to have singled us out for favourable attention and showers gifts upon us. For me, this was one of the latter moments. I knew that by any measure I had no right to be where I was. I had contributed nothing to life that I was aware of, and yet here I was being transported through this fairy-tale landscape on the other side of the world in some indescribably miraculous machine whose method of operation I could only guess at, waited on hand and foot by highly trained staff whose one aim in life seemed to be to make me more comfortable by the minute.

It was August 1968, and I was on my way to Ecuador where I was to spend two years as a volunteer. In truth, I didn't have much idea of what I was letting myself in for. My 'posting letter' had informed me that I was to be a 'public relations expert in a School of Radiophony in Riobamba' and I had accepted the offer like a shot because of my desperation to get to South America, although I can see now, on reflection, the recklessness of it all.

I had studied Spanish literature at university and knew nothing about 'public relations'; a 'school of radiophony' was not a term I was familiar with, nor could I find anyone who knew what it meant; and Riobamba, I learned from a lady who had spent thirteen years in Ecuador trying to avoid it, was 'the worst place on earth'. To make matters worse, on my arrival in Lima I had only been able to understand a few words of what the immigration official had been trying to tell me, with the result that the poor fellow had been forced to break into his already broken English, which turned out to be a class above my university Spanish. Still, I can't say that all this bothered me much – in fact, it probably added to the challenge.

I stepped down from the yellow Braniff jet onto the tarmac of Quito airport and had my first taste of altitude. At 9,000 feet you feel strange – the air is thin and oxygen scarce. Added to this was the glare. Everything seemed to sparkle and dazzle – the aircraft, the tarmac, the buildings, the clouds – making me shield my eyes.

'Richard Poole?' A Scottish voice cut through the haze; the British Consul had come to collect me. He whisked me through Immigration and Customs with the wave of a diplomatic pass, then ushered me into the rear seat of the Embassy Land Rover, introducing me to the uniformed chauffeur who was polishing an already immaculate windscreen.

As we drove into town the Consul pointed out interesting sights along the way, although not a great deal actually registered with me. I remember a diminutive woman, a member of a road-gang, hacking away at some rocks with an enormous pick-axe, and the national football stadium, an impressive monument named with unintentional irony after the last ruling Inca, Atahualpa, whose sorry fate was only a sign of things to come for his fallen people, and incidentally for a talented but unassuming national football team.

Somehow the Consul and I had got round to talking about the 1966 World Cup. Whether it came about through passing the stadium or because the Consul felt duty-bound to warn me early on in our relationship that he was a Glasgow Celtic supporter I can't say, but I soon learned that England were more than a bit lucky to win it and that what they really lacked was a Jim Baxter in midfield. I didn't take issue. It was, I reckoned, rather early in my expatriate career to be making enemies.

We reached the Embassy after half an hour's drive through suburbs of low, white houses flanked on either side by dark green mountains. The two-storey building was finely situated on a hill overlooking Quito. Such was the fatigue sweeping over me that I can remember precious little about that first evening spent with the Consul and his family. I awoke the following morning feeling better, but was disturbed to learn at breakfast that I had somehow managed to 'drop off' in the middle of the conversation. Not that anyone minded very much except that I had done so during a particularly riveting account of Celtic's 1967 European Cup triumph over Inter-Milan.

Later that day, about noon, Mr Martinez, the secretary from the School of Radiophony, came to collect me. As I was leaving, the Consul thrust a bottle of whisky into my hands.

'To break the ice in Riobamba,' he said warmly. 'And don't forget to tell the Riobambeños that not all midfield players in Britain are like Nobby Stiles,' he called after me as I walked towards the taxi. 'We have at least one genius north of the border!'

I waved back. 'That's the first thing I'll tell them,' I said, while making a mental note to do nothing of the kind, and then turned my attention to the future.

A couple of hours later, Mr Martinez and I were on the Panamericana bus and heading south through the cordillera to Riobamba. The Panamericana road stretches from Caracas to central Chile and across to Buenos Aires, and if you see it on the map you might imagine it to be a magnificent highway sweeping down through the length and breadth of the continent. In reality –

at least in those days – it was often little more than a narrow track hewn roughly from the mountainside and winding round and round in seemingly endless circles. The stretch ahead of us, however, happened to be one of the few to benefit from tarmac and the journey promised to be relatively smooth.

'Panamericana' was also the name of the main bus company on this route. The bus service, strangely enough, was one of the few things that functioned efficiently in Ecuador. Unlike the trains, the buses left on time, were fairly clean and modern, had reclining seats, and usually got you to your destination quite quickly. Some of them, on the longer routes, even had stewardesses in uniform who served you coffee and handed you a pillow the moment you sat down. Our bus wasn't one of these but it was comfortable enough and I was able to sit back, pleased when the conversation had run its course and I could lend my attention to what was going on around me.

Ecuador is small, about the size of Britain, but has an astonishing range of climate and topography. The Andes are its backbone, running from north to south down the middle, and on either side the land slopes away abruptly – to the Pacific coast in the west and to the Amazon rain forest in the east. Despite being situated on the Equator – a circumstance to which the country owes its name – Quito and the other towns of the Sierra, all of which are located in high basins, have a cool and attractive climate. In fact, the only thing I knew about Ecuador in advance of receiving my posting letter came from a single line in a school geography book stating that 'Quito has a climate of eternal spring', which is more or less true. There is also an astonishing diversity of indigenous culture which, owing to the ruggedness of the terrain, the lack of infrastructure and the stagnant economy has changed little until very recent times.

It was a spellbinding journey and one I was to make countless times thereafter, my appreciation growing all the while. From Quito to Riobamba: from the perfect cone of Cotopaxi, the highest active volcano in the world, to Chimborazo, the hunch-backed colossus of the cordillera. And in between, the *páramo*, which made me wish I could paint, or compose music, or at least point a camera in the right direction – anything, in fact, that would allow me to distil a portion of its magic. The bleak, open, windswept *páramo*, treeless and cold, endlessly sparkling in the thin mountain air, its melted-snow waters trickling softly through the grass. And its sheep almost everywhere – flocks so numerous that it was hard to believe fleecing only came with the Spaniards – often tended only by a child of tender age, usually a small girl, the very spirit and image of her Indian mother.

First impressions are often those that touch most deeply and stay with us longest, and those who have yet to visit the Andes might do well to remember this and to savour every moment of their first encounter, for the Andean spirit is, indeed, a special one. From *páramo* to *puna* it speaks to you of silence, space and peace, in limitless measure, shaped by the easy arcs of the cruising condor. Its essence is of solitude, and such transcendence as it inspires can rarely be shared with anyone.

The ancient Lords of the Andes, the Incas, were remarkable among other things for the creation of a sophisticated and complex society at high altitude. Archaeologists have noted how the rise and fall of advanced societies is often related to the presence and management of forests. Drawing heavily upon forest resources, society is able to flourish; then, as the forest starts to decline, so the economy declines with it, and often unfavourable climatic changes seal the fate of the people.

The central valley of Mexico is a good example. Anyone who has seen the gigantic pyramids of Teotihuacan will appreciate the scale of manpower required to build such structures, yet one look at the semi-desert terrain leaves you wondering just how a commensurate population might have survived in such a wasteland. The ancient city of Teotihuacan, in fact, is estimated by archaeologists to have covered something like fifteen square miles. The likely answer is that at one time the central valley of Mexico was clothed in forest and that it was over-exploitation that turned its fertile lands into arid scrub.

The Incas were a notable exception to this, however, in that much of their settlement took place high upon the *puna* above the tree-line of 3,500 metres. In fact, research carried out recently by anthropologist Johan Reinhard has revealed over one hundred archaeological sites in the Chilean Andes situated above 5,200 — religious sites perched high on mountain-tops in order to gather the first divine rays of the sun — with some, incredibly, as high as 6,700 metres; that is to say, higher than Ecuador's snow-capped colossus, Chimborazo.

Intrinsic to most things Inca, therefore, is a sense of loftiness and space — high plains bordered by treeless mountain slopes, with the moderate amounts of timber they required being brought up from below. It was an economy based squarely on certain specialized crops that did well at altitude, such as quinua and maize, and a range of potatoes and pulses; and of course, the llama and the alpaca which, while declining disdainfully to carry loads of any significance, provided wool for clothing, meat, and fuel in the form of dung. Timber was not central to this economy despite its selective use in construction and furniture, weaponry (bows and lances) and short-span bridges — the treadways of the classic Inca bridges that swung horrendously over the yawning chasms of the Andes were not made of wood but of a fibrous plaited grass that conveniently allowed the hooves of the Spanish horses to slip through.

The houses were built then as many of them still are today, with mud or grass walls and thatched roofs, and doors of plaited twigs. In the absence of draught animals, and perhaps for reasons relating to the Incas' particular vision, the wheel had not found its way into everyday use, although it existed in the form of children's toys, so there was no call for the construction of the kind of carts and carriages that were so much a part of European life at the same period. Neither, of course, did the plough exist — just a simple digging stick called a 'chaqui taclla' which served to break the earth.

An ingenious arrangement of terraces, indicating an intimate familiarity with the dynamics of water-flow and drainage, turned barren mountain slopes into flourishing grainfields and vegetable gardens capable of supporting population densities well in excess of those today's agriculture can feed. The 'roof of the world' location ruled out the cultivation of squash, so favoured in the rest of the region, and it may not have added up to the perfect diet but it was a self-sustaining economy that could have gone on for ever.

The *páramo* of Ecuador and parts of the Peruvian and Bolivian *altiplano* lie below the tree-line and are theoretically suitable for afforestation. In fact, a number of these areas were reportedly forested at the time of the Conquest, not only with trees but with bushes and shrubs also, all of them valuable species that soon fell to the European axe to make room for farms and provide fuel for the mines, and which subsequently passed from the collective memory.

Little in the way of reafforestation had been attempted before the second half of the last century when, under the Conservative government of García Moreno, eucalyptus trees were introduced to Ecuador for the first time, and until quite recently it was believed that they held the key to the *páramo's* transformation.

'They grow like weed,' a forester once told me euphorically, 'fast and strong!' This seemed like good news for the Indian and the poor mestizo because in our modern world they have come to depend on firewood and timber. But the forester's analogy proved to be uncomfortably accurate and his euphoria was short-lived. Like weed the eucalyptus did, indeed, grow – too fast and too strong – and they soon strangled everything in their shadow. The trees themselves then began to languish for want of nourishment, and what had been envisaged as dense, thriving forests turned out to be little more than gangling clumps. Subsequent plantings of pine appear to be faring better, but it is too soon to say if the experiment will succeed or not.

Change is inevitable and the days of the Ecuadorean *páramo*, and quite probably those of the Peruvian and Bolivian *altiplano* too, are almost certainly numbered. The trees will see to that, and if not the eucalyptus or the pine, then some other species that seems to fit the bill – some import from the Himalayas, perhaps, that can miraculously survive at 16,000 feet.

For the present, an impression of loftiness and space persists, despite the crowded clusters of pine, the straggling eucalyptus and the persistent urban sprawl, and a sense of the past is still there to savour a while longer. But the final transformation cannot be far away. It will come, and subsequent generations will tread heedlessly over the dust of history and revel in new scenic delights and new economic benefits; they will be right to do so, for change is badly needed. But a part of me at least is glad to have known these lands before they are rendered unrecognizable by the white man and while they still bear some resemblance to those not-so-distant times when the Inca roamed and reigned supreme in his strange, heady realm where shadows seldom fell.

With a couple of hours and Cotopaxi behind us, the *páramo* had opened up and we were in sight of Latacunga, the first town of any size south of the capital. As the bus approached the police barrier – the check-point situated at the entrance of every town where driving licences are routinely inspected and perfunctory searches are made for contraband and escaped convicts – the many illicit passengers standing in the gangway all dutifully ducked down while the policeman obligingly saw nothing. Hordes of women wearing trilbies and carrying baskets over their arms laid siege to the bus from all sides, raising the cry of 'axuxas! axuxas!'

Axuxas (the 'x' pronounced like the French 'je', and the 'u' protracted into a hooting 'oo' sound) are a large round biscuit made of wheat flour and only found in Latacunga.

The women clearly believed in their product with a vengeance. They forged up the steps before the departing passengers could get off, setting about all and sundry with their baskets and their ample hips. Meanwhile, others of equally ambitious intent attacked from the outside, thrusting brown paper bags full of axuxas through the open windows.

'Axuxas, señor! Axuxas, señora!' they cried, as if one should be desperate to buy all they had. I must confess I bought far more than my fair share in my time, from sheer intimidation, and usually ended up giving them away to some kid in Riobamba or Quito when I reached my journey's end.

The women also sold hard-boiled eggs, only here, in delegating the task to their trimmer, less assertive offspring, they employed a different strategy. 'Huevos' in Spanish, or 'eggs', is also the vulgar term for 'testicles' and the mere mention of the word is usually enough to provoke a wry smile among the passengers. Indeed, it is difficult to refuse when an attractive young girl looks you straight in the eye and asks sweetly 'if she can shell your eggs for you?' Whether it was deliberately designed as a sales technique or not, I can't honestly say, but they did seem to sell rather a lot.

Two hours further south is the town of Ambato, Riobamba's great rival. The towns are similar in size – about 30,000 population in 1968 – with similar traditions, although Ambato is considered to be the more commercial of the two. To an Ambateño, the inhabitant of Riobamba is a 'chagra' – a yokel; whereas for the Riobambeño, the inhabitant of Ambato is something of a city-slicker, someone who has no time for you and who might rip you off if given half a chance. It is all relative, and terribly innocent, of course – at least, it was in 1968 – but for me, coming as I did from the rural margins of Bristol, Riobamba seemed like home from home and this may well account for the ease I found in settling in.

Ambato's great landmark is its cathedral, reputedly built with relief money accrued in the wake of the great earthquake of 1949. It was a town that I only ever seemed to be passing through and I spent very little time there. The buses made a mandatory stop of twenty minutes, both coming and going, and as a consequence I got to know the bus station fairly well in the course of my two years. To anyone seeing it for the first time and contemplating having a bite to eat there, its dining facilities might seem to bear many of the attributes of a health inspector's nightmare. But there is an irony in the way the food is prepared in these inauspicious surroundings, one that applies to most places in the Third World. Here, everything is cooked so thoroughly – the pot kept boiling for hours on end – that no bacteria could possibly survive. On the other hand, in the kitchens of the 'posh' hotels where standards of hygiene are not always what they should be, where power-cuts occasionally defrost freezers, and where trendy chefs often only half-cook their orders, salmonella thrives.

As far as I could see, Ambato's bus station 'diner', which consisted of about twenty stalls operated by extremely good-natured, weighty women, had just about everything you could wish for. The choice of fruit, for example, which resulted from Ambato's easy access to the Oriente, was head-scratching. You had your usual bananas, mangoes, tangerines, oranges, pineapples, avocados, and pawpaw, plus a superb plum named 'claudia' after a Spanish Queen; but you also had pomegranates, passion-fruit, soursop and custard-apple; and a few things that we don't even have names for, like 'naranjilla', a delicious smooth-skinned, bright orange tree fruit used for making cold drinks; 'tomate de arbol' (tree tomato), a hard-skinned, shiny, reddish-brown fruit also used for making drinks; and 'zapote', which does exist as 'mammey-apple' but which I had never seen.

There were plates stacked high with pastries, and enormous square trays holding up roasted pig in varying stages of dismember-ment – 'fritada'; there were rows of white enamel buckets in which 'choclos' – corn-on-cob – simmered and steeped; and there were piles of soft white cheese, sliced ready for the taking. There were the old stand-bys of 'seco de chivo' (stewed goat's meat and rice) and 'caldo de gallina' – a clear soup containing potatoes, carrots, onions, parsley, and lumps of chicken; and finally there was that great *pièce de résistance* of the provinces, the pre-Columbian specialty of 'cuy' (pronounced 'kwee') – baked guinea-pig. Row upon row of the tiny golden carcasses stared at you wherever you looked, their paws forever gripping the sides of the tray and their grinning teeth having the last laugh.

I could never make up my mind on the Ambato versus Riobamba question. Ambato's mountain, Tungurahua, was no match for mighty Chimborazo, that was certain, but in other respects Ambato had more to offer. It had, for example, a certain sophistication – nicer restaurants (in addition to the bus station), hotels and parks; and it also had the Salasaca Indians. These diffident souls, easily identifiable by their long black ponchos and round white hats with upturned brim, have retained their traditional ways to a remarkable degree; and their beautiful tapestries, usually in the form of stylized birds, are instantly recognizable wherever you see them.

Above all, Ambato had its annual Festival of Fruit and Flowers, an agricultural show for which it was, and still is, deservedly renowned. But somehow it lacked the indifference to change that I found so attractive about Riobamba – a reaction that I realized was not only delusory because change is inevitable, but also quite indefensible in a 'development' worker. Still, it was a contradiction that I was prepared to live with.

Ambato, however, occupied a special niche in my affections. As a place on the way to somewhere else, it offered time out to reflect, undisturbed and free of care; it had the attraction born of transience. I have often wondered if the temporary release from responsibility while we are on a journey is at the root of the love of travel, and perhaps there are many other attractions connected with this theme. I find, for example, that travelling provides occasion for measuring spiritual progress, because in so far as our ability to conquer fear is an indication of such things, travel in the Third World is the perfect testing-ground. And I see it also as a rehearsal and a preparation for that great final journey that we all have to make one day when the emotional and material baggage that has been weighing us down for so long will be jettisoned.

There were four magnificent snow-capped peaks, the 'nevados'. First, to the north-west, there was Chimborazo – 20,000 feet and massively built, a white poncho slung casually over his bulging shoulder; and by his side was his servant, whom the Indians called 'Carihuairazo' – Man of the Wind. Out towards Ambato was Tungurahua, clearly visible from Riobamba, its truncated cone still clearing 16,000 feet. And then, to the south-east, there was Altar, its twin peaks and saddle all finely draped in a silk mantle – a shape

that hints of former glory in the days before the God of Fire blew it
to pieces.

But it was Chimborazo that commanded the land and stole the
view. Many times I have gazed at its smooth bulk from the roof of
the house or the window of the bus, inspired by its sovereignty and
finding comfort in its sheer stability. Yet how different it can look
from the morning to the afternoon to the evening! The stark
surprise at sunrise of finding it still there, as huge as the day before;
a blinding barrier across the sky at noon, obstinate and unforgiving,
a challenge and a threat; and in the evening, ghostly and remote,
almost moving, with perhaps a single strand of cloud, the guardian
spirit of the plain. And sometimes it would display itself even at
night, when struck by some wildly romantic moon, producing
insomnia and casting long shadows of memories belonging to
another age; ever silent, ever present, it was never completely out of
your mind.

If I had never reached Riobamba, the sight of Chimborazo that
first day would have made the trip worthwhile. I watched it for a
full hour in the fading light before the bus finally came to a halt
alongside the railway station, smack in the middle of town.
Darkness had fallen in the space of a few minutes and it was
getting cold. Riobamba is noted for its coldness, although it never
reaches freezing point in the town itself. The icy wind comes
hurtling down from the slopes of the Great Refrigerator and there
is nothing in the way to stop it. How often have I seen, as I
returned home in the early hours of the morning, the huddled
figures of Indians crouching in doorways, fighting to stave off the
chill with little more than a threadbare poncho – Indians who have
been driven from the *campo* by want and hunger in the hope of
earning a few sucres as labourers and who have no place to lay
their heads.

'*Cargador!*' yelled Señor Martinez at the top of his voice in search
of someone to carry my suitcases. 'Carga!' he snapped at a diminutive Indian who was hovering near the end of the bus where the
luggage was being unloaded – 'Carry this!'

Chimborazo and Carihuairazo   Photo R. G. Torske

The translation of 'cargador' – if you are fortunate enough to find it in the dictionary – is 'porter', but this term, except perhaps when it is used in an African context, comes nowhere near the meaning required here; the cargador bears little resemblance to his European counterpart. His customary attire is the red poncho and round, white, stiff-brimmed hat that certain of the Chimborazo Indians wear. He is lucky if he can afford a pair of rubber sandals made from old car tyres, and more often than not he flaps along barefoot over the wet, freezing cobbles. He has a rope wound around his shoulder; this is the line with which he ties his load and from which his life hangs. The usual procedure is for him to lean forward with his arm outstretched against a wall for support while the cases and boxes are balanced on his shoulders, with the rope going around the outside and tied in a knot across his chest. He will then trot along, bent almost double, a few feet behind the 'patrón' – the person hiring his services – his health and his dignity bartered for a pittance.

You could argue – as some have done – that as pre-Columbian America had no pack animals to speak of, apart from the weedy and temperamental llama, it would have been more commonplace and less demeaning than it appears to us today for people to carry loads of this kind. But such arguments do not impress. Few Indians, apart from those who buried themselves deep in the Amazon jungle, managed to salvage any dignity in the face of the invader and discussions based on what might or might not have been accepted norms 500 years ago are purely hypothetical. Common sense must surely tell us that if the lot of the cargador appears humiliating and archaic to us, it is unlikely that it feels much different to the man beneath the load.

Two cargadores carried my suitcases to the School of Radiophony. It was well after seven by the time we arrived and the staff had long since gone home. Señor Martinez introduced me to the night-watchman, then shook my hand firmly in a gesture of welcome and headed off in the same direction. The watchman, with a minimum of preamble, showed me to a small room with a

Cargador – Guamote, Chimborazo Province   Photo R. G. Torske

flagstone floor, half-lit by a sad yellow bulb that dangled low on a flex, and furnished with a single bed and a small metal table, by the side of which was a wrought-iron stand bearing a bowl and a jug of water. We exchanged a few words, and then he too respectfully took his leave and closed the door quietly behind him.

Instantly I knew, for the first time in my life, what it was to be alone – totally alone. That indescribable moment had arrived, the moment of truth when many a volunteer feels like grabbing his bags and running. It is the worst of both worlds – the old world is still inside your head but you are not there; and the new world is all around you, but still unknown.

I reached for the Consul's bottle of whisky and poured a draught into the golden plastic cap, and then sat for a while on the edge of the bed, experiencing the classic anti-climax, thinking back over the chain of events that had brought me there and wondering why I had been so sure all along about what I wanted. How different the reality seemed – this drab, chill room – from the llamas, volcanoes and Inca ruins I'd had in mind.

I knew I had to think my way around it somehow. Feeling not a little ridiculous, I raised my 'glass' to the night and drank to my arrival in Riobamba. To my amazement I felt a mite better, even before the liquor reached its mark. I drank a second time, to Scotland and Jim Baxter – and again I felt my spirits rise. And then, in a gesture of sheer defiance, I raised my glass a third time and drank to sock one in the eye of the cold mountain air that had caught me unawares. And then I climbed into bed and slept. I was no longer wondering what the world outside would look like in the daylight. I was inclined to believe it would still be there in the morning.

CHAPTER TWO

RIOBAMBA

RIOBAMBA LIES some four hours directly south of Quito, and like most other towns in the Sierra it is situated about 9,000 feet above sea-level in a valley or plain. 'Rio-bamba' means 'river-valley' – a mixture of Spanish and Quechua, which is an apt combination given the racial composition of its people. The province of Chimborazo, of which Riobamba is the capital, has a larger than average indigenous population and this has left its particular stamp on the town, although in general the province has followed the same pattern of settlement as the country as a whole.

Culturally, the countries of Ecuador, Peru and Bolivia are divided fairly evenly between 'blancos' and 'mestizos', on the one hand, and Indians, on the other, in a fashion that has not changed radically since the second half of the sixteenth century. The Spaniards, great city-builders that they were, and those who came to identify with them, soon monopolized the urban centres, whilst the Indians – those who survived the fighting, the forced labour and the European diseases – were confined almost exclusively to the rural areas, so that today, Spanish is the language of the towns and Quechua still the language of the countryside.

But if the two cultures are still identifiable, despite extensive lending and borrowing, the races are anything but. They form a spectrum, at one end of which you have the 'blancos' – the 'whites' – who are of pure European descent and who have vigorously defended their pedigree and their power down through the ages.

The water carrier – Riobamba   Photo R. G. Torske

These people, who represent some ten per cent of the population, have generally managed to contrive a degree of separateness and tend to reside in well-appointed houses in Quito, Guayaquil and the provincial capitals. Their interests are primarily commercial, although many of them still own farms that are managed in their absence by a 'mayordomo', and which they occasionally visit with their families for recreational as much as business purposes. And at the other end of the spectrum, you will find some pure-blooded Indians (although there are none too many of these) who live in remote rural areas and who speak and understand no Spanish at all.

In coastal Ecuador there is also a small but growing minority of Blacks who were brought over originally as slaves from West and Central Africa to work the farms and sugar plantations in preference to the Indians, who succumbed too readily to the tropical heat and disease.

The racial middle-ground – the product of liaisons between Spanish males and Indian females, always in the form of coercion and usually in the form of rape – covers the vast bulk of the population and this, in turn, falls into one or the other of two cultural groups – mestizo and Indian. The term 'mestizo' was originally a racial designation signifying 'of mixed blood', but it has come to have a predominantly cultural application, indicating someone who identifies with European values but is not 'white'. And if, from the outside, the dividing line between what is 'white', what is 'mestizo', and what is 'Indian' sometimes appears blurred, you can be fairly sure that the person on the inside knows where he belongs.

Identification of the two original races along cultural lines is still possible to a certain extent, therefore, but to try to accurately define what this consists of in hard and fast terms is a recipe for insanity. Certain traits are normally considered to be 'Indian' or 'mestizo', but in any one case some, all, or none of the generalizations may apply.

Our 'typical' Indian will be primarily a speaker of Quechua or another native language, and probably illiterate. He will live in the rural areas in a rustic dwelling with a thatched roof and mud and

wattle walls, or at best a tin roof and concrete-block walls; and he
will earn his living principally from subsistence farming on land that
is either his or held in trust on behalf of the community. At all
events, he will consider himself an integral member of that
community and will identify predominantly with it.

When he is there he will adhere to his traditional dress which, in
the Sierra, amounts to a hat, a poncho and a pair of loose-fitting
trousers for the men; and a hat, a shawl, a long dress, and a series of
woven braids and belts for the women – the colour and design of all
of which will indicate the particular group to which he or she
belongs. He will either go barefoot, or, more commonly these days,
wear sandals made from old car tyres, or cheap plastic shoes or boots.

He will be dark-skinned (compared to a European), short and
stocky, and will bear some or all of the physiological traits of his
Asiatic forefathers who presumably trekked across the Bering Strait
into Alaska between 40,000 and 10,000 BC. These traits include the
extra fold in the eyelid, prominent cheek-bones, straight black hair
which he almost never loses and which seldom turns grey, and a
smooth chin that he rarely has to shave.

The one certainty is his position as the underdog in Andean
society; his standard of living hovers just around the poverty line.
The Indian accounts for a little under half the population, the
mestizo forty-odd per cent.

The mestizo is principally a town-dweller, although he could
also be a peasant farmer ('campesino') and work a 'parcela' or
'finquita' (small-holding) in the not-too-remote countryside; he
could also conceivably be a relatively wealthy farm owner managing
his hacienda either in person or in absentia. His means of subsistence,
whatever it happens to be, is normally his own. Co-operative efforts
of one kind or another are not uncommon, especially among the
rural poor, but there is little tradition of collective land-ownership or
collective labour, any more than there is a traditional dress – he is,
after all, a 'cultural European'.

He may choose to wear a poncho, but this will be mainly for
reasons of practicality, and his usual garb, like that of the town-

based mestizo, will be European in style. In fact, the mestizo's dress should generally be regarded as an attempt to distance himself from an indigenous life-style, albeit with varying degrees of commitment. He is a Spanish-speaker and probably literate, although he may, by association, have picked up Quechua as a second language; he may even have relatives who are Indians.

Within the town, his occupation can range from that of the extremely poor labourer or artisan, who barely manages to make ends meet, to that of the solidly affluent businessman with plenty to spare. Complexion, too, can vary substantially, from the very dark ('negro'), to the very pale ('blanco'), and the correlation between wealth and whiteness is neither coincidental nor difficult to discern.

There are many complications to this picture; for example, the fact that the term *campesino* or 'peasant farmer' is used equally to refer to mestizos and Indians alike; and that an Indian can become an 'honorary mestizo' for the day by virtue of donning European dress, which he is likely to do if he goes to town on official business.

It is also possible, as happens with increasing regularity in these days of urban drift, particularly since the oil finds of the mid-seventies, for an Indian to cross over the line and become a mestizo on a permanent basis, but it would be unthinkable for the reverse to happen and for a non-Indian to become an Indian (although the odd hippie, anthropologist and volunteer have reportedly tried it). Not only would such a step be considered aberrant and retrograde, it is the mestizo culture that is the stronger of the two and the indigenous culture that is everywhere under threat, so that it is invariably the Indian who surrenders. In fact, as Ronald Wright points out in his admirable book *Cut Stones and Cross-roads*, the Indian is by definition a loser because – in what must be the ultimate form of prejudice – the moment he is successful at anything, he is auto-matically classified as a mestizo.

If Riobamba is sometimes referred to as 'an Indian town', it does not mean that its inhabitants are Indians. In any case, town dwellers, with only a few exceptions, are almost by definition

mestizo – the town being the product of extensive specialization
and the concentration of wealth, both concepts absent from pre-
Columbian America. What it means is that many of the town's
inhabitants have relatives and contacts in the *campo* and that,
supposing such things could be measured, there is probably a higher
percentage of 'Indian' blood in their veins than in most other towns.
It also means that the place occasionally gets flooded out with
Indians, especially on Saturdays – market day – when the centre is
awash with ponchos, hats and the sound of Quechua.

This, then, is Riobamba – an 'Indian' town of some 30,000
inhabitants, laid out in blocks in traditional colonial style and lined
with cobbled streets and faded white-wash walls, and surrounded by
hills and mountains, four of which are magnificently snow-capped.
It is a curious and incomplete meeting of East and West, an impoverished cultural crossroads set in an exquisite corner of the Andes.

On Saturdays the movement starts early with some of the *campesinos*
having spent the night on the pavement in the hope of securing a
pitch, or a deal, in the early hours of trading. Buses and lorries
arrive in the darkness and disgorge their loads – people, livestock,
vegetables, fruits, and large square bales of alfalfa that will soon be
lining the streets.

If you travel on a country bus on a Saturday, you will probably
be sharing space with a basket of chickens or a sack of potatoes.
You might find a pig staring at you through the window as it hangs,
miserably, upside down, swaying with every lurch and jolt; or pass
the distorted figure of an Indian woman as she stumbles along, bent
almost double beneath the weight of a sack of onions or a hefty
sheep, draped around her frail shoulders. And behind her trail her
brood, in descending order, like the pipes of Pan, or a row of
Russian dolls, with the smallest infant carrying an even smaller
infant on her back. And how quickly you get used to such sights!
Only the surprise of the visitor reminds you of the norms you left
behind not so very long ago and of the changes that have silently
taken place within you.

Riobamba market – winding down   Photo R. G. Torske

By nine o'clock the place is buzzing with noise – mechanical, animal and human; jokes, laughter, mock cries of outrage over prices, genuine cries of outrage over prices; Spanish, Quechua, English – 'Hey, meester! Hey, meestera!' (to a woman); the occasional beggar clinging, pleading in a plaintive monotone replete with diminutives, 'a little favour, little gringo, little sir, just one little sucre, for the sake of little God, don't be a little bit bad'; and the smells – food smells, animal smells, human smells, the smell of diesel, cheap tobacco and trago. Already the trago is starting to flow and will do so into the late afternoon.

Clusters of by-standers surround the various side-shows: the man with three shells and a pea whose movement you could always track easily from the side but lost sight of the moment it was your turn and you stood in front; the mystery of the 'unholdable coin', where the showman offered a whole sucre – at a time when the beggars asked for and were pleased to get twenty cents – to anyone who could hold it in his hand for a second, but all of them dropped it instantly as if it were red-hot (I never found out what the secret was); the Indians agog with wonder as a 'clairvoyant' tells a bent and crippled old lady that 'he can see she has had a hard life and many times wondered if she could go on'; and the greatest show of all, the dentist drilling teeth outside on the pavement, while scores of well-intentioned onlookers gather helpfully around to inspect the open mouth and offer advice.

As the day and the drink wear on, disputes become increasingly common, especially between husband and wife, with usually a drunken, abusive Indian woman trying hard to drag her even drunker husband to his feet so they can go home – convention has it that the woman abstain from paralysis so that she can do just this.

Drink has a terrible hold over Indians, not just in Ecuador but everywhere from Northern Canada to Southern Chile, for reasons that reputedly go back to the Conquest and the trauma it invoked. The early chroniclers relate that alcohol was rare among the Indians when the Spaniards arrived. What there was, along with the coca leaf (never prevalent in the area and abolished altogether in the nineteenth century) was 'chicha' – a stale-tasting maize beer, not particularly potent and largely restricted in its use to certain elites and specific festive occasions. The arrival of the Spaniards, of course, changed all this, creating both the supply and the demand for hard liquor.

I can't help thinking that there may be more to it than this, because although the events of the Conquest might well explain the depression and the urge to self-destruct, it would not explain the Indians' awesome susceptibility to the power of drink itself.

This same hopeless and despairing addiction to strong alcohol is seen everywhere amongst the world's indigenous peoples, from the Americas to Africa and the Pacific Islands, to an extent that I find myself wondering if it might not be a function of their heightened spirituality. Could it not be, for instance, that where the spiritual side of our nature is more attuned, with all that this implies in terms of pre-cognition, telepathy, and communion with the divine – all of which are part and parcel of their everyday lives – there is a greater susceptibility to the power of alcohol; and that, conversely, in 'developed' nations, which are invariably more

Thatching minga – Chimborazo Province   Photo R. G. Torske

materialistic, we have lost this sensitivity and thereby acquired a degree of immunity? And I wonder also if the scourge of alcohol and drugs that has traditionally afflicted North American Blacks is not purely socio-economic in origin, but spiritual also – stranded as they still are between two disparate cultures, the African and the European.

But for all their drunken wrangling, the Indians are not unduly quarrelsome or difficult people. On the whole, they are fairly amiable and straightforward, and not especially devious, as rumour would have it, except in so far as they have had to disguise their true motives and feelings in order to survive the wrath of their masters. Having suffered inconceivable hardship and injustice themselves, they have generally been prepared to live and let others live their more comfortable lives in peace, being quick to provide assistance to anyone who might need it, their oppressors included.

This sharing of life's ups and downs is instinctive even today, as evidenced by the tradition of the 'minga', a system of voluntary collective labour that can be called upon at any time when some task important to the community needs performing – a road or a bridge in need of repair, a piece of land or property in need of attention, or an irrigation ditch to be dug. The response is total and the recompense is nil. This was just one of the things that truly mystified the Spaniards, who sometimes failed to motivate the Indians with either lashes or gold, and were astonished to see them mobilized in minutes by a village headman for whom they would work for hours on end without reward.

It is important to remember in this connection that there was no private wealth before the Spaniards arrived – a concept that may not come easily to those of us brought up on consumerism and a cash economy – and that the significance of the much-revered gold was its reflection of the sun, the symbol of divinity, the source of all being. This was a more readily accessible symbol, perhaps, than a book and a man on a cross, both of which the Indians found, to their mortal cost, totally incomprehensible.

I recall an incident that took place in the market one Saturday morning when a solitary Indian woman was beaten about the head and robbed of her precious cash by some drunken thug. I remember looking at her as she sat there on the pavement, wailing and weeping, with blood streaming down her face. To those who ran to her aid, the only words she would utter were – 'es malo' – 'he is a bad man', and I wondered at her reaction, more grief than anger, and at the simplicity of her language. This single word, 'malo', sufficed to contain all the pain and injustice that she must have felt at that moment; and I compared it to the string of oaths and expletives that the average European would have uttered in a similar circumstance.

It is through isolated incidents such as this, and the insights that follow, that one can arrive at a more complete picture of what life means to the local people – insights that perhaps only just break the surface, but if you can hang onto them long enough to examine them at leisure, they can open up doors of understanding.

Another such incident took place one time when I was on the Panamericana travelling to Quito, and I found myself sitting next to a young Riobambeña – a girl of seven or eight years old, who was making the journey alone. It was a foul day, a storm was blowing outside and rain was lashing against the window-panes. The girl, I couldn't help but notice, was sobbing. Thinking that she was frightened by the thunder, I ventured to comfort her by telling her that the noise would do no harm.

'Oh no, señor,' she replied, turning her tear-soaked face towards me but still looking away, 'it is not the thunder. It is my little brother. You see he shines shoes, and when it rains nobody wants their shoes shined.' And I felt like weeping too, for the girl, and her brother, and the family he was probably supporting, and for my own stupidity.

But it was a lesson that served me well, because through it I came to see that not just the casual decision to have or not have my shoes cleaned, but a whole host of other half-conscious decisions I was in the habit of making every day bore implications I had never imagined; and through it I also learned ultimately to recognize the pale face of hunger as it stared at me from beneath the brim of a beggar's hat, and from the back row of the class I was teaching as some impoverished schoolboy struggled, manfully, to stay awake and learn.

We need a new word in the English language, one that means 'season', 'climate' and 'weather', and yet is none of them. It should represent something temporary, less regular than 'season', more precise than 'climate', and more consistent than 'weather' – something like 'spells of weather that recur at odd intervals'. Whatever the word, there were moments in Riobamba, related to the climate, that inspired a feeling of elation. It was something in the light and the air you breathed that lifted you sky-high and left you dreaming of all that you might do one day, instead of brooding over all that you had failed to do in the past. There were many times, usually in the early morning and evening, when I felt myself so transfixed by the gentleness of the light, the softness of the breeze and the scented stirrings of the eucalyptus, that I had no desire to move from where I was ever again.

Strangely enough, part of the magic seemed to derive from the people – in the same way, perhaps, that charm is the property of the unknowing – and the fact that they seemed to be wandering around and going about their daily business without the slightest awareness of this extraordinary gift that enveloped their every move – and many of them may well have been, never having travelled away to experience its absence.

There were other times too, that were not so pleasant, always in the mid-afternoon when the very air felt languid and wanting, and every movement inclined you heavily to sleep, a sleep that would remove the traces of toil and refurbish the spirit. You could resist, mad-doggishly, if you wanted, but it was hard to think of a reason why you should. It was far easier to succumb, like everybody else, and fabricate some ludicrous excuse as to why you were late, like everybody else, and trust, as always happened, that habit would eventually erase the guilt.

It was Sunday mornings that I came to enjoy most, for these were times when the survival instinct was laid to rest for a few hours and a different, kinder, more leisurely race of people took to the streets. In roped-off alley-ways, games of 'ecuavolley' – the homegrown, three-a-side version of volleyball – were contested with a passion inspired by the hefty side-stakes, but always good-humoured enough to let the occasional vehicle pass unmolested. In dusty squares, the old folks played out their games of bowls in slow motion, their reminiscences punctuated by the dull clunk of metal. And I envied them for their lifelong camaraderie, which my generation had swapped for mobility, and for the store of wisdom they kept hidden away.

In the Main Square, other senior citizens – the photographers – chatted and smoked, and only half seriously looked for business, their antique bellows-cameras posing idly, waiting for the odd gringo left over from the market and wandering aimlessly around. Just occasionally, perhaps out of lifetime habit, or deference to a wife at home, they diverted their attention long enough to look for a family outing, or a young couple on a high, or an infant who had caught sight of the faded painted pony.

Overhead, wood-smoke from the bath-houses spiralled forever skywards and then settled faintly over the town, reminding you of the nearness of the *campo*, and of the incense that would soon be enveloping the faithful as they flocked in their numbers to worship — gentry, commoners and peasants alike, filling the churches with their bodies and their passion to overflowing, in a genuinely moving, but alas fleeting, gesture of human brotherhood.

CHAPTER THREE

RADIOFÓNICAS

AMONG THE PEOPLE I met on my first morning in Riobamba was a tall, amiable Peace Corps agriculturalist named Paul who was also assigned to the School of Radiophony. It was Paul's job to advise the peasant farmers how to grow their crops. Paul, unfortunately, was just one of a number of Peace Corps casualties at that time, his problems stemming from the fact that his background was in history. The policy-makers in Washington had decided, as they still do in fact, that, on the strength of a couple of summers spent working on his uncle's farm and three months' training in the United States, he would be competent to teach Indians, who had been growing maize for several thousand years, how better to go about their business. He had only been in post for a month or so, but already the hopelessness of his situation was beginning to get to him.

He invited me to go with him for a coffee and the two of us headed off in the direction of a small restaurant called 'Monique' situated right in the centre of town on the main square. We covered the half-dozen blocks or so at his brisk pace, and sat at a table near the window. Even though he had only been in country for a short while, these few weeks gave him a head-start and a ranking I knew I should never be able to match. There is an unspoken scale of seniority amongst volunteers based on length of service, and it separates you for ever. It is a bit like being a younger brother – fate has you cast in second place and no matter how hard you try, you can never make up the ground.

'Monique' was always referred to as 'the best restaurant in town', but since there were only two, that didn't mean a great deal, and it tended to enjoy a reputation that was not easy for the casual visitor to fathom, especially once you had sampled the crude rusticity of its furniture. In the main, its position of pre-eminence derived from its location at the centre of town. From inside you could observe the daily round of activities with the sense of protected privilege normally reserved for the occupants of theatre boxes.

'Dos cafés en agua,' Paul ordered confidently in a broad non-Spanish accent, 'two black coffees'. But I was impressed all the same because the waiter trotted off instantly in the direction of the kitchen, and because his construction was substantially different from the 'dos cafés solos' I had learned at school.

'Well, how are you liking it so far?' I asked, straight to the point and confidently expecting to hear the best.

'OK now,' he replied, and then added with a laugh, 'but the sons-of-bitches threw stones at me the first day I got here.'

'What's that?' I responded with horror. 'Somebody threw stones at you? Who did for heaven's sake?'

'Oh, some kids out there in the park. Called me "imperialist". Me, for God's sake! Can you believe it? I thought only you Brits were imperialists.'

'So what did you do?' I asked abruptly, half afraid of what might come next.

'Well, I went over and told them that we are the "good guys", and after that they seemed quite friendly; I think they probably just wanted a bit of attention. Anyways, I haven't had any trouble with them since.'

'Have you seen them since?' I asked anxiously.

'Oh, sure, every day. They always wave out,' he added nonchalantly. 'Uh oh! Don't look now, but here comes Philip Marlowe.'

A formally but shabbily dressed, rotund little man in his forties came in and took up a seat a couple of tables away from us. He was wearing a dark brown suit, a green tie and a black trilby, all from another era, and under his arm he carried a copy of the daily newspaper, *El Comercio*, which he duly removed and opened out to

its fullest extent, disappearing behind it. The waiter made no effort
to serve him.

'Secret Police,' said Paul, not bothering to lower his voice. 'He
was trailing me for two full days when I first got here. He's probably
after you now.'

I could hardly believe my ears. 'What on earth for?' I exclaimed.

'Wants to know what everybody is doing here,' replied Paul
matter-of-factly; 'at least that's what he was trailing me for.'

'Why didn't he ask, for Heaven's sake? Didn't he know you were
Peace Corps?' I stammered.

'Well, he does now OK, because I finally cornered him and
asked him what he wanted. I told him what I was doing here sure
enough – here to help his country.'

'And he accepted it?' I asked anxiously.

'Seemed to. At least, I haven't seen him around for the past
couple of weeks so I guess he must have. Anyways, I get the feeling
he just likes playing the part. I mean, just look at the guy!'

Philip Marlowe had positioned himself so that he could see us
both in the mirror, and was peering around the edge of his
newspaper, checking us out with side-long glances.

'How you doing, pal?' asked Paul loudly, waving at the mirror. *El
Comercio* shifted abruptly, cutting off our line of vision, and Philip
Marlowe remained silent.

'Well, I reckon they must get all manner of weirdos passing
through here – dope-peddlers and the like, people on the run, not
to mention ex-Nazis, so I guess they have to be pretty careful,' said
Paul understandingly. 'What you should do, the first chance you
get, is to take your passport down to *Imigración* and tell them who
you are and what you're doing here, and you shouldn't get too much
hassle after that.'

As he was speaking, an old black telephone perched up on the bar
started to rattle. Its bell was so feeble I couldn't help remarking on it.

'Good heavens,' I said. 'I don't think much of their telephone
system, you can hardly hear it. Sounds like it's under three feet of
water.'

'It's probably designed that way', said Paul, 'so it doesn't wake anybody up.'

'It's for you,' the waiter said, holding the receiver out in my direction.

'Can't be for me,' I replied confidently. 'Must be for my amigo here.'

'It's for you,' he repeated, looking straight at me, and dropped the receiver down on the bar with a clunk.

'How can it be for me?' I objected. 'I've only just got here. In fact, I've been in Riobamba for less than twenty-four hours, and in this restaurant for precisely five minutes. Nobody knows I'm here. In fact nobody knows me, full stop!' I was becoming agitated.

'It's for you,' he said without humour, for the third time, and trotted off into the kitchen.

'Better go and answer it,' said Paul.

'This is ridiculous!' I protested, but got up and moved towards the bar all the same. I glanced across at Philip Marlowe as I did so and almost caught him looking at me, but *El Comercio* was quicker than I was and he disappeared from view leaving just the top of his trilby showing.

I stretched out an unsteady hand towards the telephone, alarm bells going off inside my head by the dozen, my eyes searching for the gun-barrel I was sure was about to emerge from the kitchen and spread me all over the wall.

'Hello?' I said, my throat dry and my voice quaking.

A sweet female voice answered. 'Qué tal?' – 'How are you?' 'Qué haces?' – 'What are you doing? I just wanted to say hello. My name's Tomasina.' And then there was a click, and whoever it was hung up.

I was dumbfounded. It was beyond belief. First, I hear about a public stoning, then the Secret Police, and now some insane telephone call – all in the space of five minutes. Was this what they meant on our orientation course when they warned us about culture shock, I wondered?

'Listen, Paul,' I pleaded. 'Do you think you could possibly tell

me what the hell is going on around here? I feel like I've just walked
into World War Three.'

'Just like I felt, buddy,' he replied, 'and it ain't nice. But don't let
it get to you. Once you get the hang of the place it ain't so bad.' He
spoke like a veteran, but I wasn't convinced. 'Who was it anyway,
the Gestapo?'

I told him about the phone call.

'Oh,' he said, laughing, 'so that's what it was,' and then he
explained.

'You see, they have a sort of custom around here, more of a
game, really – it goes like this. Some young chick sees a guy she
kinda likes sitting in a café. The guy, just coincidentally you understand, happens to be sitting near the window. He smiles, and she
ducks into a store half a block away and calls him up just to say 'hi'.
Or it can happen the other way round, of course; in fact, it usually
does. Either way, it's all very sweet and innocent – in fact, I kinda
like the idea. Hey, you haven't been smiling at any young chicks,
have you? Anyhow, man, sounds like you got yourself an admirer.
Did you get her address?'

I ignored his questions and breathed deeply. A flicker of light
had just appeared at the end of the tunnel. I felt confused, but
somehow relieved – not all the natives, it seemed, were out to get
me. I straightened my shoulders, swallowed, and half-resolved to go
over and confront Philip Marlowe. But I didn't go through with it. I
reckoned I'd had enough excitement for one day, and besides, I
feared that my Spanish might not be up to it.

We sat for a while longer just chatting and exchanging experiences and inspecting each other's accent, and occasionally glancing
over towards El Comercio, until eventually and much to my relief
Philip Marlowe decided to call it a day and made a sleuthful exit
from the restaurant, with El Comercio back in its rightful place
beneath his arm. Later that day, I did exactly as Paul suggested and
went down to Immigration and registered with the authorities, with
the happy result that neither Philip Marlowe, nor El Comercio, ever
returned to bother me again.

Escuelas Radiofónicas Populares, or 'Radiofónicas', as everybody called it, was the creation of a remarkable man, Monseñor Leonidas Proaño, the Bishop of Riobamba. The story went that one day he decided to use the funds that had been donated for restoration of the cathedral by the gentry of the town to set up an innovative system of education for the Indians.

He had caught on to a concept known today as 'distance education' and which, in the case of Chimborazo, meant supplying the Indians with transistor radios to take with them into the fields where they worked, and setting up a transmitter broadcasting educational programmes in both Spanish and their native Quechua. It was hoped that, with the assistance of helpers travelling out to the communities at weekends to provide some practical follow-up, significant inroads might be made into the massive problems of illiteracy and innumeracy. The concept, still revolutionary in 1968, is in common use today, and is the main means by which other indigenous groups in remote rural areas are reached, usually in their own languages as well as Spanish.

Monseñor's passage was not an easy one, as you might imagine. To preach Indian rights in the 1960s, to seek the company of the destitute, to wear a poncho and celebrate Mass exclusively for *campesinos*, was no way to gain popularity, especially among the rich and powerful, and he came in for a good deal of criticism including an alleged reprimand from the Vatican, apparently uneasy about his unilateral style of operation − others called it 'his stubborn streak'.

Still, nothing of value comes without sacrifice, as he well knew, and he weathered the long storm with courage and dignity. When he died in September 1988, the funeral in his native Ibarra was attended by many thousands of mourners, most prominent among whom were the many indigenous groups of the Sierra whom he had served throughout his lifetime. In the end, this gentle man died a hero, nominated not long before his death for the Nobel Peace prize and posthumously inspiring a national literacy campaign that is reportedly more effective than the countless previous ones.

Radiofónicas was housed in a single-storey structure with a sagging, red-tiled roof. There were half a dozen rooms set around a courtyard in typical colonial style, with the transmitter attached to the rear. The 'radio' side of the operation consisted of a fairly well-equipped workshop funded by the Belgian Government, a couple of technicians who had been trained in Belgium, and an announcer.

Also under the same roof was a dispensary run by nuns; a general store; a credit union that served only *campesinos*; an agricultural extension unit (to which Paul was attached); and an education unit, which planned the radio lessons and supervised the helpers who travelled out to the communities at weekends.

It was to this most worthy institution that I was sent as a volunteer – in response to a request for a 'public relations expert to work in a school of radiophony'. The term 'public relations expert' was as near as Radiofónicas could get to describing the person who would sell the idea of the 'school' to donors in the United States and Europe, and also advertising space to companies in Quito and Guayaquil.

At that time, with government funding about to dry up, the future of Radiofónicas looked very bleak indeed. My arrival, therefore, which was heralded with photographs and interviews by the press as I stepped off the plane in Quito, was seen as crucial to Radiofónicas' survival.

It is with painful regret that I have to confess I was not the man for the job. They had asked for 'a public relations expert' and this, more or less, was what they needed. Instead, they got a potential teacher of Spanish, a language that some two hundred million people in South America spoke infinitely better than I ever would. Every cloud, of course, has a silver lining, and in later years I was able to turn this experience to positive effect when, as a Field Director with Voluntary Services Overseas, I took the trouble to find out what people actually needed, and ensured that the volunteer was suitably qualified. This has helped to mitigate my sense of failure to a certain extent, but the bitter disappointment of those days still returns to haunt me in unguarded moments.

My first three months passed with me waiting for Radiofónicas to tell me what to do, and Radiofónicas waiting for me to act. When this little misunderstanding had been cleared up, I spent the next six months doing the rounds of companies in Quito and Guayaquil trying to drum up business – not an easy task for someone whose sales prowess was such that he usually ended up buying the raffle tickets he was supposed to sell. But there was another problem too, one that was cultural in origin and that I never came close to cracking. When a company manager told me that he thought Monseñor Proaño was doing a great job and he would be delighted to advertise on our radio, I believed him.

It seems quite laughable now, when I think back on it, but it was my first encounter with Latin American duplicity and I was totally unprepared for it. It was only when the promised cheque still had not arrived four weeks later, and I knew I could no longer blame it on the mail, that I realized I had been taken for a ride. And my carefully crafted letters to potential donors, which my Peace Corps colleagues swore had reduced them to tears, fared no better because they elicited no response at all – nothing. So it came as no surprise when the priest in charge of Radiofónicas one day called me into his office and suggested we should go our separate ways.

Looking back now, it is hard to see why I lasted as long as I did, given that I produced so little of substance. And the strain, despite the joy of being there in Ecuador, of writing letters that were never answered, making appointments that were seldom kept, and hearing promises that were invariably broken, was considerable. I was hopelessly out of my depth, both professionally and culturally, and felt so at sea in a world I knew nothing about that when the end finally came, it was something of a relief.

Radiofónicas had had a raw deal. They had paid out the best part of a year's salary which, meagre though it was, was more than they could afford, and they had received practically nothing in return. I, on the other hand, had breathed in the daily wonder of living in Riobamba, been touched to the core by everything I had seen, and had entered into a lifelong affair with the Andes. Radiofónicas may well have been a non-starter for me, but there was no way I was about to pack my bags and go home. The place was now in my blood and I knew it would take more than a single failure, even one of this magnitude, to remove it.

Over the years and the miles, I have developed the theory that expatriates are irrevocably cast in the mould of their first in-depth overseas experience, to an extent that defies time and reason. I see it everywhere I look – the young man who spent his childhood in India, or went there to work at the start of a career, will travel the world for evermore but dream only of returning one day to India. The District Officer who cut his teeth in Tanganyika will find peace nowhere except East Africa. Wave all the glossy pictures of Hindu temples you like and seduce him with the finest Tandoori cuisine, nothing for him will ever compare with the spacious beauty of the plains, the exquisite sky-scapes, the unending drama of the big game, and the elusive scents of the African night.

Such people have become geographical stereotypes and no matter how hard they try to be otherwise they remain 'an Asia person' or 'an Africa person'. Moreover the 'Asia person' is also a 'China' or an 'India' person, and the 'Africa person' is also an 'East' or a 'West Africa' person. It is a bit like a first love affair. You may have others that are more passionate, more caring and more enduring, but they will never touch you in quite the same way. Our feelings can never reproduce themselves exactly and when we open ourselves to our first embrace the imprint is indelible.

I have lived for several years in Africa and come to love the land and its peoples dearly. I have listened to old Africa hands pouring out their reminiscences deep into the night, their hearts at one with the beat of the continent; and I have heard some of them – the few who know – running down Latin America for all its faults and deficiencies, and I have only been able to nod my head in agreement, for in most categories Africa comes out ahead. Yet in spite of this, nothing pulls me quite like a thought of the Andes.

Something of the Andean spirit touched me deeply in those first few months in Riobamba. The town itself was a quiet, sunlit place, where you could walk in safety at any hour of the day or night. What misconduct there was, was usually more a question of 'sin' than crime — drunkenness, lying, irresponsibility, failure to keep one's word and petty theft. The serious crime, as ever, implicated the police, the wealthy and the senior public officials, but these were circles that I fortunately had no reason to frequent.

As much as the peace and quiet, it was the simple, everyday things you absorbed without realizing it and could never recall seeing for the first time, like cobblestones and rooftops, doorways and workshops, baskets and blankets, cauldrons and pork; and the meagre round of social activity — walking to the Post Office on a Thursday evening to see if the overseas mail had come down from Quito was the big event of the week; the old-fashioned picture houses that were empty on weekdays but packed at weekends when the public turned out in force; the old-fashioned greetings still very much in vogue, often accompanied by a doffing of the hat: 'Don' and 'Doña' — 'Squire' and 'Mistress'; 'Señor' and 'Señora' — 'Sir' and 'Madam'; 'tenga la bondad de . . .' — 'have the goodness to . . .'; 'please do me the honour of . . .' All legacies of an age of chivalry that lasted for three hundred years but today seems so remote. And always in the faces and the voices of the people, traces of a pre-colonial past that lives on in the blood and the spirit.

Paul and I hit it off really well from the start, partly because we had one enormous concern in common — our non-viable jobs — and partly because we just liked each other, and so we decided to look for an apartment together. The first one we found was situated one block from the main square, directly beneath a billiard hall. 'No, we won't mind the noise,' we told the landlord in best macho fashion — but that was before we moved in.

It wasn't so much the drunken voices, or even the music — it was the billiard balls. We never discovered what rules they were playing to, but about every five minutes or so an ivory sphere would hit the

floor – our ceiling. 'Son-of-a-bitch!' Paul would shout, and hit the
ceiling with a randomly aimed hiking boot, which, of course,
achieved precious little apart from leaving traces of mud on the
paintwork. It got so bad one night, about a week after we moved in,
that we couldn't stand it any more and we decided to go up and
complain.

It must have been close to three o'clock when we dressed and
climbed the two flights of stairs to the entrance. 'Now, how are we
going to play this?' I asked astutely, given that we didn't have any
particular plan in mind.

'I'll tell you what,' replied Paul, 'since you Brits are so smooth,
why don't you politely ask them if they would be so kind as to
consider making a little less noise – if that isn't too much trouble?'
His imitation of an English accent was appalling. And then he
added in New Yorkese, 'and if they don't, we'll send in the mob'.

I knocked somewhat half-heartedly at the door, and then stood
back a pace with Paul towering over me in his red check lumber
jacket. There was silence for a second and then the door opened a few
inches, and a youthful face appeared. It blinked and then exclaimed:

'Pablo, Pablo hermano' – 'Hey, Paul, Paul my brother' – 'What a
surprise! Hey, fellas, guess who's here – it's Pablo!'

The door swung open wide in a gesture of invitation and a
dozen more youthful faces filled the frame, all shouting 'Pablo!'
They were the crowd who had stoned Paul in the park.

There was no escape from this one. There was no way that Paul
was going to tear down the bridges he had been at such pains to
build, and there was no way they were going to let their 'dear
brother' leave without at least one swig from the trago bottle.

It must have been close to dawn when we staggered back downstairs to our apartment and flopped down onto our mattresses.

'Well, we certainly showed them a thing or two!' I slurred,
reflecting on the debacle we had set in motion.

'All in the cause of improving international relations, my dear
fellow,' replied Paul, echoing Peace Corps' philosophy, and then
repeated, 'all in the cause of improving international re-lations . . .'

There followed a three-hour interval before his next utterance.

'What's that banging inside my head – billiard balls or trago? Hey, man, we gotta get out of this place. I can't take no more of this trago stuff. What the hell do they put in it to make your head pound like this?'

And we moved out that same day. We found a place overlooking the market, which at least only disturbed the peace on Saturdays.

It was not unusual for us volunteers, as we searched among our store of family reminiscences for points of light to guide us through unknown territory, to bestow upon our absent parents a respect never accorded in their presence. Paul was particularly fond of home-spun philosophy. At the suggestion of anything unorthodox, he would say, 'Never do anything you can't get a shot for – that's what my old pappy used to say,' and then he would add emphatically: 'Sounds like pretty good advice to me.'

But he was a clean-living fellow anyway and he never did anything that you *could* get a shot for either. I recall one occasion when a couple of the other volunteers asked us if we wanted to go over to the whorehouse with them.

'Not me,' replied Paul, and then added, paraphrasing his father's words of wisdom: 'Never do anything you might get shot for – that's what my old pappy used to say. Sounds like pretty good advice to me.'

'How about you, Rick?' asked Chuck, one of the volunteers.

'No thanks,' I replied, and then added pointlessly, 'I've had my share of intellectualism for a while.'

'You'd better believe it,' Chuck came back. 'The one I had the other night was so dumb, she reminded me of the joke – you know, the one about the whore who couldn't spell and went to work in a warehouse. Man, that chick was so dumb, I don't think I could take another night like that. Think I'll give it a miss too.'

We never did get to see the whorehouse, not even from the outside, which is not altogether surprising given that it was situated a few respectful miles from town and hidden away behind a clump of eucalyptus, and I feel as if we might have missed out on something fundamental about Riobamba. After all, it was here that half the male population, usually at the behest of an uncle or an elder brother, learned the facts of life. It certainly wasn't at school, or anywhere else in this sternly regimented society where family honour still depended on a woman's chastity. But 'the Paradise Hotel' was always there, lurking in the background, even if seldom referred to by name, and consequently the opportunity was always there as well, but we never did go, and I occasionally find myself wondering whether our 'education' might not have suffered as a result.

But Paul was in love – madly in love – with a girl back home. He loved her so much that I could never work out why he came to Ecuador in the first place. He wrote to her at least once a day and received as many letters in return – though all of them arrived in a bundle on Thursday evenings; and he would lie on his bed for hours, listening over and over to his tape of *Man of La Mancha*, a show they had been to see together shortly before he left for training in Montana.

Seeing him smitten like this put me in mind of the old war films and how the 'boys overseas' would cling to their photos of the 'girl back home', and live from one letter to the next – but they had no choice. Paul did, and still he chose to come. I always assumed – I never actually asked – that Peace Corps was something he just felt he had to do and that they had decided between them that he'd better go and get it over with, rather than spend the rest of his life lamenting a missed opportunity.

I guess neither of us wanted it said, but we both knew he wouldn't be staying long. If his job with Radiofónicas had been up to scratch he would probably have soldiered on for a while longer, but as it was, he had no real reason to stay. He was a serious, church-going fellow, with a strong sense of responsibility. There was this great magnet up north pulling at him and there was no counterforce down south to hold him back; and his Peace Corps pay cheque, which kept arriving with embarrassing regularity, only served to remind him how little he was actually doing.

I knew when the moment had arrived. When the Peace Corps Director came to visit, as he did every so often, Paul requested 'early termination'. It came as no surprise to the director, since his volunteers were terminating in large numbers all over the place, largely because most of them, like Paul, did not have a genuine job of work to do. He gave the nod of approval and Paul immediately set about organizing his exit.

The first thing he did was to empty his trunk — mostly in my direction. He had always been concerned by the fact that the one British volunteer in the country had arrived without a medical kit (his was the size of a suitcase), twelve injections, a sleeping bag or a locker with over a hundred books in it — not to mention the infrastructural support of four Field Offices, a doctor, and several nurses. He put to rights as much of this deficiency as he could, and then we spent the next couple of days filling his trunk again with the best that Ecuador had to offer in the way of tapestries, ponchos, shawls and carvings; and then we sent it back whence it had come only a few months earlier, to upstate New York.

A group of us went with him to Quito to put him on the 'Ten o'clock Braniff' — the morning flight to Miami that had become both the symbol of escape from a frustratingly unproductive existence and the promise of a long-dreamed-of home-coming. It all seemed so simple, and I found myself reflecting on the fact that so much preparation, commitment and goodwill had been allowed to end so unceremoniously. Like many others he had come in like a lion, in a blaze of attention and excitement, and now he was going out like a llama, in quiet anonymity.

We watched him climb the steps to the aircraft, then turn and give a final, perfunctory wave and disappear inside. We turned also, in silence, and headed back into town to the bus station, feeling as if part of our heritage had been taken from us.

When I reached the apartment several hours later, the place felt indescribably empty. Every floorboard seemed to creak with loneliness, and I realized how much I was going to miss having him around. But I realized too that for the first time in my life I was about to live alone, and I wasn't at all sure if I liked the idea.

It's funny how things come together sometimes. I received a letter
from Paul some nine months later, the very day I was pulling up
stakes to leave Riobamba myself. It was his first in reply to several I
had written – and his last. It was little more than a note, which said
he had returned home to find that his girl had been carrying on
with someone else. He sounded thoroughly depressed, and with
reason. In one fell swoop, he had lost Peace Corps, Ecuador, and
the woman around whom his plans for the future revolved. And I
wondered too, if he suspected, as I did, that he had missed out on a
friendship that would have lasted a lifetime.

PART II

NATIVE AMERICANS

CHAPTER FOUR

AN INDIAN
PERSPECTIVE

MONSEÑOR PROAÑO'S concern for native Americans was well-founded, though precious few of his fellow countrymen could see it at the time. The Indians sensed in their bones that the order of things was somehow wrong, horribly wrong, and they flocked to Radiofónicas in droves for the helping hand that was being extended to them for the first time.

For once there was an institution for the Indian farmer which, instead of treating him with disdain, actually welcomed him, dirty and unkempt as he invariably was, and made him feel as if he belonged. An institution that offered him help of the kind he badly needed, with no strings attached – a health centre run by friendly, efficient nuns who charged next to nothing; credit on the easiest of terms to buy seed, fertilizer and tools for his farm, and technical assistance to go along with it at no extra cost; a store where he could buy basic commodities – food, soap, kerosene for his lamps, batteries for his radio – at prices lower than elsewhere; a radio station that broadcast programmes for him and him alone, and in his own language. Quechua, he had always been led to believe, was of no consequence for it had never been written down and was the language of a backward people. But here was an institution that offered him the chance of escaping from the scourge of illiteracy, an incontrovertible proof of his inferiority in the eyes of the world; above all, it offered him hope that things could, despite all the evidence to the contrary, get better.

Those who feared the consequences of Monseñor's radicalism were right in a sense, for the social order was never to be the same again. The seeds planted in the sixties, reinforced by the Agrarian Reform Act and supported by a number of national and international agencies thereafter, were to bring forth a new awareness of social justice that has changed the face of Ecuador, and to the country's credit the violent clashes so commonplace and ruinous in neighbouring Peru, and to some extent in Bolivia too, have yet to happen here.

But at the same time the final reckoning has yet to be made, and one would be foolish to predict the outcome in advance, for although considerable progress has been achieved over the past thirty years, there is still a long way to go. Some of the basic questions have yet to be answered, and the relative calm of today could easily turn into the all-consuming conflagration of tomorrow. One such question, that of to whom the continent actually belongs, has never been fully resolved as far as the Indians are concerned – especially some of the Amazonian groups who were never conquered at any time – and it needs to be, if true integration and stability are to be attained.

Radiofónicas was at the vanguard of this process and sought by peaceful means to bring about what others elsewhere have tried to bring about by violence. The state has also been supportive and there is probably not a great deal more that it can do from a legal perspective, given that the Indian, in theory, has just about the same rights as everyone else. Converting these rights into equal opportunity is what really counts, however, and this is another matter entirely, and depends upon the extent to which ordinary citizens, and the judiciary, are prepared to recognize the justice of the Indian cause and back it with affirmative action.

Those with the power to implement change invariably have most to lose, and they may well choose to allow personal interest to override any sense of right or wrong. Even now, there is a paranoia emerging amongst the middle and upper classes as they imagine having their homes, businesses and daughters snatched from them by hordes of machete-wielding Indians. In some quarters, therefore, a hardening and a polarization of attitudes is taking place.

There is no denying that the Indian is still treated badly, although the abuse he suffers now is usually more subtle and is becoming more akin to the silent discrimination that Blacks have come to know so well in Europe and the United States. Such is the state of Indian distrust and subservience, especially amongst the older folk, that an Indian will seldom look you in the eye when you are talking; he will either look past you, or more likely, at your feet. And neither has he forgotten the primary rule of the serf's trade – always give the answer that the 'patrón' wants to hear. He knows only too well that he still has bosses, even if they come in the guise of government officials and expatriate development workers. I discovered this habit early on in my time at Radiofónicas when I asked a *campesino* what language they spoke in his village, which we were about to visit.

'Castellano, pues, patroncito,' he replied, but I barely heard a word of Spanish all the time we were there.

Twenty-five years ago abuse was openly verbal and physical, and the humiliation that went with it was equally open. I have seen Indians deliberately left miles from their villages simply because the bus driver couldn't be bothered to stop; I have seen fare-paying Indians made to give up their seats to 'blancos' and sent to the back of the bus; I have seen sober, work-soiled Indians thrown out of shops as if they were drunks, and at other times I have seen them reviled publicly for no reason at all. And all of this – in days when not just in theory but also in practice they had access to land titles and basic rights of citizenship – they suffered in silence. But it was not the silence of dignity; it was the silence of a people who have been stripped of every vestige of self-esteem.

I don't recall ever having seen an African or a West Indian so visibly cowed as a result of humiliation suffered at the hands of their colonial masters, and certainly nothing that can compare to the behaviour of an Ecuadorean Indian in the presence of virtually any 'blanco'. He will instinctively call you 'doctor' or 'engineer', and accord you the corresponding respect, simply because your skin is lighter in colour than his and you happen to be wearing a half-decent set of clothes. Indeed, even the most deprived, under-represented Africans and West Indians have always struck me as being impressively self-assured by comparison. And the North American Indian too, while admittedly wrestling with serious identity and alcohol problems, appears to have fared somewhat better.

This overt degradation of a whole people is a curious phenomenon to witness and you wonder just how the people cope. Theirs is a state of mind that results from living for five hundred years without hope and energy. For some people it is incomprehensible and they condemn the Indian for it — 'a feckless rabble', as a university lecturer of mine once called them. But such people, like those who confidently state that 'the underdeveloped nations of the world should pull themselves up by their boot-straps', have never experienced such a condition even momentarily, and lack the ability to imagine it.

Such short-sighted criticism is not restricted to the remote and the academic. I have heard educated Ecuadoreans criticizing the United States for its racism, without realizing that the abuse of the Indian in their own midst is many times worse. For me, the real tragedy of the Indian has always been that there has never existed, in any Latin American country, a ruling class with a conscience.

Although the British bore a heavy responsibility for the abomination of slavery, it was the white ruling class and their representatives in Parliament who eventually put an end to the practice. Of course there were a number of outstanding black leaders, and sustained, imaginative and telling resistance by the masses; also, industrialization and changing economic patterns undermined the demand for slaves. But the Slavery Bill, which was first presented to the British Parliament in 1810, became a reality in 1833 because enough people among the privileged classes cared sufficiently to do something about it.

The same cannot be said of Spain and Spanish America. In Cuba, for example, slavery was not abolished until some half a century later when the Spanish Empire was on its last legs. And in Ecuador, although officially abolished in 1852 – under direct pressure from Britain – this really only applied to those Blacks who were willing to enlist in the army or who had sufficient resources to 'go it alone'. True emancipation did not arrive until the Liberal Revolution had finally run its course in 1911, and the abolition of the *huasipungo* system – an alternative form of slavery whereby resident Indian peasants belonged body and soul to the property owner – only came with the Agrarian Reform Act of 1964.

In Latin America there has never been a significant element among the privileged classes prepared to extend a hand to the Indian and take up his cause. There have been isolated protests from a handful of brave clergymen and women, and from a number of equally courageous political and human rights activists. There have also been sporadic outbursts from students – for as long as they have remained students – and the eternal promises of the politicians, designed to disguise their spiritual bankruptcy, their unfailing graft and their total lack of interest in Indian affairs. In a sense, the courageous few who stand out like bright stars in a very dark night make matters worse, for without them there would be nothing to believe in at all and the charlatans would be stripped of every last thread of credibility.

Cultural idiosyncrasy must surely also play a part in this question of subservience – perhaps the long-suffering Asiatic, steeped in fatalism and imbued with a sense of hierarchy from time immemorial, is forever conditioned to obey without question the absolute power of the Incas and their successors. Was this the real explanation for the numerical impossibility of the Conquest – not the horses and the guns, nor the awesome sight of the Europeans, nor even the freak coincidence of a civil war that was dividing the empire, but the unthinkable seizure of the divinely ordained ruler, the Inca Atahualpa, without whose authority society could not function, so hierarchical had it become?

Yet there seems to be resistance in some quarters to taking such matters seriously, with those who perhaps fear being labelled 'racist' flatly refusing to acknowledge either that there are such things as 'cultural traits' at all, or that they can shape the destiny of a whole people. Salman Rushdie, for example, some time before his fall from grace, wrote that such generalizations as 'Blacks have rhythm' and 'Asians are hard-working' should be shunned on the grounds that they promote racial stereotypes. Anyone who has spent as little as half a day in Africa, however, can hardly fail to have noticed that Blacks do, indeed, 'have rhythm', in a way that Europeans and Asians generally do not. Admittedly, such observations may not hold good in every case, but then generalizations never do.

What I think we have to beware of is entering into a different and more damning type of prejudice by refusing to recognize the obvious because it does not fit in with some idealized view we have of the world. It is absurd to deny that there are cultural differences that set people (beautifully) apart. Racial stereotypes in themselves are harmless, and only become threatening when they are associated with prejudice. It is the emotions behind them that one needs to focus upon.

In the case of the Indian, there is the enduring effect of the collective trauma, the impact of which we cannot even begin to imagine, of seeing a whole world, a show-piece empire of some nine million – with a military elite that had conquered all before it – turned upside down, complete with gods, and reduced to a state of serfdom, virtually overnight. How would Europeans react, one might ask, if they awoke one morning to find that their social order, their science and technology, and their cosmology – such as it is – no longer existed?

I have also wondered about another possibility, as suggested by Richard Luxton in his intriguing book *Mayan Dream Walk*, that the Andean Indian might have been aware of something that still eludes us Europeans today. Perhaps, like the Maya before him, he understood from his prophesies that there would come a catastrophic defeat that he would be destined to endure until such time as he was released and returned to his rightful place among men. If such a conviction still exists among the Indians of the Ecuadorean Sierra, I suspect that it is more a matter of instinct than the conscious belief it apparently still is among certain of the Maya. Anyone who has spent much time among the American Indians will have discovered that they are tuned into something we know nothing about, and may well have wondered what it is that keeps them going in spite of everything.

Throughout Latin America from Mexico to Paraguay, wherever the Indian has survived in sufficient numbers, the most exquisite textiles are to be found. Traditional weaving techniques, most notably the back-strap loom, still operate in many areas, although European innovations have taken over in others. The vegetable dyes of ancient times have often managed to hold their own against modern chemicals, but vegetable fibres, with the notable exceptions of cotton and the ubiquitous sisal, have generally been replaced by alpaca, llama and sheep's wool, and – with increasing insistence – modern synthetic fibre. But the same animating spirit, skill and care, and often the same designs, are still much in evidence.

Traditional practices are deeply woven into the fabric of everyday life, from the tending of the sheep and llamas to the selling of finished products on the streets and in the markets. Weaving has traditionally been done at home by both men and women, while the animals are tended by the women and children, and the spinning left exclusively to the women and their daughters. It is rare to see an Indian female of any age in the *campo* who does not have a stick of raw wool protruding from her belt, like candy-floss, which she works constantly with both hands as she walks. Indeed, the abiding image of an Indian woman that I carry with me is of someone diminutive in stature, ageless, and secretive, with thick black hair falling liberally down from the brim of her hat over parchment cheeks, leaning forward under a burden of sorts – a child and some merchandise perhaps, both securely bound and hidden under a single wrap; her bare, cracked, usually trotting feet are just visible beneath the folds of a long black skirt, and there is the inevitable spindle, constantly bobbing and twisting.

Campesino woman – Guamote, Chimborazo Province   Photo R. G. Torske

It was the cotton mills of Lancashire with their cheap machine-produced textiles that first set in motion a trend still apparent today. Imported in bulk through Lima and the River Plate from the early nineteenth century onwards and distributed throughout much of South America, these textiles amounted to a death sentence for the ancient ways of the Indian, so that today it is as common in some communities to see baseball jackets, caps and shoes from Taiwan, as ponchos, hats and sandals from Ecuador.

It was not a sudden death, however, and for well over a hundred years it was business as usual. With a strong instinct for survival, and with precious little cash at their disposal, the Indians persisted and their compromised industries prevailed, turning out masterpieces one by one and in their own good time as if nothing had happened. Occasionally they even sold off their surplus wool to the very people who were threatening them with extinction. With the arrival of tourism in the 1950s and 60s, sales started to climb and there came a 'boom' of sorts, although this appears to be levelling off of late, and even to be in something of a decline.

Tourism has now become the victim of North American and European fears of drug cartels and terrorism; and, as Ronald Wright points out, tourists now have an obsessive fear of being 'ripped off', so they will often haggle for hours over the price of an exquisite blanket that costs no more than one night in a hotel, took weeks to make and will last a lifetime. In response, the Indian has tailored his work to accommodate this meanness, with the predictable result that a certain amount of what you see today lacks class. And with the revenue gained from the sale of his textiles to westerners, he is tending more and more to buy western clothing in return.

When the textile giants of Lancashire started complaining that their industries were being destroyed by cheap imports flooding in from the Far East, it was almost as if the wheel had turned full circle. Columbus may well have been hopelessly mistaken in thinking that he had reached India and referring to the inhabitants of the Americas as 'Indians', but from an ethnological point of view he was not too far off course because it was from Asia that they originally came.

The Chimborazo Indian has no name – he is called after a province which is called after a mountain. What collective identity he had was largely political and this easily gave way before the advancing armies of Inca Tupac Yupanqui, and then fell apart completely under the covetous gaze of the Spaniards, who soon took possession of his fertile land, established farms and set him to work. All that was left was a collection of odds and ends, the mere remnants of what had once been the Puruha Kingdom.

Even today there is little cohesion and sometimes no communication at all between neighbouring villages; and Indian dress reflects this fragmentation. There is a poncho that should be red but could easily be another colour; a hat that by custom is round and white, but is usually otherwise; and a hair-style that is frequently the creation of the nearest person with a pair of scissors.

In the Amazon region, where the Indians were able to remain beyond the reach of the invaders, their distinctive customs and languages stayed largely intact, although the missionaries and a dozen or more oil companies are currently doing their best to change all this. In the Sierra, however, it was a different story, and a curious one at that. The Incas did not impose their own language (probably Pukina) on the Empire, but preserved this among themselves as a royal prerogative, and chose instead to adopt a language already in use as a lingua franca throughout much of the Central Andes – Quechua. The presence of Quechua, which appears to have been developing for several hundred years before the Inca expansion of *circa* 1450, would tend to indicate the existence of a more extensive trading network than was originally supposed.

Hardly a trace of the original Ecuadorean languages of the Sierra, apart from a handful of place-names, survived the Inca presence. The Inca domination of the region was relatively short, ranging from a mere forty years in the case of the Cañari Indians to a maximum of eighty years elsewhere, and yet this appears to have been sufficient for the local languages entirely to disappear. We know that the Inca made the speaking of Quechua compulsory, and were not averse to shipping people *en masse* around the empire, and this can hardly have helped the survival of language; we know too that Spanish priests later took it upon themselves to learn Quechua and promote its use for the purpose of evangelizing. All the same, this does not adequately explain why these languages were surrendered so easily.

The local languages disappeared under what was admittedly a despotic but still a relatively constructive rule compared to that brought by the Spaniards later on; yet the adopted language of Quechua is still widely in use today after five centuries of uninterrupted Spanish presence. One might try to explain such a phenomenon as 'a deeply rooted instinct for cultural survival' or the 'marginalization of the rural classes' and the need of enslaved peoples to retain a language unintelligible to their masters. But the mystery remains. It is interesting too that so many groups, other than the Chimborazo Indians, retained their cohesion and much of their tradition despite this loss of language – language, along with land, is often seen as a primary condition for cultural survival.

Remnant or not, and despite the erosion of virtually every tangible aspect of his way of life, the Chimborazo Indian, like his indigenous cousins elsewhere, knows only too well that he is still an Indian and he chooses to remain apart from an existence that is not his and that he cannot trust. His resistance is both physical and psychological. For as long as he can, and until there is no alternative, he will resist the pressures to go to the city or the coast to live and work; and then, when he does, it is usually for the season only and, as if to prove something to himself, he dresses in his normal garb, in clothing that is conspicuous and often hopelessly inappropriate for the climate.

But sometimes the pain is too great and the struggle becomes a lost cause, and he is forced to cast in his lot and cross the divide once and for all. He moves to the town on a permanent basis, or, in more recent times, he migrates – illegally – to the United States. Such things would have been unthinkable twenty or even ten years ago, but today they are everyday occurrences.

Throughout the Sierra there are communities with hardly any adult males. They have all taken the Varig flight to Costa Rica and

made the hazardous trek north overland to Mexico and the Rio
Grande, entrusting their all to the 'coyotes', the men and women
who exploit their desperation and make capital from the traffic in
human lives. Such migrations are almost certainly without parallel
since the original trek south many thousands of years ago; what the
end result will be, and whether or not the Indian will survive his
total immersion in materialism, remains to be seen.

What we are really talking about is the survival of the human
spirit, both individual and communal, for although the former may
be ultimately indestructible the latter is not, and wherever the
economic base has been seriously compromised and normal living
rendered impossible the individual has become powerless to prevent
the break-up of the community and the dispersal of its people. It is
not a problem specific to the Americas, of course, but one that
afflicts the entire world, for the great tragedy of our time has been
the overwhelming triumph and spread of materialism and the conse-
quent damage to the spiritual side of our nature.

There is another side to the Indian character that reveals itself only
very rarely but causes the earth to shake when it does. It is a mixture
of popular justice and mob rule. Chimborazo is especially prone to
such convulsions and it was shortly before Easter in 1969, in one of
its more remote areas, that I saw it myself for the first and only time.

A number of communities had formed a co-operative and had
pooled their scarce resources so as to set up a communal store. The
idea is that the farmers buy in bulk and sell to individual members at
a price lower than they would have to pay elsewhere. One of the
commodities on sale was cooking gas, of the sort that is sold in
heavy metal cylinders. The gas itself didn't cost very much – no
more than fifty US cents – but the cylinders cost about twenty
dollars each. The co-operative had received a donation of several
thousand dollars from an American foundation and had purchased
eighty of these gas cylinders.

One night some thieves drove up to the unguarded store in a
truck and made off with all eighty cylinders. It is not difficult to

imagine the consternation of the farmers when they discovered what had happened – it was a tragedy of the highest order. They reported the theft to the police in a nearby town, but had little hope of the culprits being brought to justice or the cylinders being recovered. A few nights later two thieves attempted to rob a second community belonging to the same co-operative, with the intention of making off with a recently installed grinding mill, but on this occasion they were apprehended by the farmers, who promptly marched them off to the police station to be remanded in custody.

Criminal suspects are, to the police in Latin America, as flies to wanton boys – they use them for their sport, or their gain. Depending on how the mood takes them, they either beat them systematically, hang them from their thumbs and apply electrodes to tongues and genitals, or, if the suspects have enough money or influence, release them at once. Ecuadoreans say that 'la ley es para el de poncho' – 'the law only applies to those who wear a poncho'. On this occasion, influence prevailed because one of the accused happened to be related to one of the police officers. Both suspects were released the following day, because 'there was insufficient evidence to warrant their further detention', despite the fact that they had both been caught red-handed.

The Indians were enraged, and decided to take matters into their own hands. They seized the two for a second time and took them off to the room in their co-operative store where the gas cylinders had been kept, and there they bound them hand and foot and had someone stand guard over them until nightfall.

At one o'clock in the morning all the male members of the co-operative and some of the female members assembled at the store. They dragged the culprits to their feet and marched them off to a nearby lake which, being at an altitude of some 10,000 feet, was near freezing. They stripped the two of their clothes and plunged them into the water, and kept them there for a good few minutes until they confessed. Not only were these two the same ones who had stolen the gas cylinders, they were also part of a gang that had been operating up and down the Sierra for ten years or more.

Triumphant over the confessions, and still in the hours of darkness, the farmers returned to the police station to have their prisoners re-arrested. Their euphoria did not last long, however, because they learned that an order had been issued for the detention of their own co-operative leader and that he was to be placed under arrest 'for the abduction of two innocent citizens'. Not only were the two culprits not taken into custody but they were instantly released, and the co-operative president was locked up instead.

Word spread like wildfire through the communities and the Indians began to mass; and then they began to move. Like the first small stones dislodged from the mountain-top, they started to trickle down the hillsides, gathering volume and momentum as they went. Everywhere the call went out, and everywhere the call was heard. Men, women and children filtered in, swelling their numbers as they went, until they had become a veritable avalanche. The word 'hanging' was on everybody's lips. The hour of reckoning had come.

By the time they reached the police station, they were over a thousand strong, and the police sergeant was quaking in his boots. He sensed the mood of the lynch mob and began to plead – for reason, for justice, for his life. He reversed his two previous orders, having the co-operative leader released and the two suspects arrested. The Indians were partially appeased but still not satisfied. They would not trust this wretch of a law-enforcement officer any further, and so they seized the two culprits for a third time and dragged them off to the Criminal Investigation Department, where they handed them over to the state-sanctioned 'disciplinarians' whose methods of operation make the police seem quite reasonable.

The end result was that the accused confessed and, after the usual interminable bureaucratic delays, were given long prison sentences. The co-operative leader, on the other hand, was not troubled again. Now you may or may not feel that justice was done in this particular instance, but I think most people would agree that such behaviour can hardly be termed 'feckless' – 'a rabble', perhaps, but not 'feckless'.

Chapter Five

ALEJANDRO

I FELT AS IF I KNEW Alejandro well even before I met him, so frequently did his name crop up in conversation. Some of what you heard was fact, and some of it was fiction, but all of it was complimentary in one way or another. He was the 'golden boy' of both Radiofónicas and the Catholic Church at a time when the Church was keen to promote 'development' among the Indians, and he was the Indian with whom they felt they could do business. He was not only the village headman, he was also intelligent, articulate and good-humoured, and without any political ambitions that were liable to distance him from his benefactors or remove him from the local scene. He was first and foremost a Chimborazo Indian, and that was what he was likely to remain.

Among the volunteers who, admittedly, were somewhat prone to romanticize things Indian anyway, Alejandro was something of a legend. Somehow things just seemed to happen to him that served to create a mystique. There was the time, for example, when his children and his animals started to die off one by one. First the baby, then the next youngest, and then the calves, sheep and chickens, until he was at his wits' end, not knowing what to do, and convinced that he had been cursed.

As was the custom among his people in times of trial, he called in the local 'brujo' – the shaman – who lived in the next village and who also happened to be his uncle. The shaman arrived promptly and began to inspect the house and the farm like a hawk looking for vermin, bending low to the ground and staring intently at object after object, but being careful not to touch anything. After an hour or so he declared with confident authority that the problem was a sack of salt that was in the wrong place. The offending sack was immediately moved from one corner of the house to another and thereafter no more deaths occurred.

Later on, when I had come to know Alejandro a little better, I asked him if the story was true. His face wreathed in smiles as ever, he replied, 'Yes, Don Richard, it is true, quite true', but somehow I wasn't convinced. It seemed unlikely that the version as I heard it had not been embellished in some way or other, and yet he offered no correction, and added no detail. It was almost as if he was saying, 'Yes, my dear little gringo friend, that is about as much as you will ever understand of such things, so let us leave it there.'

I had calculated that he was probably in his late twenties, although it was never easy to judge the age of an Indian, so completely did childhood, adolescence and adulthood merge into a single process. From infancy they had their work to do, whether it was tending sheep or tending siblings, and recognition of their contribution was reflected in their dress, identical to that of adults – the girls with their long skirts, braids, shawls and women's hat, and the boys with their long trousers, ponchos and men's hat. And they were usually so muffled up against the elements that you seldom saw enough flesh to give you an inkling of how old they might be. What you did see – hands and face – was always so weather-beaten as to tell you practically nothing.

I doubt if Alejandro could have told you how old he was. Indians don't normally care very much about their age, tending to worry more about everyday realities than abstract measurements, and if you were insensitive enough to ask, he would probably tell you whatever he thought you wanted to hear. If you registered surprise, he would most likely revise it up or down by a few years, just to make you feel better. Such practices are so common that one feels bound to question a good many of the statistics contained in government documents, not least because quite often the Indians will not let the census-takers into the village in the first place, thereby compelling them to fill in their sheets with any old figures, just to save face.

Some years later I attended a lecture given by a prominent social anthropologist specializing in Andean affairs, who admitted his confusion over a particular set of statistics relating to Highland Peru, in which all the inhabitants of a certain village were given to be either 5, 10, 15, 20, 25, 30, 35, 40, 45 or 50 years old; and he concluded: 'Unless there has been some age-selective disease affecting the population, I feel a certain degree of doubt must be cast upon the accuracy of these figures.'

It was through Alejandro that many of us made our first contacts with the villages and subsequently established the friendships that meant so much to us. The first time I went to the *campo* myself was within a week or two of my arrival in Riobamba, when I attended the showing of a film on 'Mother and Child Health Care' that Radiofónicas had borrowed from the United States Information Service. We set out late one Friday afternoon in the Land Rover, loaded to the roof with projector, screen, generator, diesel, kerosene and people, and headed out from Riobamba along a narrow dirt road.

After an hour or two of slow, jolting motion, we ran out of track and had to get down and complete the rest of the journey on foot, hauling the equipment with us as we went. We were about ten in number when we set out, a mixture of mestizos, gringos and Indians, but as soon as we started to unload a couple more joined us, miraculously, from out of nowhere. Some sort of bush telegraph must have been at work because, as we trekked single file through the gathering darkness, our crocodile became ever longer. Whistles, shouts and torches signalled to huts I could not even see, telling where we were going and why, and all the while our number continued to grow.

We walked for three quarters of an hour or so, with the Indians, at their insistence, hauling the heavy equipment most of the way — we gringos occasionally flexed our muscles for a minute or two, then dropped our load with a melodramatic display of weakness that brought roars of laughter from the *campesinos*. I walked with Alejandro, intrigued by the softness of his and the other *campesinos'* voices as they chatted and laughed among themselves, just breaking away now and again to send a word or two of Quechua into the darkness in the direction of a friend. I learned my first words of Quechua that evening – 'Mayma ringi?' – 'Where are you going?'; 'Ima nallatakangi?' – 'How are you?'; 'Ima shutakangi?' – 'What's your name?'; and 'Allcu canicu!' – 'This dog bites!' – phrases that seemed charged with magic and have stayed with me over the years.

When we reached our destination we set the equipment down in the school and immediately lit half a dozen kerosene lamps of the sort made from soldered coffee tins that you could buy in the market. In the yellow flickering light I could see that the building was little more than a hut with a thatched roof and a beaten earth floor, and a dozen roughly cut wooden benches arranged to face the front. But at least the village *had* a school, and it also had a teacher, something even more surprising given that the majority of teachers usually refused to work outside the towns.

We fixed up the screen at one end of the schoolroom and balanced the projector on a bench at the other, and then waited for the place to fill up, which didn't take long, since we had brought most of the audience with us.

Alejandro introduced the meeting, speaking first in Quechua, and then in Spanish for our benefit. 'Good evening brothers and sisters,' he began. 'These kind gentlemen have come to our little community to show us a nice little film that tells us how we must keep our little children and ourselves in good health.'

The place was now packed and everyone was eager for something to happen, although they probably didn't know what exactly – most of them never having seen a film before. We managed to start the generator after half a dozen agonizing pulls at the starter cord and then switched on the machinery. The spools jerked into life, the speaker spat and crackled, and the lights flashed on with painful brilliance. 'Thank goodness', I breathed to myself, 'it's working.'

Campesino family – Colta, Chimborazo Province   Photo R. G. Torske

The film had been shot in a small Peruvian village high in the Andes. Its message, reinforced by white giants dressed in what looked like moon-suits and divers' helmets, was that little insects that hide in the mud and thatch can cause disease, and so the best way to deal with them is to fumigate everything in sight. For a few minutes there was a fragile silence as the campesinos adjusted to what was going on – and then the dam broke. Seeing their fellow Indians with their little ponchos, their little children and their little animals, up there on the screen alongside the gringos, was just too much. The nudges became giggles, and the giggles became snorts, and the snorts became guffaws, and soon the whole place was convulsed in hysterics. And that was how it stayed for the full thirty minutes of the film.

Alejandro moved to the front to address the crowd, the yellow light of the lamps barely picking out his aquiline features as he spoke. 'Well, my dear brothers and sisters, did you like this good little film that these kind gentlemen from Radiofónicas have brought us?' he asked.

Another outburst of excited laughter told us that they had, although whether their appreciation had anything to do with the object of the film was extremely doubtful. Still, who cared? A relationship had been formed and history had been made in the community. The *campesinos* would talk about 'the day the movies came to the village' for generations to come, and that was surely enough for one day.

When everyone had gone home, Alejandro led us to a small concrete-block house that he told us belonged to the teacher, who had gone away to spend the weekend in his own community. Half a dozen of us who had travelled out from Radiofónicas bedded down in the same room, rolling out our sleeping bags on the rush mat over the earth floor, and rolling up another such mat to use as a communal pillow. I didn't sleep a great deal, although it was more the excitement that kept me awake than the spartan conditions. I lay there wrapped in my sleeping bag under a blanket of darkness, reliving the moments of the day and trying hard to recall and interpret every detail of what I had seen. And when I did finally drop off, it was not for long. I was awakened by a scratching sound close to my ear – directly beneath it, in fact. I tried to ignore it, but it wouldn't go away – at least not very far, and then only to return a few seconds later.

I never did see the culprit, but I deduced that a mouse, or something like it, must have found its way into the rolled-up tube of the mat and was scurrying back and forth from one end to the other. I smiled and thought kindly of the little beast, telling myself that he was probably as upset about the intrusion as I was, and then allowed myself to float away on a cushion of contentment until the morning came.

The day dawned damp and cold. We had climbed several hundred feet in the darkness and you could feel the difference in the biting freshness of the air. I stepped carefully over a sleeping body, trying not to wake the others, and slipped outside to have a look at our surroundings.

What I saw was eerie. Everywhere about me cloud was snaking up from the ground in twisted spirals, as if the grass was on fire. Dark green valleys plunged down and out of sight, swallowed up in the banks of mist that clung limply to the contours of the slopes below. Over to my right, wood-smoke was seeping steadily through the thatch of a rooftop, winding its way upwards and into the leaden mass that hung ominously overhead.

I was about to turn back inside, when I caught sight of something moving through the mist down below. I fixed my gaze on it for a second and was able to make out the form of a man climbing awkwardly up the slope. He appeared to be carrying something large and cumbersome on his back, making the ascent difficult. A few feet more and I saw clearly what it was – it was a table, and a large one at that, tied in such a way that the legs were pointing outward from his body. He was also carrying something in his hands. Since he was heading in my direction, I decided to climb down the hundred feet or so to meet him, and offer some assistance. As I reached him, he smiled apologetically, and said, 'Good day, patroncito. How has the day broken for you?'

'Good morning,' I replied, 'I am fine. And how has the day broken for you? Can I help you at all?'

'Don't trouble yourself, little gringo. Thanks be to little God I am almost there,' he answered breathlessly.

We completed the last stretch of the climb together and then, unfastening the large knot that was tied across his chest, he released the table, which I took and righted just outside the door of the house. What he had been carrying in his hands was a canteen of hot milky coffee. This he placed on the table and turned immediately to make his way back down the slope.

'What a miracle of God!' I exclaimed, to express my deep appreciation for his kindness – there was nothing in the world I wanted more at that moment than a cup of coffee. 'Are you not going to drink with us, little brother?' I asked, knowing full well what the answer would be.

He hesitated for a second, being careful as always to keep his gaze from mine, then replied, 'May God reward you, little sir,' and then added as an after-thought: 'So that you do not think too badly of us.'

And with that he turned and headed back down into the valley from whence he came. I stood and watched him as he picked his way over the rough terrain, nimble now without his load, until the mist had finally claimed him.

It has become something of an axiom in the field of community development to say that one should work through existing structures. As the colonial powers discovered, you are far more likely to get results if you incorporate the local chief into your hierarchy, than if you by-pass and alienate him. The development agencies and the Church generally understood this, but they often overdid it.

Among the Indian farmers the headman was just a man like all the rest who had earned a degree of trust from his fellows that authorized him to speak on their behalf. It was understood that this responsibility might bring the odd bonus now and then, like being invited to a conference in some other part of the country, but nothing that would compromise the brotherhood and unity that prevailed among the villagers. The respect that his position carried, in fact, was derived in great part from his humility, and this quality, so deeply rooted in Indian life, was the guarantee of stability.

The development workers, particularly the expatriates, often misread the nature of this leadership role and sought to 'reward' it – as was the custom back home – and caused a good deal of disruption in the process. Where the attention and favours shown to the headman were excessive, the initial embarrassment could very easily turn to jealousy and then schism, threatening the survival of the very social fabric the development workers needed to build upon. The problem was invariably compounded by the fact that these same workers were rarely around long enough to see the fruits of their labours, so that each new generation of 'helpers' would arrive and stay just as long as it took to repeat the mistakes of their predecessors.

About six months after our 'film show', Alejandro was flown to the United States to assist with the orientation of Peace Corps volunteers. The predictable result was that, having seen 'Paree' he was

no longer quite so interested in 'the farm', and he soon began to
show signs of restlessness. The Church, too, was dangling all sorts
of quasi-political carrots in front of him, and although none of it
actually amounted to a salaried post, it all served to undermine his
standing in the community and to sow seeds of confusion in his
soul.

Unfortunately, it did not stop at Alejandro, because other
Indians were also invited abroad, and not just by the Peace Corps
but by a variety of other organizations too – all of them believing
that there was much to be gained from such visits. All sorts of apoc-
ryphal stories began to spring up around these visitors, like the
Shuar Indian who disappeared from his hotel in Los Angeles only to
be found a day later hunting for deer along the freeway with his
blow-pipe. Such stories are nonsense, of course, and insulting at the
same time, but they are not without a point – the point being the
astonishing insensitivity of 'hosts' who had no idea what life would
be like for the Indian returning to his village.

Such gestures of 'co-operation' are, thankfully, no longer fash-
ionable, and the realization is taking hold that development,
whatever path it happens to take, needs sensitivity, patience and,
above all, respect. The conclusion I finally came to is that the
bridge of communication for all the skills and knowledge necessary
to a people's empowerment must be built painstakingly of friendship
and trust. It takes time and it demands the sharing of experience at
first hand. There is no room for short-cuts, and communication will
surely never come about if the 'developers' and the 'developed' move
in circles that barely touch.

This has been the case with daunting regularity until now, I
believe, firstly because most expatriates, for reasons of privilege and
opportunity, hail from middle-class backgrounds and have scant
understanding of the poor man's perspective in their own country,
let alone in someone else's; and secondly, because a good many have
been attracted overseas for the wrong reasons, most notably good
salaries, exotic settings, pleasant climates and the opportunity for
travel – with little genuine interest in relieving the plight of the

poor. When the hunger and want finally disappear, as one day they surely must, each and every one of us will be called upon to look to his condition, for at the heart of development generally I believe I can detect a murmur of escapism.

In some ways the missionaries came closer to 'getting it right' in that many of them were prepared to roll up their sleeves and work, and indeed live, side by side with the local people; unfortunately their dogma frequently got in the way and prevented them from seeing the native people as true equals. The disastrous attempt to evangelize among the Huaoranis in the mid-fifties led to the deaths of several protestant missionaries and the near destruction of an ancient way of life in the Amazon rain forest. Rachel Saint, the sister of the late mission leader, is known to have expressed her regret about the whole enterprise some twenty years later – a view that was echoed in impeccable American English by a Huaorani who had been removed from his home environment when still an infant by this same mission and taken to the United States to be 'educated'; thereafter he was trotted out before congregations as a shining example of a 'saved soul'.

I fear, however, that we are in for a new wave of protestant zealotry as North American evangelists, promoting a bewildering number of sects, seek to spread the Gospel to the furthest corners of the earth in a way that they believe will hasten the return of Christ. Their presence in Latin America is growing by the day.

Alejandro was more fortunate than his Huaorani counterpart. In time, the focus of the development agencies switched elsewhere and he was allowed the space he needed to return to normal living. When I visited him many years later, I found him still working his farm and representing his fellow *campesinos* in a number of useful ways.

He greeted me cordially but politely, exhibiting the diffident courtesy that Indians always reserve for Whites.

'Thanks be to little God that you have returned safely,' he said calmly, as if I had just returned from a trip to town.

'It has been a long time, Alejandro,' I said, 'over twenty years. Many times I have wondered about you and your dear family. I have thought of you often.'

'Ah, we are fine, little Richard, we are all very fine – thanks be to our dear Lord Jesus Christ.'

We did not have a great deal to say to each other in fact, and in the event we did little more than exchange a few courtesies. I did not strive to rekindle old memories, nor to reactivate a friendship that I knew had been largely circumstantial, for I well understood that the gap between us was not so much twenty years as twenty centuries. And yet, as I stood there listening to the rise and fall of his Indian Spanish, the thought flashed through my mind that twenty years had not passed between us at all, nor had twenty days, nor even twenty minutes – in fact, no time had passed between us. It was a feeling that I was to have over and over again as I found acquaintances from the past, and it was only by looking at the children who had come along in the meantime that I was able to reassure myself that the calendar had not lied and I had not dreamt the whole thing.

My reunion with Alejandro was framed in classic Indian surrealism. He was perfectly well aware of who I was, and his recollections were every bit as good as mine, yet there was nothing in his manner to indicate that he found anything unusual in my reappearance after so many years. I began to wonder whether he and his fellow Indians might be operating in some other dimension, where time is meaningless and relationships are forever, and that this was the reason they seldom seemed to express surprise at anything.

Within their predominantly spiritual scheme of things there is no separation of either time or space, living or dead, and all things belong together in an eternally meaningful present, as is believed to be the case with certain other indigenous groups in the world, such as the Australian Aborigines and the Kalahari Bushmen. But the Andean Indian had once evolved a sophisticated and complex society, and his sense of the past was acute, all of which indicate a breaking away from a sense-dominated relationship with the environment towards the ascendancy of the intellect. This was cut short in 1532 with the Spanish landfall, and thereafter nothing was ever the same again – the very earth on which he stood was no longer his to control. The tiny parcel of land that he owns and works today has been his for barely twenty years and who knows who might come along tomorrow and take it from him again? With his material world in ruins he no longer has the measure of time – his historical clock has stopped and he is left adrift in a hostile land, with his only avenue of escape a retreat into the intuitive values of the spirit.

In some way or other, therefore, Alejandro had seen it all before – and if not any one particular set of circumstances, then the sum of what these circumstances added up to; and he had become conditioned to accept, with the same unruffled acquiescence, whatever befell him, whether it was the announcement of Judgement Day or a drop in the price of potatoes.

I should have been prepared too, for the fact that he barely looked a day older. Indeed, the more I thought about it, the more astonished I became – the man was ageless – and it was only with the greatest difficulty that I managed to convince myself that twenty years really had passed by.

CHAPTER SIX

THE GAME AT
COLUMBE

ISTILL REMEMBER the photograph that Jethro took. Ten diminutive Indians standing in line, their hats removed for the occasion, their faces wide open with honesty, their arms tightly folded with earnest intent and their chests puffed out with obvious pride. Of what were they so proud, I now ask myself? Of being in the team, perhaps, and having all the kit except the boots? Of having laid out the pitch and found goal-posts for both ends? Or perhaps it wasn't pride at all so much as a kind of gratefulness of being, like the nightingale when it sings at dawn, bursting with the excitement of the new day.

And there I stand among them, like a monument to western decadence, anaemically white, hair unkempt, hands thrust somewhat obscenely down inside my shorts in the latest macho fashion, and the Donald Duck tee-shirt that I wore out of some misguided sense of carnival and which provided apt comment on my relevance to the occasion.

But in spite of it, I can still look back with thankfulness on a day that sparkled with freshness like few others, and on the lessons that it brought.

The Indians of Columbe village had formed a soccer team and the Peace Corps Volunteer who worked there, Jethro, had asked me if I would come over one day when I had nothing better to do and give them some coaching. Jethro knew next to nothing about our variety of football – although he tried hard to learn – and now that I had joined a local team and was playing in the national league, he thought that a 'guest appearance' might provide some useful encouragement. At all events, it seemed an agreeable thing to do, to spend a few hours kicking a ball around in the peace and quiet of the *campo* and teaching a few of the basics of a game I had loved for so many years.

And so it was that, at the crack of dawn one public holiday in early November, I took leave of Radiofónicas and met up with Jethro at the railway station where we boarded the six-o'clock train for Guayaquil, getting off in Columbe, some fifteen miles away, three hours later.

There was always at least one major breakdown somewhere between Riobamba and Guayaquil, and the general feeling was that the company liked to get it over with as soon as possible – preferably before they reached Columbe – so that the passengers could then sit back and enjoy the rest of the journey in peace. Our delayed arrival, therefore, surprised no one. Furthermore, our sluggish pace and our triumphant whistle-blasts gave the *campesinos* ample warning of our approach, and by the time we pulled into the station, which was a surprisingly serious brick and wrought-iron affair, just about every male inhabitant of Columbe was there to greet us.

I should have suspected, then and there, that it would turn out to be more than just a simple coaching session, but I didn't, and we strolled off across the dew-drenched grass through the morning mist into the village, gaily chatting and laughing, and covering the 200 yards or so in better time than the train.

Columbe is a fairly ordinary village in most ways except that it is a little bigger than average, with a population of about a thousand. It did not strike me as anything unusual, therefore, that a number of people should have been milling around at that time of the morning; and it was only when we reached the square and the band struck up that I realized something was afoot. The suspicion was confirmed a moment later when a reception committee appeared from nowhere and the village headman stepped forward

and launched into an interminably long speech, addressing every
dignitary within a hundred miles, and thanking me for the honour
that this 'famous footballer from the United States of England' had
bestowed upon his humble village by agreeing to come and play an
'exhibition match'.

'Jethro!' I exclaimed. 'What is this? What did you tell them? I
thought I was coming here to give them a spot of coaching.'

'Beats me,' he replied, sucking in his cheeks and looking
skywards. 'That's exactly what I told them – that a friend of mine
who plays for Olmedo was coming down to organize a spot of
coaching. But you know how things are down here, they always get
so excited about everything. They probably announced it over the
radio and then got carried away with it all. These local radio
stations make a big deal out of everything. I mean, the other week
they even announced that the padre's donkey had broken its leg, for
heaven's sake. And anyway, man, let's not be too modest about it; I
mean it's a big thing, you know – a gringo playing in the national
league. I mean you British are supposed to be the champions or
something, aren't you? Didn't you win some soccer competition a
couple of years back?'

'The English, Jethro – the *English*,' I replied coldly. 'The British
don't have a team. And it was the *World Cup* – and no, I wasn't
actually on the team.'

'Anyway, man, just enjoy it. This is a big day for them, so we'd
better not let them down.'

'*We?*' I said incredulously. 'Just what part are you playing in all of
this?'

'Listen, amigo, I'm out here living with these people – five days
a week. If we don't produce the goods it's going to look bad. I mean,
I'm going to have to face them tomorrow. You'll be OK. You'll be
back in Radiofónicas advertising batteries and fertilizer over the
radio. But not me. I'll be here, in the thick of it. Just think about
that. And anyway, what's the big deal? A bunch of Indians who
don't know one end of a ball from the other – you should be able to
run rings around them.'

'The ball doesn't have ends, it's *round*, Jethro!' I retorted, and then turned my attention to the pitch.

It was clearly undersized by a long way and was distinguishable from the surrounding terrain only by the rustic poles standing at either end. The playing surface consisted of cow-pats and rocks, mounds of earth, great tufts of grass every few feet, pot-holes, and a megalith near where the penalty spot should have been.

'They didn't, by any chance, say where it was the donkey broke its leg, did they?' I asked miserably as I headed off in the direction of the schoolroom where the rest of the team were now beckoning me to go and get changed.

By the time I emerged a transformation had taken place. Along one side of the pitch, as if to mark the touchline, was a row of Indian women, all wrapped in their red *bayetas* and wearing round, white, stiff-brimmed hats. They sat peacefully on the damp grass, talking in hushed tones, undisturbed by the innumerable children of various sizes who hung about them – always in complete silence. Along the other touchline were the men and the boys, dressed similarly in red ponchos and white hats, laughing and chatting noisily and passing a glass around, many of them puffing heavily on rough cigarettes.

Over behind one of the goals, where a couple of cauldrons stood steaming over wood-fires, the mingled scent of pork and eucalyptus was floating into the morning air. The sun was now piercing the mist, bringing welcome warmth; and then, almost imperceptibly, the women started their soft Quechua songs, gently, politely, in unison, but with the sadness that haunts all Indian music. I could feel my resentment and apprehension ebbing away from me until I no longer cared whether I lived up to expectations or not – and I felt a little ashamed that I had ever cared in the first place. I was now inclined to believe that the day would be writing its own version of events, regardless.

A team from a neighbouring village had been invited as the opposition, and I had been drafted into the Columbe side. I protested to the captain that I ought to take the whistle, or at least

change sides at half-time, but he seemed so upset by the suggestion
that I dropped it at once. I was to play for Columbe, and that was
the end of it; and besides, it had been announced over the radio and
that somehow made it legal.

The captain, who also happened to be the village headman,
looked to be in his forties, although as ever, he probably couldn't
have told you how old he was. And it is a curious thing – something
I saw on various other occasions too – that he played with the
energy and vigour of a man half his age, right to the very last
minute of the game, so that I couldn't help wondering whether
there might not be a fairly strong case to be made in defence of
innumeracy.

He called the two sides together and spoke to them like a
boxing referee.

'Now, we all know the rules, so we want a good clean game. OK?'

'Ari! Ari!' they cried unanimously. 'Yes! Yes!'

'Right!' said the captain, and at his bidding both teams took off
the hats they were still wearing, linked arms and formed a big circle,
and then, bowing their heads towards the centre, chanted 'Amistad!
Amistad! Amistad!' – 'Friendship! Friendship! Friendship!' at the tops
of their voices.

'OK,' said the captain, 'let's go!'

'Hold on a second,' I interrupted. 'What position is everybody
playing? And what about a referee?'

'Just play wherever you want,' replied the captain obligingly.

'Well, what about the referee, then?' I insisted.

The captain looked puzzled. 'What do we need a referee for?' he
asked. 'We all know the rules.'

A spectator threw the ball onto the pitch, everyone ran after it,
and the game was under way. The men on the line started cheering
but kept on drinking, while the women on the other side switched
to hymns but kept on singing, and all the while hordes of eager
Indians, their hats miraculously stuck to their heads, wheeled freely
around in pursuit of the ball like a flock of migrating swallows in
search of its bearings.

'My God,' I thought, 'I can't play like this. I'll get murdered.'

I decided to withdraw from the line of battle and make encouraging comments to the others, as if I had understood my role to be that of honorary coach with the interests of the locals at heart. But it was no good. The ball was hoofed in my direction, the crowd became ecstatic, and it was instantly clear that I was to be Columbe's not-so-secret weapon. I controlled the ball after a fashion and was immediately ambushed by eleven frantic pairs of feet, all snapping away at my ankles like piranhas. I pivoted deftly, tripped over a grassy mound and went headlong in the mud, besmirching Donald Duck in the process.

I looked over in Jethro's direction with murderous intent, but he was busily chatting to someone standing next to him on the line and didn't even notice.

'I'll get him,' I told myself icily, as I picked myself up; 'I'll get that yankee son-of-a-bitch if it's the last thing I do!'

But things got better after that. The charge of the dark brigade eventually lost some of its steam, leaving me just enough room to manoeuvre, and towards the end I even managed to score. I struck a loose ball from about where the half-way line would have been and watched with relief as it sped goalwards. A deeply rooted and panic-stricken goalkeeper waved his arms in a frantic kind of semaphore designed to send the ball elsewhere, but to no avail. The ball whistled over the 'keeper's head and ran out into the swamp behind him. I suspect that the presence of a cross-bar would have ruled it out, but the crowd was uninterested in such niceties.

'Goooooooool!' yelled the whole of Columbe. 'Goooooooool!' yelled the opposition; and twenty-one players descended on me, slapping me on the back, congratulating me and waving their hats in the air — all of which was extremely gratifying. What concerned me a little, though, was the fact that one of the most vocal among my fans was the opposing goalkeeper; that seemed to undermine the point of it all somewhat.

I don't think anybody ever really knew for sure what the score was, but it must have been in the region of nine—all when the

Columbe captain decided to call it a day. We all shook hands, chanted 'Amistad!' a few more times, and walked off in the direction of the fried pork. Jethro came striding over to tell me that the spectators were already recounting my exploits and that I was about to enter local mythology.

'Worst game of my life,' I confessed truthfully.

'Are you serious?' he exclaimed with disbelief. 'Another goal like that and you'd have been up there with Atahualpa.'

From the reaction of the people, I could see that he was telling the truth; they seemed determined to applaud whatever I did, presumably thinking that, if *I* did it, being from the land of the world champions and playing in the national league, it had to be good – even if it included tripping over a grassy mound and sprawling head-first in the dirt. I could have fallen asleep on the touchline and they would still have been pleased. Jethro was right – I needn't have worried; but I felt uneasy about it all the same. I couldn't work out which was worse – disappointing their expectations or being accorded a reputation I didn't deserve. In the end, I decided to live for the moment and opted for the latter, and strolled casually over towards the acclaiming fans, and my plate of pork and potatoes.

The din was almost deafening as spectators and players alike vied with one another in recounting their favourite moments amid gales of unremitting laughter; my own name, I noticed, cropped up time and again amid the excited babble of Quechua, although in what connection exactly, I was unable to discern. And needless to say, mixed in with it all, there was the customary element of Indian enigma.

'I knew it was going to go well for us', I overheard our jubilant captain confidently informing a captive audience, 'when I dreamt last night that the pigs were eating tall grass.'

We had a few hours to wait for the evening train back to town and so we took our time. We gratefully devoured the food, and launched ourselves wholeheartedly into the dancing, but we declined the ever-circulating glass of trago, hiding behind the only available excuse that 'we were on medication and that it was against doctor's orders'. It was only on the grounds of probable and imminent death that one might be excused from this relentless descent into paralysis. Jethro even carried a small bottle of white pills around with him to produce on such occasions as evidence, and he had perfected a traumatized look to go with it that managed, in one astonishingly agonized grimace, to convey both his regret at not drinking and his unspeakable contempt for the medical profession. It was a masterful performance.

Shortly after nightfall we headed back down towards the railway track and settled ourselves on our bags, alongside a couple of *campesinos* who had also been at the game and who were now on their way into town, somewhat the worse for wear. The train was several hours late of course, and we whiled away the time just chatting, and occasionally exploding with laughter as we thought back over the events of the day, savouring with particular delight the image of the players reverently doffing their hats every time they went to head the ball. In the distance we could hear the revelry as it continued into the night, and even detect the changes of mood as the trago took hold.

By the time the train arrived the music was still going strong but the voices had become quieter and the conversation was well into the 'earnest' stage – when reflection sets in and the accidents of life are analysed and assessed; when the mediocre are made mighty and their exploits are embellished. It was the hour of the historian and I knew that the evening would not end until their work was complete and an 'authorized' version of the game was established. But I reckoned that by then, if my luck held good, I should be safely back in town, and who was to say when I might visit Columbe again – if ever?

Chapter Seven

MOSCABEL

I HAD DECIDED to take advantage of one of Ecuador's many national holidays – by custom a one-day holiday that falls in the middle of the week somehow stretches to the weekend – and gone down to Puyo, in the Oriente region, at the invitation of a Peace Corps friend named Bob. I was to spend a couple of days with him trekking through the rain forest. To be honest, I needed to get away for a while to escape the frustration of trying to do meaningful work for Radiofónicas. I had been there almost six months by this time and the full realization of my irrelevance had hit me. I felt a need to put some space between myself and the project for a short while, therefore, so as to be able to see my predicament more clearly and try to make sense of it.

Bob was a good person to be with, being the thoughtful, philosophical type, and I felt that he could probably be relied upon to provide some fair comment, not least because he had been through something similar himself. He was in his mid-thirties, an electrical engineer by trade who had been sent to work with the Ecuadorean Electricity Company in a small town in the south of the country called Gualaceo. His job had been a non-starter. No one had been expecting him, there was little or no work to do, and he decided to call it quits after six months when, while trying to set up some coloured lights for the annual festivities, he slipped, electrocuted himself and fell from a twenty-foot pole. He decided that if he was going to risk life and limb, it might as well be in pursuit of something worthwhile – hanging up fairy lights wasn't what he'd had in mind when he applied to the Peace Corps.

He was now based in Puyo and had indeed found something worthwhile to do, although it had no connection with power supplies. He had turned himself into a surveyor of the lands of the Amazonian Indians, in order to register them with the Land Reform Office before they could be taken over by the oil companies and the settlers who were arriving in increasing numbers from the Sierra. It was something of a race against time, and it was a cause that appealed perfectly to his humanitarian and political instincts. I think we all realized that, when push came to shove, the land titles probably wouldn't mean a great deal, but it was the kind of gesture that we felt needed to be made, if only as an 'awareness-building' exercise for the Indians.

I had sent a message in advance of my arrival asking if there was anything I could usefully bring down with me, meaning for Bob and his house-mates, but in his customary selfless manner he had interpreted my offer as a request for information about the trip we were planning. He sent me a one-line reply that read, 'Bring something to protect your head from the vampire bats'. I thought he was joking.

Puyo, in the native language, means 'cloudy', and the place was almost permanently under a layer of cloud. The town was built mainly of wood, and the streets, apart from the one that ran through the middle, were unpaved and without drainage, so everywhere and everything seemed to be permanently saturated. The air was thick with the heavy scent of plants, the whirring of insects, and the smell of mildew – in the walls, in the beds and in the pillows; and, for the brief moments that the sun shone, Puyo became one huge steam-bath.

The change from the Sierra was unbelievable. In just a few hours, you had exchanged ice-cold winds and dusty streets for heat-waves and quagmires. Curiously, the volunteers felt that they had 'lucked out' in coming to Puyo – which came as something of a relief to me because I was about to feel sorry for them. Clearly their regional preference had already been set, as had mine, which surprised me no end, for I had no idea that I had developed a bias in favour of anywhere.

Bob shared a wooden, two-storey house towards the edge of town with three other volunteers, two of whom were also working with the Land Registration Project. The third was attached to the Ministry of Education and bemoaned his fate at every turn, complaining endlessly about his frustratingly unproductive job.

Contrary to the fashion of most Puyeños, who were rather more status-conscious, the volunteers had taken to sleeping in hammocks. This was the ideal response to the climate, avoiding as it did any bodily contact with mattresses. They also had special mosquito nets to ensure that nothing other than the air reached their skin during the night. I had neither, so I cleared a space on the floor between the rubber boots, wooden crates and machetes, and rolled out the sleeping bag that Paul had left me, then climbed inside and prepared myself for the hottest night of my life.

'How's it going down there?' came a voice from the darkness. 'Hope the scorpions and the snakes don't bother you too much. Haven't seen a mamba for a couple of days, so you should be OK.'

'My dear fellow, we didn't conquer half the world by being frightened of a few little beasties,' I reminded him, while pulling the zip up tight; and then added, in my best Roger Moore accent: 'Sleep well, gentlemen.'

The day broke with a slow, leaden light, and scarcely any difference in temperature from the night before. Needless to say, despite the absence of any uninvited bed-fellows, I had found it impossible to sleep. I ended up alternating about every half-hour between the sleeping bag, until the heat drove me out, and nothing, until the mosquitos drove me back in.

We breakfasted perfunctorily on plain rice and black coffee, and then, as Bob and I had planned the evening before, the two of us grabbed our rucksacks and headed straight for the bus station. We were fairly heavily laden. We each carried a change of clothing, an oilskin, a full canteen of water, a machete, a flashlight, a couple of bags of sweets, biscuits, a few tins of cheese, rice and sugar, and some cigarettes for the Indians; and, in my case, a sleeping bag stuffed into a plastic bag and tied on the outside. We covered the eight blocks at a brisk pace, stopping to pick up some fresh bread along the way, and then handed our packs to the driver's young assistant, who was hanging from the steel ladder on the back of the bus, so that he could store them on the roof with the rest of the luggage.

The bus was already quite full and we were obliged to take seats near the back. This was something we had hoped to avoid because we were going to have to get off in the middle of nowhere and it would mean fighting our way past crowds of standing passengers, many of whom would have baskets and sacks.

'A Tena! A Tena!' shouted the young boy on the ladder enthusiastically, as if there could possibly be anyone in Puyo who didn't know where the bus was going.

After ten minutes or so, the driver moved in behind the wheel and started the engine, revving it authoritatively to advertise his imminent departure to any dawdlers. It was also the signal for the 'stand-by' passengers to get on – the ones who were only going a kilometre or two and didn't have the right to occupy a seat. They always had to wait until the last moment to see if the driver was going to take them. He always did, of course, partly because there were always a few relatives amongst them, partly because Ecuadoreans find it hard to put regulations above people's needs, and partly because the fares went, unticketed, straight into his pocket.

Finally, when just about every spare inch had been filled and there was barely room for a humming-bird to fly in, and with the tarpaulin pulled tightly over the luggage on the roof, we lurched off in a cloud of smoke and headed out of town along the rain-sodden dirt road – the driver's assistant still hanging from the ladder on the back and advertising his destination to the world at large.

We jostled along for what seemed an age in the creaking, ramshackle heap, bouncing up and down with every bump and pothole, and straining our necks to avoid the baskets that swayed from

the arms of the women who
crammed the aisle. Our destination was 'Kilometre 47',
which was about two-thirds of
the way to Tena. Those forty-
seven kilometres – what with
our chugging pace and the
frequent stops – took us nearly
three hours to complete.

'Kilometre 47' was marked
by a single wooden stake
about two feet high that had
once had 'K 47' painted on it.
This was the only remarkable
object – that I could see at
least – in an otherwise
unbroken wall of dripping

The author in the Oriente
Photo R. Yeates

greenery to indicate the start of the track to Comata, the village
from which Bob worked and where the survey equipment was kept.

It is remarkable how quickly the trappings of civilization
disappear. It was a seven-hour walk to the village, climbing two
hills, wading through thick mud, crossing a couple of rivers, scrab-
bling up slippery slopes on hands and knees, and all the while
cutting back thick foliage with machetes and keeping an eye out for
snakes. The heat and humidity got to you in no time, sapping your
strength and making your movements heavy and imprecise.
Disappointingly, we saw virtually no wildlife apart from the
hindquarters of a startled deer and the occasional blaze of a parrot
in flight, and I soon realized that the Tarzan films of my youth, in
which anacondas and pumas lay in wait behind every bush, had
been somewhat exaggerated.

We reached Comata by the late afternoon, and bedded down –
or in Bob's case, 'strung up' – in a room in the Captain's house, a
fairly large bungalow built on stilts to keep it above the rains and
the snakes, with a wide veranda running along one of the sides. I

was impressed. The Captain was the village headman who had, unusually for an Indian, served in the army, and the experience had obviously opened his eyes to the possibilities of a different life-style. He had been one of a number of Indian children who had been abducted by Catholic missionaries and taken to religious boarding schools in the town, in the interests of 'saving their souls'. He had moved on to the army from there. His had lost his right hand during his time in the military, as the result of an accident while dynamiting fish.

He asked me if I would take his photograph standing to attention with his rifle in classic military pose. He cut a fine figure, his back straight as a ramrod and his chest swelled with pride. I sent a copy of the photo down to him a few months later by the hand of a friend of a friend, but I have no way of knowing if it ever arrived.

We drank some water, ate a few peanuts that the Captain had recently harvested for sale in Puyo, and sat chatting for a while with the family on the veranda until the day was just about done. It was barely six o'clock but we were both tired and anxious to be in the sack before the mosquitos came out in force. There was also the question of light, for it looked from the heavy cloud as if we were in for a dark night and we didn't want the Captain to be using up his scarce supply of candles; nor did we want to be needlessly using up our flashlight batteries. We handed over some rice and cheese to the Captain, so that his wife could cook up some breakfast with it in the morning, and took our leave. I lay there for a while listening to the sounds of the rainforest, but not for long. The next thing I knew it was daybreak and I realized I had slept right through – mosquitos, heat and all.

Soon after breakfast Bob, the Captain and I loaded up the equipment, which in addition to the Captain's rifle consisted of half-a-dozen poles, a tape-measure and a theodolite, and started off in the direction of a small village where the surveying was to start. It was a couple of hours' walk further into the forest, over flatter terrain this time, and again the trek proved zoologically uneventful, although the Captain did disappear at high speed on one occasion in hot pursuit of a deer. He came back empty-handed without a shot being fired.

The only other sign of life was a pair of Indians who appeared from nowhere and without a sound, and who would have startled the living daylights out of me, had the Captain not been with us. They wore just loin-cloths and head-bands, walked barefoot, and each carried a bow, quiver and blow-pipe. They were Huaorani, true nomads of the rain forest, and they were out on a hunt, although they had not had much luck either and had strayed some short distance from their usual territory. I wasn't sure if they were acquaintances of the Captain, for they showed neither surprise nor friendship at meeting him and merely exchanged a few words in Quechua, presumably about the state of the path ahead, and moved on. As they disappeared into the foliage, I looked across at the Captain and reflected on the difference a shirt and a pair of trousers can make.

We stumbled upon the village quite suddenly and without warning, so abruptly did the rain forest end and the clearing begin. The place must have had a name, but I never found out what it was. At all events, it was the village where Moscabel lived. I say 'Moscabel', although I cannot be sure this was her name. It sounded like it, and for the next three days I called her by it, but I couldn't be certain. Whatever she said to me on that first morning somehow registered in my head as 'Moscabel', and that was the way it stayed. At all events, she didn't seem to mind.

She was just one of a dozen children who flocked around us as we strode in, but I noticed her straight away. Her eyes followed my every move, and she cocked her head confidently to one side as if to say, 'You might come from another planet, but don't think I'm frightened of you.'

I reckoned she was about nine years old, a dark, scrawny, wide-eyed little girl, with a brilliant smile and long, straight black hair. She and the other villagers were dressed in European clothing, although in her case it amounted to nothing more than a shabby little cotton dress falling well short of the knees. She grabbed my

The Captain   Photo R. Poole

hand and marched me off to her parents' house, where she had obviously decided I was to spend the night. I didn't resist, and although I doubt that her parents had much say in the matter, they received me cordially and showed me where I could put my pack. It was an interesting beginning and it did not take me long to appreciate that I was in the company of another type of Indian altogether – ones who had not been conquered by either the Incas or the Spaniards, and who were a very different race indeed.

The village was really a mere 'settlement', for it was situated in a clearing that measured no more than 200 yards across and had only five dwellings. Except for the small vegetable plots – groundnuts, yucca, sweet potato and tobacco – the earth was flattened and completely bare, no doubt to make it easier to spot any reptiles that might creep in, and the forest began at the edge of the clearing in a solid wall of vegetation. The dwellings were rectangular and spacious, with walls of loosely bound bamboo cane and steeply sloping, thatched roofs supported by stout upright poles and crossbeams lashed together. An array of hammocks hung between the beams and it was here that people sat, sideways, when they were not working. The furniture, such as it was, consisted of a couple of cane benches raised about two feet above the ground, and a wide sawn-off tree-trunk served as a table. A few items of earth-stained clothing hung from a single nail – and that was about the sum of it.

Away from the house under a loose canopy of banana leaves a wood-fire smoked beneath a big clay pot resting on three triangular stones; and a collection of smaller pots and utensils stood on the ground nearby. I handed over some rice, sugar and cheese to Moscabel's father as a gesture of friendship which he graciously accepted; he directed me to one of the cane benches and told me that this was where I could sleep. I thanked him and rolled out my sleeping bag on top of it, as if to stake an immediate claim to such a fine bed, and then I stretched myself out, somewhat ostentatiously, to illustrate both my fatigue and my pleasure at being among friends.

My repose did not last long, however, for Moscabel grabbed me
by the hand and began entreating me to go with her to the other
side of the compound. Her Spanish was almost non-existent, as was
that of all the women, and we communicated as best we could with
the usual mixture of mime and monosyllables. But she had
something she wanted me to see, of that I was certain, and she
hauled me off to the vegetable plots. For a moment or two I couldn't
for the life of me make out what she wanted to show me. All I could
see was a thin bamboo cane bent over under tension and a piece of
fine twine attached to it that reached down among the yucca plants.
She motioned me to be quiet and sit still. I obeyed, squatting down
on my haunches as Moscabel was doing, until my legs ached and I
could hardly bear it any longer. 'Shhh!' she whispered, 'shhh!'

Suddenly there was a lashing of the air as the bamboo cane shot
upright, quivering like an arrow that had hit its mark, and right in
front of me, flapping like mad with its foot caught in a noose, was a
small yellow bird. She leaped up and down, clapping with delight,
then raced across to free her panic-stricken prey and take it to her
mother for the pot. She returned in a flash to reset the trap and
urged me to sit through another performance, which I did, only this
time sitting on the ground for the ten minutes or so that it took for
another unsuspecting creature to come along. I was really quite
impressed with the simple efficiency of it all, and, as in the Sierra, I
was touched to see even the young children taking an active part in
the economic life of the community.

We walked back, bird in hand, to the house and sat down on
the bench, where we got into conversation with her father, who had
been joined by Bob and the Captain and a couple of the other men.
Moscabel sat by my side and held onto my arm, doggedly resisting
her father's attempts to shoo her away.

The Spanish was a little stilted but we managed to communicate
after a fashion, with just a little help from the Captain, who stepped
in now and again to translate some of the less obvious bits into
Quechua. Moscabel's father had taken down a wad of tobacco from
a nail above the fire and was slicing it on the table with a sharp

knife. I noticed that juice was oozing from the dark brown compres-
sion of leaves. He rammed some of the shavings into a wooden
pipe, lit it with an ember from the fire, puffed on it for a second,
then passed it round. I tried to handle it with aplomb, but the stuff
was strong — very strong. It made my throat burn, my eyes water
and my head spin. I handed it to Bob, who gave a perfunctory puff
without inhaling and passed it on.

Some pretty appetizing smells had been emanating from the pot
all the while, and now it was the mother's turn to produce
something special. She served me first as the newcomer and handed
me a fine enamel plate with a large piece of meat and some yucca in
a rich gravy sauce. I was deeply touched.

'Wanta,' said the Captain proudly. 'They shot it this morning.'
And I realized, as he said it, that he had been hoping to shoot
something himself so as not to arrive empty-handed.

'Excellent!' I replied. 'Magnificent,' not having the faintest idea
what 'wanta' was. When the others had been served, I turned to Bob
and asked him what we were eating.

'Wanta,' he replied shortly.

'Yes, I gathered that much, but what is it exactly?'

'Well,' he started, choosing his words carefully, 'you might say
that it was a sort of cross between a bush pig and a rat.'

I chewed more slowly. 'A sort of pig, you say?' I replied after a
few seconds.

'Well, to tell you the truth, it's more like a sort of rat. I mean, it's
a rodent, so you probably ought to call it a rat. Yep, I reckon I'd
probably have to call it a rat, if I was going to call it anything — a
large rat. It's pretty good though. High in protein.'

And he was right, it was pretty good, and since the family had
gone out of its way to provide us with a local delicacy, we empha-
sized how good it was. It compared especially favourably with what
came next.

Moscabel had been sent off with a calabash shell and she
returned with it full of a bitty, off-white liquid. She wiped the inside
rim with a clockwise sweep of her thumb and held it out to me.

'Take a swig', said Bob, 'and pass it on.'

I did as I was told. It had a stale, cidery sort of taste that was not altogether unpleasant.

'Te gusta?' asked the father. 'Do you like it?'

'Sabroso,' I replied. 'Delicious.'

It came around again of course, and again and again; and under Moscabel's watchful eye, I did more than just sip, and pretty soon I was feeling a warm glow inside.

'I suppose this is chicha,' I said, turning to Bob.

'That's right. But the real thing. You won't see any of this up in the Sierra.'

It was thicker, whiter and slightly sharper than the Chimborazo version. The Indians of the Oriente still make it as they have done for centuries – not with maize, as they do in the Sierra, but with yucca, which they boil then masticate and spit back into the brew to cause it to ferment. They leave it for a day or two until it acquires its potency.

I reckoned that if it had turned to alcohol – which it obviously had – then all the germs had probably been killed off at the same time. In any case, after downing several bowls of it, I didn't really care too much either way. The pipe continued to circulate, and the calabash along with it, and the fluency of our impromptu language continued to get better all the while as we launched into one topic after another, occasionally falling about with laughter as our confidence grew and the bonds between us strengthened.

With the heat, the chicha and the fatigue of the journey, I was about ready to keel over, even though it was only mid-afternoon. The others had already reclined into their hammocks and so I stretched out on the bench and closed my eyes. Several hours later I suddenly awoke in a state of panic. There was something clinging to my face like a warm rag. I smashed it off frantically.

'Vampire bats!' I muttered, spitting with disgust. I knew exactly what it was, although I had never been near one before. 'So he wasn't joking after all!'

I felt my forehead – it was bleeding profusely. I reached for a handkerchief from the pocket of my jeans and applied it to the wound. I knew bats could carry rabies, but what bothered me most was the thought of having this revolting thing on my face, calmly drinking my blood. I was angry that no one had warned me about it – though no doubt somebody would have done if the chicha hadn't got in the way.

I felt like waking Bob and telling him what had happened, but he was far away in the land of dreams, secure inside his bat-proof net, and I thought better of it. I fumbled inside my pack for my rubber poncho, took it out and pulled it over my head. But with the sleeping bag underneath and the poncho on top, I started to suffocate and sweat like a pig.

'This is ridiculous!' I told myself emphatically. 'There has got to be a way out of this. I mean you can't live your whole life in fear of some stupid bat, for heaven's sake!' And I removed the poncho from my face to get some air. It felt unbelievably fresh and sweet, and it was not long before I was feeling better and my thoughts were turning to other things.

For some good while – perhaps an hour – all was quiet, and I was just about managing to convince myself that it was probably a freak attack and it wouldn't happen again, when back it came, fluttering around my head like a black newspaper caught in the wind. I lashed out madly with my fist but merely struck air.

I sat up on the bench wondering what on earth I was going to do next. Everyone seemed to be sound asleep, including the Indians who didn't have nets. Only the smoke from the fire was stirring. I decided to put the sleeping bag away and lie on the cane surface of the bench in the hope that some air might reach me from underneath. It helped a bit but with the poncho back over my head, sleep remained a forlorn hope. I lay there waiting for the return of the bat, wondering if it was capable of drilling holes through rubber.

Shortly before daybreak the youngest child, a baby of about a year old, started to cry loudly, and the mother stretched out a sleepy hand towards the little hammock that hung by her side to rock it back to sleep. But the baby kept on crying, and I watched as the mother eased herself to the ground, picked the baby up and carried it over towards the still smouldering fire. Blood was streaming down the child's face and I could see that it had been bitten quite badly. I learned later that vampire bats inject an anti-coagulant that keeps the blood flowing. The mother reached into the ashes and selected a small ember from the fire which she very gently applied to the wound. The bleeding stopped instantly, and with it, the child's crying.

We were all a bit hung-over the following morning but we still managed to put away a breakfast of rice, cheese, cold yucca and black coffee – albeit when the sun was showing above the tops of the trees. Bob was planning to leave immediately with the Captain and two other men to do some surveying out in the forest and, as they would be gone for five days and I had to be back in Riobamba in four, it was decided that I should spend the rest of the day in the village and then make an early start for Puyo in the morning. I reckoned that if I left at daybreak I could probably manage it in a single day, although I was quite worried that I might get lost somewhere along the way.

In the meantime, Moscabel had decided that I ought to learn something about jungle survival and that the very least she could do was to teach me how to use a blow-pipe. She selected one from the family's collection that stood propped up against a beam – three of them in a row, like billiard cues – then lifted down from a nail a quiver filled with lethally sharp slivers of bamboo and a calabash stuffed with the white fleece of a cotton-wool tree. We walked over to the vegetable plots, a safe distance from the houses, where she proceeded to instruct me in this ancient art of her people.

She balanced a bunch of green bananas on a tree stump and retreated about twenty yards. This slip of a girl then selected a dart of about the same proportions as herself from the quiver and pulled off a tuft of the fleece, which she proceeded to wet and roll between thumb and forefinger until it was the same size as the bore of the pipe. She then wrapped it around the shaft of the dart and gently slid both into the white bone mouthpiece. Without further ado, she levelled her enormous, nine-foot weapon at its target and spat contemptuously down the barrel. I saw nothing in flight but instantly realized that the dart, still wrapped in its cotton wool, was now imbedded in one of the bananas.

'Now you try!' she said, holding the pipe out to me.

I got to be quite reasonable at it after a while, without actually hitting the bananas – even at half the distance. But I could see that it was a lethal weapon, even without the optional extra of a curare tip.

The forest Indians are well schooled in the science of poisons and drugs of all kinds, and we in the West have learned a good deal from them and are genuinely in their debt, not least for quinine, novocaine and the contraceptive pill. They also have a plant called 'barbasco', the leaves of which, when mashed and thrown into the river, will cause the fish to float helplessly to the surface, and without any side effects to harm the consumer – although others arriving from the outside and lacking the Amazonians' feel for the link between conservation and survival have subsequently learned of its existence and abused its power, seriously depleting the stocks of a good many rivers.

The blow-pipe is back in England now. I have it displayed on a wall at home. It is probably my most prized possession. My engineer father expressed astonishment that something nine feet in length could have been fashioned from purely natural materials, with no implement more complicated than a knife, and yet be so perfectly straight, smooth, rigid and light. He doubted that anyone in the West, given the same materials, could match it, even with modern equipment. I hadn't looked at it that way and have been grateful for his comment ever since, for it brought a dimension of scientific respectability to something that had simply been an object of love. He was astonished even further when, while demonstrating what Moscabel had taught me, I pierced a Sunday newspaper clean through, colour supplement and all, at twenty paces. But what he couldn't see, as I carefully removed and inspected the dart, was that my heart was aching for that little girl and her people so far away in the Amazon jungle on the other side of the world.

I spent the day playing games with the children and handing out sweets, and now and again, with Moscabel's consent, talking to her father. He asked if he could buy the sleeping bag from me and I instantly offered it to him as a gift, although I wasn't sure at first why he would want it. Later on I realized that it was probably for the attacks of malaria and other fevers and chills that assail them periodically and leave the body racked with cold, despite the oppressive heat. He, in turn, and without any prompting, offered me the blow-pipe, together with the quiver and the supply of cotton wool, and I was more than happy with the barter.

That night after dinner, as we sat beside the smouldering ashes of the fire and passed the pipe around, the parents informed me that Moscabel would be accompanying me back to Puyo. At first I would not hear of it – the idea of having a small girl leave her family and take me on a day's journey through the rain forest seemed quite preposterous; but the parents insisted. They argued that she regularly walked with the other children to the Captain's village, where they had a makeshift school, and that she had accompanied her father into town on numerous occasions and was well acquainted with the way. The plan was that she would stay with her uncle in Puyo for a few days and then return with him on his next visit.

I also learned that the mother needed some medicine for a liver condition, and with this I capitulated, for I could see that the offer was not solely on my account. I, in fact, would be looking after Moscabel, while she was showing me the way. She was to take with her one of their handful of chickens to sell in the market, so as to have money to pay for the medicine, and had already been instructed – the parents informed me most pointedly – not to part with it for less than thirty-five sucres – about two dollars.

We set out early the next day as planned, Moscabel with a small bag over her shoulder containing a bound and gagged chicken, a couple of bananas and a wad of tobacco for the uncle; and me with my pack now lighter by one sleeping bag, and with a nine-foot blow-pipe.

We started off in fine form, but a pattern soon emerged with Moscabel in charge and me at heel. I can still see her now, standing with hand on hip, encouraging, admonishing and occasionally giggling, as I slithered about, trying hard not to snap the blow-pipe in two. But in fact we made much better time than Bob and I had done on the way in and we reached the road, with only a couple of stops to drink from streams, eat and rest, in less than eight hours. It was still only mid-afternoon and we didn't have long to wait before a Land Rover drew up and offered us a ride into town. The driver dropped us off at the uncle's – still in the hours of daylight – and then, having promised to call first thing in the morning to help her with her shopping, I took my leave and headed off in the direction of the Peace Corps house.

She was ready and waiting when I got there next morning, bouncing up and down with excitement at the prospect of going shopping in the 'big city'. The chicken was duly re-bound and gagged and put back into the bag, and off we went to the market to see how much we could get for it.

Unfortunately, the top price we were offered, after half a dozen attempts at hard bargaining by Moscabel, was only twenty-five sucres and I could see she was becoming despondent. I had to think of something fast.

'Listen,' I said, 'we need a chicken back at the house, so why don't you let me buy it. It looks like a pretty good chicken to me.'

She seemed quite pleased with the idea and so I gave her the thirty-five sucres; and then added, 'No, on second thoughts, you put that thirty-five sucres in your pocket and give it to your mother, and you buy the medicine with this,' and I handed her another thirty-five sucres – no doubt thinking what a generous gringo I was.

She accepted it quite happily and we headed over to the pharmacy, which also happened to be a general store that sold everything from rice to bicycles. She marched cheerfully up to the counter and asked for the medicine. She then proceeded to point to a whole range of other items, asked how much they were, and took possession of them one by one until the other thirty-five sucres that

I had given her for her mother were gone too. In this way she acquired a plastic comb, a band for her hair, some coloured pencils and a note-book, half-a-dozen candles, a box of matches, and a couple of bars of soap. And the whole thing had been carried off with such aplomb that I couldn't help laughing, in spite of myself.

'Moscabelita!' I said to her when we were outside, using the diminutive to soften my indignation, 'that money was to take back to your mother – not to spend on odds and ends! Now take this', I said, giving her another thirty-five sucres, 'and *give it to your mother!*' I was quite emphatic.

But she was gone again, and emerged this time with a scrubbing brush, a Chinese towel, two enamel cups, a canvas bag with an elephant on it and a plastic bucket.

'Ah!' she said, 'I just love coming to town!'

'This girl's dangerous!' I said to myself. 'Thank goodness they're running low on chickens.' And realizing that if she wasn't taken into custody soon she might well be the ruin of all of us, especially me, I took her back to her uncle's. But when I told her that it was time for me to say goodbye and go back to Riobamba, she flatly refused to let go of my hand, and followed me down the street.

'You must come and see me again,' she said, pleading with those wide black eyes of hers, and she made me promise to return as soon as I could.

I told her that I would do my level best, and that if God willed it, I would be back to see her in a few months – which is what I sincerely hoped, although I knew that the odds against it were high. I took her back to her uncle's once again, gave her a big hug, ordered her to stay where she was, and walked steadily away in the direction of the volunteers' house where I intended to deposit the chicken with a note attached to its neck, pick up my pack and my blow-pipe, and head for the bus station. I didn't dare look back.

I began to feel better almost at once – somehow relieved, despite the sadness of leaving Moscabel. Even the air felt suddenly less oppressive. In a few minutes I would be on the bus and heading for the open spaces and the cool breezes of the *páramo* where I now knew I belonged, even if the job I was going back to was not all that it might be. The heat and the bats – even the people – would soon be a thing of the past.

'After all,' I reasoned to myself, 'you can't carry relationships around with you for ever. It's silly to even try.'

But then suddenly I heard footsteps behind me – hurried, anxious footsteps, like those of a child running in earnest. I stiffened, unsure what to do, whether to turn and rebuke her, or hasten my step and outpace her. I stopped, ready to take issue; but when I turned round there was no one there; not a soul in sight; nothing – just an odd banana frond flapping idly in the morning breeze.

Some years later, while sitting in a Pizza Bar in New Jersey with Bob, and reminiscing at length about our experiences, I asked him whether he thought the family would remember my visit.

'Oh, I should think so,' he replied slowly. 'I mean it isn't every day that a gringo passes through their village, let alone one who trades a sleeping bag for a nine-foot blow-pipe, and then buys the same chicken three times.'

CHAPTER EIGHT

THE INDIAN AND
DEVELOPMENT

IT IS WELL KNOWN that outsiders, and perhaps above all the British with their curious mixture of elitism and identification with the underdog, will fall into one of two camps when confronted with the Indian. They will either revile him or put him on a pedestal. This owes much to the fact that there still exists a separate Indian identity after five centuries of uninterrupted exploitation, and somehow, as when a defeated boxer just won't go down, we can't work out why. In *Mornings In Mexico*, D.H. Lawrence sought to explain the contradiction in the following terms:

> It is impossible for white people to approach the Indian without either sentimentality or dislike. The common, healthy, vulgar white usually feels a certain native dislike of these drumming aboriginals. The highbrow invariably lapses into sentimentalism like the smell of bad eggs. Why? – Both reactions are due to the same feeling in the whiteman. The Indian is not in line with us. He's not coming our way. His whole being is going a different way from ours. And the minute you set eyes on him you know it. And then, there are only two things you can do. You can detest the insidious devil for having an utterly different way from our own great way. Or you can perform the mental trick, and fool yourself and others into believing that the befeathered and bedaubed darling is nearer to the true ideal gods than we are.

The Indian way of consciousness is different from and fatal to our way of consciousness. Our way of consciousness is different from and fatal to the Indian. The two ways, the two streams are never to be united. They are not even to be reconciled. There is no bridge, no canal of connexion. The sooner we realise this, and accept this, the better, and leave off trying, with fulsome sentimentalism, to render the Indian in our own terms.

It may seem at first glance that Lawrence is overstating the case, but I am not sure that he is. A separate consciousness there is indeed, despite massive acculturation on the part of the Indian – the adoption, for example, of cows, pigs, chickens, sheep, horses, oxen, the wheel, the plough, various metals, money, a variety of musical instruments, and a certain amount of literacy. In fact, it would appear that, under favourable conditions, the Indian has a near-infinite capacity for absorbing western paraphernalia without surrendering his essential 'Indianness'.

To a certain extent, something similar might be said of the white man, for he has also absorbed a comprehensive range of things American into his life-style, most notably potatoes, tomatoes, maize, cotton, chocolate, tobacco and turkeys, plus a number of medicinal plants that have given him quinine, strychnine, novocaine and the contraceptive pill. And yet, the result is not the same because at the end of it all the culture of the white man remains unassailably strong while the culture of the Indian is everywhere under threat.

There are a number of serious questions that need to be answered if we are to understand what is at stake here. It is easy to say, for example, that the European has usurped the space and the resources of the Indian and that this is the reason why indigenous American culture is languishing. And yet this cannot be the whole story. Why is it, for example, that an anthropologist entering an Amazonian village with a tape-recorder and a camera will change the lives of the people he meets for ever, whereas an Amazonian Indian arriving on the streets of New York, typically dressed and armed with the most prized artefacts of his culture, will have nothing like the same effect? He might raise an eyebrow or two, but most likely his appearance would be shrugged off by the locals. Is it that our technology represents some higher form of truth that is, in itself, irresistible? And was this a further reason why 160 Spaniards were able to defeat the military elite of an empire of some nine million? In other words, irrespective of their number or their moral conduct, did the Spaniards represent some higher civilization that was ultimately irresistible, and was their victory necessary, perhaps even pre-ordained, so as to correct the bias of a people who had strayed too far into the realms of the immaterial?

Nowhere in the Americas is there a happy union of the two cultures. The Indian does not seem to be able to live happily and at peace with a foot in either world. To understand why this should be we need to look at the paths that the two cultures – the European and the Indian – have taken. This may shed some light on the steamrollering spread of western civilization and on some of the more insoluble aspects of the development puzzle.

The dominant trait of the European is intellectual power, the recent origins of which are generally believed to date from the time of the Renaissance when reason began to take over from intuition and faith as the main instrument of enquiry. Certain Islamic texts clearly indicate that various 'European' discoveries such as planetary motion (Copernicus/Kepler), gravity (Newton), and the circulation of the blood (Harvey) were already well documented by Arab scholars by the twelfth century; but let us assume that the emergence of 'rational humanity' begins with the Renaissance and it represents the dawn of a new age.

The emergence of the intellect in this primary role meant that Europeans were able to dissociate themselves from the objects of their attention and thereby gain a degree of detachment, and this in turn allowed a measure of ascendancy and control which has subsequently confirmed the value of science. Certain risks were inherent in this development, however, in that humanity began to lose its intimate contact with nature, and hence an instinctive reverence for the order of things. We had, in fact, started out on the long road towards what we recognize today in its more negative aspects as 'materialism' and 'the cult of the individual', and this brought into play a whole host of moral, spiritual and metaphysical considerations, most of which we have successfully managed to ignore.

Indians, on the other hand, are non-intellectual and non-assertive. This does not mean that they cannot be endowed with great intelligence, wisdom and insight, but that their relationship with their environment is still largely characterized by intuition and submission. They do not have, nor do they seek to have, control over material reality based on a cause and effect analysis. In fact, their general attitude implies an acceptance of whatever befalls them and an obligation to bend to the exigencies of circumstance rather than to seek to impose their will upon it and change it. Their basic stance, therefore, is fatalistic.

Social organization is founded on communal living and sharing. Indians identify with the smell of the earth and recognize the existence of a life-spirit emanating from the source of all being and running through the whole of creation, uniting rocks, trees, animals and humans. The Indian does not see himself as separate from the rest of existence, much less does he see himself as superior to it. Humility is at the core of his being.

Looked at in these terms, it is difficult to see how the two cultures can be reconciled, and from a developmental perspective there are a number of factors that make collaboration difficult. It is odd that so little attention should have been given to what is clearly a matter of supreme importance. Religious belief, cultural practices and the general question of consciousness, all of which must surely be at the very heart of the priorities of any society, have yet to find a place in the 'development' forum.

This, I assume, is because those concerned have lacked the interest, or the sensitivity, or the linguistic ability to recognize and understand what is at stake. The normal tendency is to assume that American Indians or Africans or Pacific Islanders are simply poorer versions of ourselves — which is, of course, what they will be if current trends are allowed to go unchecked – and then proceed to apply European prescriptions to problems that are not European in essence. Finally, we throw up our arms in exasperation at what we think is the inherent ingratitude or incompetence of the 'natives' as our efforts prove futile and the aid millions pour down the drain.

It is true that, in the face of repeated failure, the development agencies have recently been forced to look closely at what they are doing and to re-examine their strategies, but this has yet to lead to any penetrating analysis of cultural differentiation.

Examples of developmental myopia are not hard to come by, such as the attempts to introduce settled agriculture among certain nomadic tribes who consider the earth to be sacred and the breaking of it to be sacrilege; to introduce animal traction among peoples who have consciously chosen, over thousands of years, to reject both the wheel and the plough; to promote the widespread cultivation of rice for consumption among groups for whom rice has a purely ritualistic significance; to impose a decidedly western invention, like the co-operative, on people who have scant or no experience of handling money and no concept of share-ownership; to advocate mining in communities whose reverence for Mother Earth makes such activities seem like acts of rape; to implement complex irrigation systems in lands where to divert the course of a river is to tamper with the divine order; and to construct a high-tech beer factory in a country where alcohol has been proscribed by both civil and ecclesiastical law – such practices have been the norm rather than the exception in the short history of development.

The developmental status of any society can be defined in terms of its relationship with the environment, that is to say, whether the community dominates the environment ('developed'), or whether it is the environment that is the dominant partner ('underdeveloped'). Development is all about the control of resources, whether for our enrichment or our security. The availability and accessibility of these resources are important too, but generally speaking the signif-icance of this has been over-emphasized at the expense of other, equally important issues. That there is much more to development than economics and politics is shown by the pockets of agricultural plenty in the midst of vast seas of want, which occur wherever independent communities of Mennonite and Japanese farmers are to be found throughout Latin America. It is a question of attitude of mind, therefore – of perception – and this has proven to be the greatest stumbling block until now.

The European's intellectual leap and the power it has given him over his environment, as contrasted with the Indian's fatalism and powerlessness, fundamentally separates the two cultures. The recognition of this is crucial to any attempt to understand where we have been going wrong, because seen from this perspective, nothing we have to offer is likely to make much sense. Our technology, and our prescriptions in general, are the product of a particularly aggressive, purposeful and analytical psychology that has been developing, with constant reinforcement, for centuries and has no immediate relevance to the world's indigenous peoples, most of whom have been intimidated by circumstances and events for so long that they dare not even raise their voices for fear of invoking some sort of retribution.

If we look in the broadest possible terms at what the 'European way' consists of (this of course includes North America and all the other 'developed' nations), we can see that it amounts to a technological assault on the environment. Europeans have seldom questioned their right to conquer, plunder and shape the planet according to their will, and this they have done with spectacular irreverence, the consequences of which they are only now beginning to face.

Other cultures have not assumed such a separate and ascendant stance, but have seen themselves as an integral part of a harmonious and benign whole, showing humility and reverence before what they see as a mystical 'Mother Nature'. Not many indigenous peoples in Africa, Asia and America, for instance, have shown a consuming passion for planting flags on the tops of mountains in the way that Europeans have done. Conquest and the exploitation of resources have not figured to anything like the same extent among their priorities. To supply such people with a tractor, therefore, and expect it to produce the same results as it would in Europe is to misunderstand the nature of their relationship with their environment.

This is why so many 'crucial' western inventions lie broken, discarded and unlamented in the developmental graveyards of the Third World. It is not simply a question of the farmers failing to appreciate the material value of our products (how could they?), nor is it necessarily a question of any inherent lack of aptitude. The fact is that the tractor is not the appropriate expression of their need. It is the product of a different dialogue – a foreign language – that can only be acquired at the expense of the native tongue.

There are other significant perceptual differences, and if we look at one issue in particular – the question of money and the cash economy – it may help to illuminate the picture as a whole, for it is a fairly cômplex business.

Money is an abstraction – one that purports to represent the value a society places upon its labour and production. But in itself, of course, money is quite worthless. This is patently obvious to anyone in a subsistence economy living a hand-to-mouth existence, but it may not be quite so clear to those of us who are familiar with only a cash economy.

Pre-Columbian society had no money and commerce was trans- acted largely on the basis of barter; in the case of the Incas, with certain essential items of food and clothing emanating from a central government store. This situation did not really change until the Agrarian Reform Acts of the 1950s and 60s when, for the first time, the Indian had cash at his disposal and entered the market economy. In barely a generation, therefore, he has had to get used to the concept and practice of money, although its abstract nature runs counter to all his time-honoured traditions, and indeed, his common sense; he has had to learn to put his faith in it, which, given the Spaniards' track-record for honesty, cannot have been easy.

Another, perhaps more important, problem with money relates to the question of precision, for nowhere in indigenous society – beyond the symmetry of arts and crafts – can precision, as we know it, be said to exist. It must have been there to a fine degree in pre-

Columbian times, at least among certain elites, as the architectural and scientific record clearly indicates, but it is not there today. If, for example, a farmer ploughs a furrow a bit crooked, or drops a few extra seeds in the hole, what difference does it make? And if he arrives a couple of hours late for a meeting, who cares or even notices? And what does 'late' mean anyway?

Precision is a characteristic of western culture and is a function of the level of control we exercise over resources. Most of our technology, and this includes the circulation and manipulation of money, depends for its effectiveness on an instinctive grasp of the importance of precision, and yet this is glaringly absent from indigenous societies around the world. So many prescriptions we have held out to them have presupposed a capability for being precise, whether it is in the operation and maintenance of vehicles and machinery, the measurement of medicines and fertilizers, the keeping of accounts and records, or the use of the contraceptive pill – and yet virtually nowhere in the Third World does such precision exist.

The lesson to be learned from all of this is that the question of development is complex. It involves the availability of resources and access to them in the first place; it involves technical expertise; and equally important, it involves an attitude of mind that believes in its right and ability to impose its will. The transition from 'underdeveloped' to 'developed' will only come about when this perceptual change takes place, and until then, whatever solutions we hold out to the underdeveloped peoples of the world are destined to fail. What we have been doing until now is trying to reproduce our own successes in completely different conditions; we have, to borrow a Spanish saying, 'been asking the oak-tree for pears'. But to understand more fully why it is that so many of our efforts to export successful technologies have met with insuperable problems, we need to examine in greater detail the relationship between technology and culture.

One of the enduring myths in western thinking is the notion that progress is predominantly the product of individual genius – the belief that a Freud or an Einstein happens along and single-handedly pushes back the frontiers of knowledge, thereby enabling a groping humanity to emerge from darkness into light. If we look closely at the environment from which the genius emerges, however, it becomes clear that the process by which significant change takes place is not so simple. For a person's ideas to gain acceptance, insight alone, no matter how valid, is not enough. He or she must also be part of a wider movement supportive of the same endeavours and aspirations. History is littered with inventions that arrived before their time and were subsequently consigned to the scrap-heap. Any successful technological innovation, therefore, and indeed any great leap forward in human awareness, presupposes something of a symbiosis between the pioneer and the environment.

If a given discovery had not been made by X, it would have been made by Y, for there is no force as great as that of an idea whose time has come. Given the need, the resources, and a favourable, non-repressive social climate, the technology will appear spontaneously like the fruit on a tree. It does not take a freak of nature miraculously to appear and invent something out of nothing; it needs a keen and gifted observer to see what is already in the process of ripening and to pick it from the tree of life on behalf of humanity.

We need to readjust our vision of world history so as to see humanity as a single organism that has been evolving into ever bigger social units – from the family to the clan, to the tribe, to city state, to the nation state, and finally to the stage that we are now about to embrace, the world community. From there, we can take the further step of recognizing that our technology has been developing all along to support this higher social purpose.

This is why certain monumental discoveries, such as settled agriculture, metal-working and the concept of zero, appeared in different parts of the world at approximately the same time, with no apparent means of connection. And this has continued to be the case right through to the present day with such inventions as photography, radio, television, the internal combustion engine and the jet engine appearing in different places more or less simultaneously with a great deal of rivalry and not much collaboration going on between the inventors.

When we see humanity as an organic whole evolving according to a predetermined social pattern, instead of as a collection of individuals whose survival has been left to chance, locked inexorably into competition with each other, then our purpose as a species begins to make more sense. Our brothers in the 'underdeveloped' world have no problem with such a thesis, that there is a single indivisible purpose, at once all-embracing and benign – what surprises them is that anyone should think otherwise. It is we who have become separated from the natural order of things who do not see that our progress has only ever been a series of 'gifts' from the world of spirit to the world of matter.

There is a special relationship, therefore, between the inventor and his or her environment, as close as that between artist and environment, which is why the arts and sciences always flourish hand in hand. Not only is the inventor unconsciously representing the aspirations of his or her fellow citizens, these aspirations are instinctively translated into a cultural framework that is, by definition, appropriate. Any invention is appropriate to its mother culture, and the inventor is both the interpreter and the spokesman for a people. What is special about the inventor is not so much 'creativity' as the ability to perceive and articulate what is already there.

This is of immense importance when we consider the question of technology and its appropriateness to developing countries, because we tend to imagine that all technology is potentially universal in its application, when in reality every innovation is the culmination of an extremely long and idiosyncratic process that has its roots deep in the history and the traditions of the people. When our technology is seen for what it is, namely the fruit of this process, then it becomes clear why it cannot be transplanted and reproduced successfully elsewhere without those same primary conditions that caused it to appear and flourish in the first place. This is the reason why there are still two quite separate and distinct cultures in the Central Andes after five hundred years of enforced co-habitation – they don't have anything in common. There is no point of contact, no 'bridge, no canal of connexion', as D.H. Lawrence wrote.

The greatest failure of the development agencies has been their inability to recognize that the dialogue between the underdeveloped peoples of the world and their environment is fundamentally different from our own, and that the solutions of the developed nations are idiosyncratic to the point of being unexportable.

Fritz Schumacker took an enormous step in the right direction when he introduced us to the concept of 'intermediate technology', a term that has subsequently been replaced by the more semantically accurate one of 'appropriate technology'. He saw the need to adjust our technology to a level that would make it readily assimilable in the recipient communities – and thereafter sustainable with minimal or no external support. He was, however, speaking of *technological* appropriateness rather than cultural, and concentration on the latter seems to me to be the next logical step.

I believe we must recognize that there can be no development without western notions of science and technology. Certain African intellectuals have argued the case for a hypothetical and totally different type of development – something as yet undefined that might have evolved along traditional lines in the absence of colonization. But this, I believe, is wishful thinking. There never has been, nor ever will be, an Arcadian paradise in which even the meek and humble enjoy a reasonable standard of living. Without western science and technology the productivity necessary for this affluence, and the social services it involves, is not possible. A good deal has been said about the superior health of those indigenous peoples who have been left undisturbed in their natural habitat, and although their health is undoubtedly superior to those whose way of life has been disturbed, it is still inadequate compared with the standards of western medical science.

We need to respond to pleas for help – and the world's poor *are* calling for assistance, loud and clear – with predominantly western solutions, but in a technologically and culturally appropriate way. We need to devise strategies with their understanding and consent, in a way that will enhance their control of the environment and bring about improvements in living standards in a manner compatible with their values and traditions. This will take time and close co-operation at the village level; the solutions that count will not be those designed in western universities and applied by expatriates from the safe distance of a capital city. They will be worked out *in situ* with the central actors of the drama taking part at every step. The ground is becoming increasingly fertile for such co-operation, for there is a growing recognition on all sides that, with the right approach, significant advances can be made.

This is the ideal scenario. The other, less attractive version sees the Indian being drawn ever more closely into the vortex of our material ways, and languishing miserably as a result, although less so with each subsequent generation as the indigenous identity becomes progressively diluted.

In all probability it will not end quite like this because western civilization cannot survive much longer the way it is going. The selfishness and the greed, the prejudice and the exploitation, the arrogance and the insensitivity, and the wholesale destruction of our planet are weighing too heavily against us. A society without a spiritual base cannot last; the West, I believe, will soon follow a similar path to that of Eastern Europe and undergo an internal collapse of some kind, so that we will be left with the same problem of having to re-establish order from chaos.

If we are fortunate, what will emerge from all this is a new world order and a new world culture, with a multitude of regional variations, in which the poor will discover the value of science and technology and apply it appropriately, and the rich will rediscover the value of the spirit and apply it intuitively. There are sure to be a few traumas along the way, but if this is the price that has to be paid, then, so be it. Personally, I can't wait to get there.

PART III

GRINGOS AND LATINS

Chapter Nine

VOLUNTEERS

THE PEACE CORPS apartment in Riobamba was located on the top floor of a five-storey building next to the food market. It was owned by the ironmonger whose shop was downstairs. Soon after taking over the place in 1966 the volunteers had caused a sensation by offering to pay more rent in line with a pay-rise they had received. Such happenings were unheard of in Riobamba and consequently caused a good deal of confusion – but the landlord handled it well. He said 'thank you very much' and broadcast it far and wide, which did the Peace Corps a power of good. As a public relations strategy it was a stroke of genius, and the volunteers soon found that their appearance in the market, previously met with suspicion, was now greeted with smiles, and that their monthly food bills were falling dramatically. The 'gringo tax' to which they had been unknowingly subject had been silently abolished.

The apartment had four bedrooms, a large living room, a good-size kitchen and an extensive patio where the evenings were often spent politicizing and philosophizing, or just tracing the outline of the hills against the heavens.

The furnishings were home-made, which meant that they were little more than a collection of wooden 'rafts' with mattresses placed on top. The floors were covered with a network of overlapping rush mats that seemed as permanent as the building itself, and the walls were decorated with the usual posters of Bogart, Hendrix and 'Che',

and the odd quotation from Dylan and Lennon. But despite its spa-
ciousness you had to negotiate your way around with care, being
ever watchful not to step on the eternally full ashtrays, the casually
discarded boots, and the inevitable record player that stood, surrounded by a debris of records and sleeves, in the middle of the
floor. All in all, it added up to everything you might have expected
from non-conformist young men in the late sixties.

They were happy days, and not just because they were good
times in themselves, but because there was something special about
being associated, however indirectly, with the United States at the
height of its golden age. Some of the magic seemed to rub off on
the people. Later on I realized how fortunate I had been to have
landed in the company of the seven Peace Corps Volunteers living
in Riobamba – the four in the apartment, a married couple living
apart, and Paul – because their general enthusiasm for everything
they saw around them was contagious.

When you first arrive in a country you are inevitably dependent
on other people for a whole host of practical information just to
find your way around, and this can extend, if you are not careful, to
other areas as well, including personal opinion. You will hear such
comments as, 'don't go to so and so – he's a crook'; or, 'don't bother
with so and so, he's a waste of time', and since you probably don't
have the time to go and find out for yourself, you accept it, and so
conventional wisdom is formed and passes, unchallenged, from one
generation to the next. Such prejudice does not necessarily stop at
individuals either, but often reaches out to the people and the
country at large. Which expatriate has not, at some time or other,
been tempted to join in with a session of character-assassination
aimed at his host country, lampooning the locals for everything that
comes to mind, from the quality of the telephone service to their
alleged IQ?

Fortunately such was not the case with this particular group of
volunteers, and I find it seldom is the case with North Americans
generally. They do not seem to be as cynical as Europeans, and do
not favour a humour that depends for its edge on the disparagement

of others; they are usually prepared to believe the best of someone until they know otherwise. Whether this is the characteristic of a youthful nation whose ideals are still pretty much intact, or whether it comes from looking outward with a favourable eye in the direction of the rest of the world from whence their forebears came, I cannot say, but it strikes me as an especially healthy frame of mind.

The volunteers were devoted to the 'Indian cause' and talked about it endlessly – who was working for it, who was against it, if change would come, how and when it would come, and so forth. And they opened up their homes to the *campesinos* in a way that was truly admirable and at times set them at odds with their neighbours.

It was an interesting characteristic of the Indians that, having exchanged greetings, they would often be quite content just to sit, doing and saying nothing. It took some getting used to for those of us who were conditioned to feel uneasy at silence, but the Indians could sit for hours on end staring into space and feeling no compulsion to communicate.

It took me a while to learn to be a good host to an Indian. I had trouble with the silences at the beginning and had to force myself not to let them bother me. I learned also that you should not ask an Indian if he liked something before you served it, because the question is meaningless. He would probably think there must be something wrong with what was offered, for why else would you ask? It would never occur to him that you were referring to 'taste' – individual taste, and choice generally, along with such things as vegetarianism and keeping pets, are quirks of an affluent society and have no place in the Indian way of things. Everything he has and does is related to survival – it is functional rather than decorative. Animals are there to be eaten, or milked, or to guard the property, and not to brighten up the place. But it does not mean that he has no affection for them – he does, in abundance – and every time he slaughters a cow or a goat, or drinks milk, he thanks God, and also the animal for surrendering itself so that he might live another day. So you just serve up the food and drink without preamble and wish him 'buen provecho' – 'bon appetit'.

A good many of these things I learned from the Peace Corps, either listening to them or watching them in action. They acted with sensitivity and sincerity towards the Indians, and if the Peace Corps as an organization was sometimes lacking in such qualities, a good many of the volunteers were certainly not. The Riobamba volunteers invariably spoke well of the Indians' courage and stamina in the face of malnourishment, lack of medicine, and the long hours from sunrise to sunset spent working in the bitter cold of the *páramo*. Their capacity to endure seemed only to be exceeded by a readiness to disguise pain with a smile. All the same, you did see the pain at times, when the trago started to flow and guards were dropped, and then it would pour forth in torrents, the wailing of a soul in torment for 500 years, escaping through music and song, and especially through the plaintive notes of their many flutes – straight, simple reeds cut close to the ground that depend for their life on the Andean wind, and are fashioned to play a solo melody.

I recall one time, while enjoying the revelry at a village dance, commenting casually to a *campesino* girl who worked at Radiofónicas that I could not make up my mind whether the music was happy or sad. She turned to me abruptly and stared at me in blank amazement: 'Can you not see, Don Ricardo?' she asked incredulously. 'Can you not *hear* that they are very, very sad people trying to be happy?'

Among the activities that the four who shared the apartment promoted under the heading of '*Campesino* Leadership Programme' was a game called '*Huasipungo*', which was a kind of Monopoly played out in a *campesino* context whereby the players – the *campesinos* – were cheated by all and sundry and lost everything they had. Such 'role-play' games are fairly common among the voluntary agencies today but they were still something of a novelty then. Everyone enjoyed it immensely and invariably fell about laughing, but none of us was really sure if it was achieving its objective of 'raising consciousness'.

One day, one of the volunteers received a cheque for a couple of hundred dollars from his church back home as a contribution towards the Leadership Programme. The church did not specify how the money should be spent and we agonized for ages over the various uses it might be put to – a hand pump, a health post, a community centre, courses in animal husbandry and first aid, and so on – without coming to any real conclusion. In the end, we decided that it was paternalistic for us to make the decision, and that if we were to be true to our ideals of partnership and co-operation we should just hand the money over and let the *campesinos* decide for themselves how best to spend it. They, after all, were the best judges of their own needs.

And so it was that one Friday morning Chet, the volunteer in question, handed over a wad of sucre notes to the headman of the village in which he was working, explaining that the money was a gift from the people of his village back home to the people of this village in Ecuador and that they should decide for themselves how the money might best be spent. The headman gratefully accepted the gift, and we, in turn, sat back and eagerly awaited the outcome of their deliberations.

When Chet returned early Monday morning, he found the village deserted. There was no sign of life anywhere; no *campesinos* working in the fields; no kids herding sheep; and none of the wood-smoke seeping through the thatch that normally signalled the stirring of life and the start of the new day.

'Hey, where is everybody?' he asked anxiously of a solitary old man whom he eventually found sitting on the wet grass, propped heavily against a mud wall.

'Chuchaqui,' replied the old man, dragging a limp hand across his brow in a manner that betrayed complicity, 'hangover'.

And that, in a word, was where the money went – one riotous, weekend-long binge. But the exercise was not entirely wasted, I might add, because we, at least, learned something from it and concluded that what their consciousness really needed was not so much 'raising' as a little 'redirecting'.

Riobamba's second restaurant, the 'Botecito' or 'Little Boat' as it is called, is situated two cobbled streets back from the Parque Sucre, the main square in Riobamba. These days there is no sign outside announcing its presence, and the clientele, in so far as it exists, are the few Indians who come in from the *campo* now and again for a spree. This is some change from the old days when the gentry of the town brought their entire families, all decked out in suits and frilly dresses, to take over the place and spend liberally, leaving an enormous debris of empty plates, tall brown bottles, and crumpled serviettes behind them. In those days the Indian did not dare set foot inside and the few that you saw were threadbare, half-cowed beggars who came to the door to ask for alms, which were nearly always given.

It was in the 'Botecito' of its heyday, in late 1968, that I first met Alfredo – a meeting which, contrary to expectations, was to leave a lasting impression. I was with two of the volunteers from the apartment at the time and we had gone there for the 'churrasco' lunch – the steak, rice, chips, fried eggs and onions – that was to become something of a ritual with us on Saturdays when the 'Campesino Leadership boys' were in from the *campo*. The meal itself was fairly cheap – about five sucres in those days – although you were never really sure what the final toll would be because the proprietor charged for ketchup 'by the finger'. When you asked for the bottle he would stand in front of you and, with perfect fairness, draw a line on the label to indicate where the level was, and then calculate accordingly. When the ketchup had not gone down far enough to reach the label he had no way of marking the bottle, but we never quibbled in earnest.

Alfredo was just sixteen at the time; a fresh-faced, enthusiastic boy, mad keen on weight-lifting and physical fitness and, in the fashion of most Ecuadorean youth, eager to speak to foreigners to learn about their countries. His very first words to us, right out of the blue, were to ask if we liked 'Jinetes en el Cielo'. It took us a while to work out that he was referring to the old song 'Ghost Riders in the Sky'. He was learning the guitar, he told us, and was sure he would be able to play 'Jinetes' in no time. Somehow he seemed to assume that we, and presumably all gringos, were accomplished musicians. It was an instinctive faith in our expertise and our resources that cropped up time and time again.

Alfredo was the waiter in the 'Botecito' and he had been working there for three years. It was a common enough story – a bright young lad with no father at home, obliged to take up a dead-end job to bring in money to support innumerable younger brothers and sisters. He worked long hours, six days a week, for next to nothing. But he was energetic and ambitious, and his idealism was still pretty much intact. He told us that 'the restaurant was just temporary, until he found a real job', and, sensing that we might be able to give him the kind of advice that his poor mother was unable to give, he used us as a sort of careers' advisory board. Over the weeks we went through a whole range of job possibilities with him until he finally decided that he was going to become an electrician. The future was sure to be in electricity, he prophesied (quite rightly, as it turned out), and that was where he wanted to be.

It seemed a long shot at the time, there being no facilities for part-time study in Riobamba, and Alfredo having no way to finance himself. But this did not seem to deter him at all. He knew where he wanted to go, and the means of getting there was of little consequence. He plotted feverishly to seek out a way, and eventually, against all the odds, he found one.

We could see, the moment we entered the door one Saturday lunchtime, that he was orbiting somewhere near the moon. His every look told us that he had been dying for our arrival, and it made us feel good to be needed that much, if a little uneasy at the responsibility it entailed. He detoured swiftly from the table he was serving and whispered urgently, 'I've got it! I've got it right here! I'll be over in a minute. Don't leave without talking. OK?'

His good humour and his sense of duty did not desert him in his excitement, and he continued about his work, casting side-long, conspiratorial glances in our direction. Of course we felt good in any case, but we tried hard to show it so as not to detract in any way from his great moment. It might, after all, be the turning point in his life, and I suspect that deep down we all felt a little privileged to be sharing in this moment of personal history. We tried not to let our interest flag as we waited for the customers to depart and Alfredo to come over and tell us his news.

It was a correspondence course that he had stumbled upon – 'The George Woodbridge School for Personal Advancement' – and he held out a cutting from a newspaper and a brochure that a cousin living in Quito had sent to him. The literature told the story in pictures – a smiling, grey-haired gentleman was seen handing a diploma to a successful, dark-skinned student, and the following pages testified with photos and signed statements to scores of satisfied customers throughout the world for whom George Woodbridge had been the 'doorway to a brighter future'. Alfredo was well and truly hooked. He no doubt saw a photo of himself there along with all the others, affirming with beaming satisfaction that 'George Woodbridge had been the right connection to a career in electrics'.

I guess we all felt a little shamefaced at the cynicism that the crude brochure provoked in us, but who were we to judge? We knew nothing of this particular institution and, in any case, the lad was riding high and we had no wish to bring him earthwards. We read through the fine print and as far as we could see it was fairly straightforward. The Correspondence School, based in Miami, promised on receipt of US$50 to send a small electrical tool-kit and the first of twelve monthly lessons that were to lead to 'The George Woodbridge School for Personal Advancement Basic Proficiency Certificate'. It was simple – you sent off the money, applied yourself to your studies, and within a year, you had a qualification in electrics from the United States. There were one or two additional payments to be made along the way, but Alfredo would cross those bridges when he came to them. For the present, he could hardly contain himself. 'Los Estados Unidos!' he said with an incredulous, triumphant yelp, and repeated it just to make sure that he had heard himself properly the first time – 'The United States!'

He got the $50 together fairly quickly, somewhat to our surprise. We helped him a bit but didn't want to remove the sense of achievement by making it too easy for him. Where the rest of the money came from we didn't know and never asked, but we suspected that he, or his mother, must have gone the rounds of family and friends. At all events, it can't have come without a struggle, even though foreign currency itself was not difficult to come by at that time. The money order was duly sent off to Miami, along with the enrolment form, and we all sat back to endure the three weeks that we reckoned it would take for the reply to arrive. The suspense was killing enough for us, so heaven knows what it must have been like for Alfredo. I wonder what incredible schemes he plotted during that agonizing wait, for he had no doubt that his ship had finally come in.

We continued going to the 'Botecito' on Saturdays even after the three weeks were long gone, although it hurt us to see him trying to disguise his disappointment. We needed to show him that we still believed it would work out, and we persevered despite our growing sense of foreboding and the shadow that had fallen across his face.

'Hey, come on man,' said Chuck, one of the volunteers. 'Take it easy! The mail gets held up – everybody knows that! Hell, I've waited up to three months for a letter from my girl back home. They dump it in Quito somewhere and get around to sorting it whenever they feel like it. It'll get here soon, you take my word for it, buddy. You just take my word for it!'

But it never did, and finally we ceased to mention it altogether. When I was about to leave Ecuador in the middle of 1970 I went back to Riobamba and called to see Alfredo a last time. He was still there in the 'Botecito', working and running between the tables as seriously and efficiently as ever, but I fancied that some of the spring had gone from his step. He smiled warmly, and gripped my hand.

'Please will you write to me?' he asked.

'OK, I'll write,' I said.

But I never did. I justified not doing so by the fact that scores of people had asked me to write, as they always did whenever anyone was about to leave, and I knew I couldn't write to them all. And besides, everyone made promises that they never had any intention of keeping, and I was just doing the same. But all the same, I knew it was wrong. Alfredo was special, and I should have written.

When I returned to the 'Botecito' twenty years later, the owner, Señor Zambrano, lamented the passing of time and trade and recalled approvingly how the wealthy used to spread their cash around. Today the gentry go elsewhere and the Indians have taken over. 'The Indian is tight with his money,' he says without malice, 'no afloja' – 'he won't let go.'

The old boy is nearly eighty now and doesn't much care. His lack of concern shows in the primitive kerosene stove that still burns in the smoke-blackened kitchen, even though the town is now fully electrified and gas supplies are good, in the squat wooden chairs that have not been replaced in maybe two generations, and in the cats that chase each other, unhindered, around the dining room.

Talking to him again after so many years, I had the feeling that he would be content with his memories from now on. The Indians might well take over – he didn't mind. In its heyday the 'Botecito' had seen the very best that Riobamba had to offer and its revenue had provided a living and an education for eight children – a 'rondador' of children as the Ecuadoreans call it, after the graduated pipes of the pan-flute. He had no cause for complaint; God had been good to him.

I asked Señor Zambrano what had become of Alfredo. He seemed surprised that I should remember him.

'Oh yes, of course, young Alfredo,' the old man recalled. 'He joined a small firm down the road; became a carpenter. But he wasn't reliable. He didn't honour his commitments. He became very slack and made his customers wait for their orders. Eventually he got into debt and ran off with some money. Quite a lot too, if I remember rightly, although I don't recall how much it was exactly. They say he went over Santo Domingo way, about seven or eight years ago now. That was the last I heard of him. Turned out to be no good I'm afraid. No good.'

Recounted thus, and with hindsight, it sounded all so inevitable, and yet I couldn't help wondering. Later that night I tried to think through what might have brought about this change in Alfredo's character, for unreliable and dishonest he certainly was not in those days. I could not help feeling that part of the blame was mine. Why had I not taken the trouble to write as I had promised, instead of merely adding to the multitude of falsities that were the common currency of his and everyone else's daily existence? He had, after all, confided in us volunteers as in no one else, and a letter at the right moment might – just might – have made the difference between keeping on, and giving up.

And then, of course, there was George Woodbridge and his 'School for Personal Advancement' – if it really existed. Who knows what might have become of Alfredo if he had actually completed his electrician's course? He was certainly bright and ambitious and none of us doubted the seriousness of his intent for one second. An entrepreneur, I could have imagined him – but a thief on the run, and in disgrace? Hardly! For all anyone knows he might have been some local bigwig by now, a respected and successful member of the community with his own thriving electrical business; chairman of the local Rotary Club perhaps.

It does no good to speculate in this manner, of course. What's done is done, and common sense tells you it is more than likely George Woodbridge had nothing whatsoever to do with Alfredo's fall from grace. Perhaps the whole affair was just another fad which, like his guitar-playing and his weight-lifting, was destined from the outset to sink without trace. This is the conclusion I finally came to – this, and the recognition that no one is his brother's keeper. And yet, I have to admit that I still occasionally catch myself wondering what might have become of Alfredo if that package from George Woodbridge had ever arrived.

CHAPTER TEN

PEACE CORPS

FOR A LONG TIME I was unsure as to what I really thought of the Peace Corps as an organization. It was never easy to cut through all the propaganda, the euphoria, the goodwill and the sheer scale of the thing, to get to the heart of what was actually going on. I certainly felt gratitude from a personal point of view for the volunteers' company, and for the assistance that the staff unhesitatingly gave me on a number of occasions, especially when I was sick, but at the same time I thought I sensed something approaching chaos about it. What made it all the more confusing was that hardly anyone else seemed to notice, or if they did, they appeared not to be bothered by it.

The Ecuadoreans seemed to be ambivalent about the whole thing, with the government happily agreeing year by year to the arrival of scores of new volunteers, while the political Left accused them of being spies for the CIA – an accusation which, as Philip Agee implies in his book *Inside The Company: CIA Diary*, was not altogether without foundation. I recall one occasion when a volunteer had his camera snatched from his hand by an angry citizen as he tried to photograph the six o'clock train leaving Riobamba for Guayaquil, and was told that 'spies were not welcome in Ecuador'.

There were problems all around me. If some of the volunteers I knew, like Paul, at least had nominal jobs to do, then others did not and did not pretend to have. The four who shared the apartment and who managed the '*Campesino* Leadership Programme' spent their weekdays out in the villages living in thatched huts, trying to organize what was loosely termed 'consciousness-raising activities'. None of them actually believed they were being effective (although they would occasionally comment wryly that 'it was doing wonders for their own consciousness'), and they became increasingly frustrated by their inability to bring meaningful change where it was desperately needed. It also led to a growing cynicism towards Peace Corps Washington, whom they saw as responsible for a policy that put volunteer numbers above results, and by extension towards the United States government, since the Peace Corps is a government agency.

The combination of frustration and cynicism frequently proved too much and had a good many opting for the 'ten o'clock Braniff' and the 'green, green grass of home'; except when they got there they found that the grass wasn't quite as green as they remembered and that they no longer 'belonged' in quite the same way that they did before. For some the long-awaited home-coming turned out to be traumatic and they found it impossible to adjust, with the result that they either 'dropped out' completely or became advocates of violent change – an irony that will not have been lost on the State Department.

One of the more pathetic cases I heard of was that of a former Riobamba volunteer who, back home in the States, was visited by his enthusiastic successor to the project just before he was due to fly out. The volunteer-elect, who had travelled half-way across the country in his eagerness to be fully briefed, found his mentor shut away incommunicado, staring at the colour television, listening to rock music through headphones and steadily drinking whisky. His mother said he had been this way ever since he got back.

Returning home after two years is difficult for any volunteer, firstly because you don't realize how much you have changed in the meanwhile and just how different 'home' is going to seem when you get there, and secondly because the experience forces you to ask more questions about life and the world than your own culture can answer. Ultimately, if you see it through, you end up becoming a 'citizen of the world' with a primary allegiance to the whole human race, which is fine except that, like any birth or rebirth, the process can be traumatic. The situation was made worse in the case of Peace Corps Volunteers by a sense of betrayal that many of them had about the organization, rather like the disillusionment of soldiers returning home from Vietnam.

My association with the volunteers was the first time I had come across people being paid a regular salary (which was several times my own) without having a job of work to do. I can still remember my confusion when, newly arrived in country, I asked one of the volunteers what his project was hoping to achieve.

'Hell man, I don't know,' he replied. 'I've been here six months now and I still haven't got the faintest idea what I'm supposed to be doing.'

At the time I thought he was being evasively modest and it was some while before I discovered that he had been simply telling the truth. A good many of the 200 or so Peace Corps Volunteers in Ecuador at that time did not have genuine jobs and this resulted in a process of migration from one place to another as they sought, earnestly and honestly, for worthwhile things to do. The ones on the coast thought that the Sierra might have something to offer; and the ones in the Sierra thought that the coast might be the answer; and the ones in the north thought that the south was where it was happening, and so forth, so that you ended up with a constantly shifting volunteer population. The end result of this was that well over half the volunteers did not finish their two-year terms, even though they were well aware that their early termination might render them eligible for 'the Draft'.

It seemed clear to me that the Peace Corps, which was only six years old at the time, was in trouble and I could not for the life of me work out why the decision-makers in Quito and Washington kept on bringing in new volunteers to replace the ones who were leaving prematurely. One day it dawned on me that perhaps, for them, these early returns did not necessarily constitute failure and that what seemed like a fairly heartless exercise in the survival of the fittest was just an everyday expression of the national psyche.

After all, was this not the way that the country was settled in the first place, and is this not the principle on which the nation prides itself today — on courage and determination, and individuals making it alone? How many wagons actually made it to the West? How many miners actually struck it rich in the Gold Rush? And what percentage of business ventures today actually cross over into the black, compared with the many that go under, and what happens to the ones that fail? I suspect that no one really knows for sure or cares very much either, especially about the ones that don't make it. What are Americans told by their Embassies when they report that all their cash and their belongings have been stolen? 'To find their own way home.' The notion of state-sponsored safety nets has never gained much favour in the US.

Having met many volunteers and staff who convinced me of their good faith, I had discounted early on the widespread, cynical notion that the volunteers were merely agents of cultural imperialism with a mission to promote the American way of life, and that this was the reason it was so important to keep the programme intact regardless of performance in developmental terms. Even if one acknowledges that there were, and probably still are, senior officials within the State Department who thought the same thing — one Secretary of State is on record as having said that 'the Peace Corps is the cheapest way of advertising the United States' — and that funding (in copious amounts) may well have been made available on this basis, it does not mean that those on the ground subscribed to the same view; nor does it mean that this is what their contribution actually amounted to in practice.

What the Peace Corps was really concerned about, it seemed to me, was providing opportunity, and after that it was pretty much left to the individual as to whether he sank or swam. And if they judged performance at all, it was by the ones who made it to the other side. It is an approach that contrasts sharply, of course, with that of the Europeans, who seem forever more concerned with failure and the ones who drown. It is the difference that separates the two continents — the one, a risk-all, socio-economic Darwinism in which the strong survive and the weak go under; and the other, a play-safe, welfare-state protectionism in which the weak survive and the strong go overseas. This difference of priority must surely be at the root of much of the antagonism that exists between the two.

What is certain is that the Peace Corps has changed little in the meanwhile. They continue to send volunteers by the score to unvetted, non-viable projects and the volunteers continue to leave in large numbers, many of them nursing a deep sense of failure at what they see as their inability to 'measure up'. My feelings towards the Peace Corps are largely irreconcilable – a mixture of love and sadness: love for the volunteers themselves and sadness for their predicament. The whole organization seemed to me to be flawed somehow or other, despite the nobility of its aims and its unfailing generosity of spirit. Whatever it tried to do seemed destined to misfire.

The problem derives in large part from a lack of self-awareness. A young country that has been so brilliantly successful in solving its own material problems finds it hard to understand the impediments that stand in the way of a developing nation. In the case of the Peace Corps the condition has been rendered more acute by the fact that the United States has never known, and still does not know, what it is to fail materially, so that its every move has been bolstered by an irrepressible optimism. This goes some way to explaining why the same inappropriate solutions have been thrown at the problems of underdevelopment year after year, regardless of the cost in terms of finance and morale.

To be perfectly fair, however, one has to recognize that no one has yet come up with the right answer to development questions, and every country and organization has its own record of heroic failures. We seem to be learning more and more about what does *not* work rather than what does, which is progress of a sort. But somehow the Peace Corps seemed to invite criticism by its very existence, and often in a way that had nothing to do with its performance. This was primarily a question of visibility. It was the product of an unyielding refusal to consult with others in the same field, and the fact that its aims and means were always so much more grandiose than everybody else's, so that its disasters, when they came, invariably turned out to be all the more spectacular.

There was another and even darker cloud hanging over the Peace Corps in the late sixties, and this was Vietnam. The great nation had run in pursuit of righteousness and met with tragedy, thrusting itself gauchely into a war it did not understand and a land where it did not belong, and now it was paying a terrible price. Today, we can see clearly that US involvement was a tragic mistake. If this genuinely Christian nation had only had a little more faith in humanity and a little less faith in weaponry then some 55,000 North Americans and countless Vietnamese need not have died.

As it was, a most miserable and benighted confusion reigned over the nation. Many people sensed that the whole thing was wrong but lacked the moral ammunition necessary to win the war of words. The apologists had no end of arguments at their disposal, and the machinery with which to churn them out. A good many of the volunteers openly admitted that they had joined the Peace Corps to avoid the Draft, while others could not make up their minds whether they had or hadn't; either way, it served to undermine their commitment to the organization and to Ecuador. Many were sick at heart, and it showed.

The war, as has often been said, wounded the nation as nothing else ever could, and the dilemma was all the more acute because in the late sixties and early seventies people still clung to idealism. Innocence had not yet become a crime, and people still believed in politicians; the lines between good and bad were clearly drawn. People believed in the way things were and it felt good.

I read in *Time* magazine of a comment made by a Vietnam veteran who, at the inauguration of the War Memorial in Washington, stood tearfully tracing the name of a fallen buddy now inscribed in gilt in the black marble ribbon. It made me think again about my Peace Corps friends, some of whom had also been the casualties of a miscalculation.

'Good soldier, bad war,' wept the veteran, and I thought how his words might be paraphrased to apply to them: 'Good volunteer, bad Corps.'

CHAPTER ELEVEN

LOS JETS

MOST OF THE INSIGHTS I gained into the Ecuadorean way of things came from a single Riobambeño family that I got to know very well and for whose friendship I shall be eternally grateful. It was the middle one of the five charming sisters who attracted me to them in the first place and who remained the true object of my attention thereafter, but just occasionally I would find myself being dragged away by one or more of the three brothers, who apparently thought that my time could be better spent in their company.

The three of them belonged to a gang called 'los Jets'. There was nothing sinister about it, just a group of lads inspired by *West Side Story* to give themselves a name, and whose activities rarely strayed beyond getting too drunk, smoking their lungs out and occasionally serenading some unfortunate señorita from the back of a 'borrowed' pick-up at three o'clock in the morning. It was all solid Andy Capp stuff and perfectly harmless. There were eight full members and any number of associate members of the gang, which really included just about anybody who felt like going for a drink on a Saturday night. I was tacitly accorded 'honorary member' status, which meant that I only went drinking when I couldn't think up an excuse fast enough to get out of it.

The bar they frequented, the 'Manabita', which the owner had named in a rare flight of romantic fancy after his wife, from the province of Manabí, was unremarkable in every sense except for the regularity with which its customers used to congregate. It was a corner shop that had been converted into a drinking house and was situated just two blocks from the family home, on the eastern edge of town – the dusty part where the cobblestones hadn't yet encroached. The bar was always dark even in the daytime, an impression reinforced by the nicotine-stained benches and tables, the unpainted walls and the well-trodden wooden floor, which handfuls of sawdust did nothing to enhance. The drink on these occasions was the 'canelazo' which, roughly translated, means 'a cinnamon assault', the mixture being composed of the ubiquitous local spirit, trago, and hot cinnamon water. In the cold Andean nights it went down quite well.

We would assemble around the table and the eldest brother, Mauricio, would call authoritatively to the landlord for the glasses and the bottle of trago. The kettle with the cinnamon water was kept boiling on a charcoal stove outside the door and was brought over on demand by the Manabita herself. The small tumbler glasses were carefully and ceremoniously filled by Mauricio to about two fingers, with the Manabita hovering within earshot, ready for the signal to pour.

The protocol was clearly laid down and you had to know how and when to drink. There was no asking 'what's it going to be then?' or opting to go 'on the wagon', it was canelazos all round and that was it. And you drank together, the same amount, at the appropriate signal from Mauricio, the unanimity underlining a sense of brotherhood. The conversation, although its limits were defined with some stringency, was relaxed enough, at least at the beginning when it revolved around the various events of the week just gone. Later, as the drinking and the themes got heavier, I would invariably find myself being called upon to come up with some definitive statement about the meaning of life.

Occasionally, friends from the past would return from the United States for a visit and they would be whisked off to the 'Manabita' at the first opportunity. Everyone wanted to know what life was like up there – if there was any prejudice against Hispanics, how much cash was to be made, how much crime there was on the streets, how easy it was to obtain residence, and so forth. Most Riobambeños headed for the East Coast, to the New York/New Jersey area, and the answers were already well known but undoubtedly worth listening to again.

Yes, there was some prejudice but it was tolerable, and yes, there was lots of money to be made, if you were prepared to work and boy, do those gringos make you work! Yes, there was crime and violence, and drugs, and you had to be careful where and when you walked, especially at night. And as for residence, you had to lie low after your tourist visa expired and then look for a good lawyer, but the visitor always seemed to know 'just the person' so it was 'really nothing to worry about'. I don't think I ever came across anyone with serious regrets about going; in fact, they all seemed to affirm that it was a great move and encouraged others to follow in their footsteps, always extending liberal offers of finance and accommodation to facilitate the process – offers that, I subsequently learned, were usually genuine.

Within each of the listeners there was probably still a part that hoped to hear they were better off where they were, but this battle had long ago been fought and lost and most knew deep down that they would be heading north just as soon as the moment was right – when they could get the passport, the tourist visa and the fare together. I must have witnessed half a dozen instances in the 'Manabita' when the decision to emigrate was taken, and I sometimes wondered if the landlord ever really understood – beyond his diminishing returns – the part he was playing in shaping the destiny of his clientele and the demography of the district in those latter years of the 1960s.

I had the opportunity twenty years later to visit some of these *emigrés* and to judge for myself whether or not the move had been positive. In a couple of cases there remained some unanswered questions, but for others there was no doubt of their success. They had left one country at the age of eighteen or nineteen, where there was virtually no hope of work or further education, and had gone to another where they had applied themselves night and day to their endeavours until they eventually 'made it', some in private business (haulage and car-hire for example) and others as professionals – computer specialists, accountants, mechanics and so on. For such people who were now legally resident with full rights of citizenship, the benefits were obvious and they expressed their gratitude for the opportunity the United States had given them at every turn.

But there were others I could never be sure about, although they professed themselves to be happy with their lot. I am thinking of two in particular, both of whom had worked in government. One had been a secondary school teacher in Riobamba and was now working at the check-out of a supermarket in downtown Newark; and the other had been an agriculturalist assigned to coastal Ecuador and was now a labourer in a garment factory. Notwithstanding the higher cost of living, it was plain that they were both a good deal better off financially than they had been at home. Furthermore their pay cheques arrived regularly every week, something that seldom happened in Ecuador – government employees often had to wait several months for their pay to come through. But there were also such things as job satisfaction and status, particularly in a country like Ecuador where status is an obsession, and the contrast of life in a noise-filled, crime-ridden ghetto with the space, tranquillity and scenic beauty of the Andes.

Of course immigrants, anxious to save face, are prone to exaggerate the advantages of their new home, sometimes to the point of tolerating conditions palpably worse than the ones they left behind, but I do not think that this was often the case. Perhaps the real appeal of life in the United States remained its opportunities, the possibility of being able to 'make it' one day, even if you never actually managed it; or perhaps it was the experience of living under a fairer, less oppressive system of government that provided vastly superior services for its citizens; or perhaps it was the excitement that derived from living in the foremost nation on earth during its heyday.

One Saturday evening the Jets received a visit from an old acquaintance, a man in his early thirties who claimed he was working as a singer in a night club in Atlantic City. He was somewhat older than most of the members, but they welcomed him with characteristic affection and cordiality and gave him the customary 'long-lost-brother' treatment. It soon became apparent, however, despite the display of brotherhood, that if he had ever really been friendly with any of them he had never been anybody's particular favourite, and that little had changed in the five years he had been away. Perhaps it was his pretensions that set him apart — the 'local-boy-made-good' who had come home to see how the 'old town' was doing; or perhaps he lacked the basic personality credentials for this strict macho club. Whatever the reason, there was a certain amount of tension in the air that night.

He seemed determined to speak to me in English, presumably to impress the others with his newly acquired skill, and I was torn between offending him by replying in Spanish and offending everybody else by replying in English. I decided to feed him a couple of sentences in English first to let him show off his stuff and then switch promptly back into Spanish, but his English proved to be extraordinarily interesting. Whereas he appeared to speak with considerable fluency and an excellent East Coast accent, when you analysed what he said it added up to little more than a string of the most impeccably delivered obscenities.

'So, you like the States, then?' I asked.

'You bet, man. Too . . . . much! You better believe it. Those sons-of-bitches, man. Too much!'

'Good money?'

'Good money? Better . . . . believe it! Too . . . . much! Everythin' you want, man. Those sons-of-bitches, I tell you!'

As the conversation progressed it became clear that his vocabulary had a range of about fifty words, half of which were obscenities, and yet he managed to sound convincingly like some second-generation Italian American marine sergeant. It was a remarkable performance.

With a few more canelazos inside him and with a bit of nudging from the Jets he was ready to perform, despite his protestations that it wouldn't sound the same without the six-piece band that backed him every night in Atlantic City. Tables and benches were pushed back to make space and we sat around attentively while he churned out a couple of the old standards, 'El Reloj' – 'The Clock', and 'La Barca' – 'The Boat', both nice songs that tell, inevitably, sad tales of lovers forced to part. He murdered them both. He followed this up with 'My Way', in English. At least I think it was in English but I couldn't be absolutely sure, since much of it was incomprehensible, even though I knew the words. Still, I was impressed because it was the first time I had heard him put more than four words together without using an obscenity.

Los Jets were ecstatic and applauded like mad. I turned to Mauricio. 'Not bad, eh?'

Mauricio leaned forward and whispered in my ear, 'Canta pésimamente mal el cojudo, pero es del barrio' – 'Can't sing a note, the pillock, but he's one of the lads.'

He didn't stay too long after that, supposedly because he had somewhere else to rush off to, and no one made much effort to get him to stay. As we shook hands I wished him, in English, a pleasant stay and a safe return to New Jersey.

'You bet, man. You bet!' he replied effortlessly, then added, 'Hey man, let me tell you somethin' . . . Ecuador's too much. Know what I mean? I mean *too much*! But those sons-of-bitches up there, man, I tell you – too . . . . much man, just too . . . . much!'

I told him I knew exactly what he meant and gave him a real bear-hug, because I was actually getting to like the fellow. It wasn't just that his phoney linguistic ability appealed to someone who couldn't speak a foreign language properly either; there was something delightful about his ludicrous pose. His blatant lack of musical talent struck me as being quite commendable. It was so disarming.

'Hey, take it easy man,' I said, slipping into the jargon and kicking myself for it at the same time.

'Are you serious? With those sons-of-bitches up there?' he replied – immaculately – and then made a rapid and well-polished exit.

I was never a great lover of these evenings, mainly because I didn't like getting even moderately drunk. I never displayed the effects of the 'assault' until the next day, with the result that I gained quite a reputation for being a 'man who could hold his drink', something that counted for a lot in those circles. What no one ever saw was the long hours I spent the following morning with my head in the toilet bowl. I saw this as the penalty for my stupidity and knew I was getting my just deserts.

Once you were at the table, convention had it that no one left until the group as a whole was ready to leave, so the prospect of a retching dawn hung over every slug of canelazo. But it was hard to resist such group pressure and at that time independence of spirit was beyond me, even if I had wanted it.

Sometimes the conversation would take a less pleasant turn and I would be pilloried, on behalf of 'gringos' in general, for everything that Europe and North America had done for the past 500 years. The joke was that, despite their Spanish language and their Catholicism, they always spoke as if they themselves had nothing whatsoever to do with either Europe or the destruction of the native American way of life — a self-deception that is even more pronounced in Mexico, where Spanish-speaking Catholics will tell you that 'the Yankees stole Texas from us'.

I could tell when the moment was getting near and I would brace myself for the attack, always giving something in return but never enough to provoke outright violence. At the root of it all I sensed a need to be respected. It always ended up friendly enough, as we weaved down the street in the early hours of the morning, arms around each other, brothers to the death, each having gained respect for his capacity to take and inflict pain within the rules. But the aggression was always there, the other side of the brotherhood coin and the result of the harsh conditions in which the people lived. Machismo is a survival technique for bearing the unbearable with dignity; it protects the ego from the daily round of frustration and humiliation. It will exist as long as the violence of social injustice exists, and with it will go all the paraphernalia of a violent

culture – the boxing, the football fanaticism and the rock and roll –
all of which are the necessary channels for pent-up aggression.

As the social injustice disappears so will the machismo, but until
then, ugly though it may be, it is preferable to anarchy and
mayhem. Precious few among the middle and upper classes seem to
understand the fragile system of checks and balances that control
these destructive forces, and much less do they seem to appreciate
that their tranquil and ordered lives, their refined tastes in music,
theatre, art and the like, have usually been defined and paid for by
the masses.

The rules of the game were quite complicated, although no
more so than in England where every pub has its social language, its
taboo subjects and its inner and outer circles. The players had to be
their own referees and be constantly monitoring the temperature of
the discussion – most cliques have a 'fire-fighter' or two. I soon
learned – the hard way – of the impossibility of talking about the
female family members of present company; and there was another
rule, every bit as binding, that whatever was agreed upon between
drinking partners in these moments of celebration bore no relation
to the real world.

Once we were comparing the relative stamina of Europeans and
Latin Americans. The discussion turned somehow to mountaineer-
ing, and a whole series of boasts and challenges were thrown up in
the heat of the cinnamon assault with the result that we all agreed
to meet the following morning to climb Tungurahua. Everything
was planned – the time, the place, how we would get there and
what we would need to take.

'Now, we are all serious about this, aren't we?' I asked. 'I mean,
we're all going to turn up for sure, right?'

A battery of indignant, unbelieving stares turned on me. 'Are
you doubting my word?' retorted one of the Jets. 'Listen, if I say I'm
going to do something, I do it. Right?'

Early the following morning, I arrived at the agreed time and
place only to find myself alone. I waited for an hour or so for
someone else to show up, but eventually it became clear that no one

was going to. And so, feeling pretty fed up – although also secretly relieved because the cinnamon assault had taken its usual toll and left me feeling totally wrecked, without the least desire to go climbing anywhere except into bed – I went back home. When I tentatively reminded my fellow 'mountaineers' about our arrangement later, I found myself up against a wall of impenetrable and unforgiving silence. The subject was never mentioned again.

These were the less pleasant times and they were few and far between. For the most part the friendships were warm and uplifting, and if you ever had a problem they were the best people in the world to be with. So often I have seen in developing countries how quick the people are to rally to each other's assistance. The same woman who told me that Riobamba was the worst place on earth also told me that Ecuadoreans are much kinder than Europeans. Although I can't bring myself to believe that any one group of people is kinder or less kind than another, they are certainly more openly sympathetic and responsive to need than we Northern Europeans are, even if the assistance offered frequently turns out to be more promissory than real, and seldom extends beyond a close-knit circle of kith and kin. Nevertheless, it is a society that prides itself in and survives on the strength of its relationships and you see its warmth everywhere – among members of seemingly never-ending families, towards friends, and often towards complete strangers. You see it also in those not infrequent moments when a thwarted lover is contemplating ending it all by throwing himself into the river.

I would not be so bold as to suggest that Latin romantic behaviour is no more than a piece of theatre, but the suicide threats do tend to outnumber the corpses rather. At all events, whenever someone is contemplating curing a broken heart by taking the plunge into the River Guayas, it is the job of his best friend to enter into the melodrama and talk him out of it.

'It's no good brother,' the wounded lover may say. 'I'm not going to get up from this one. This is the killer blow.'

'Is this Pablo Jiménez I hear speaking?' the friend will reply, his face a picture of shock and indignation. 'The same Pablo Jiménez who took on and defeated the whole Santo Poco gang single-handed? The same Pablo Jiménez who has had more women in a week than most men have in a lifetime? The same Pablo Jiménez who can down a bottle of trago in ten seconds and walk straight out the door, his head held high? Because if it is, I do not recognize him!'

'Ah, my brother, you speak of the man I once was, before I met this Angel of Death who poisoned my very soul, stripped me of my senses and left me broken, like a wounded sparrow, in the dust.'

'And since when does a man fall to his knees for a woman? You have been too soft with her, my friend, and she has abused your kind heart. Stand up like the giant that you are and take her in hand, for I swear that this is all she desires – to be tamed by the man she loves, and no one in the world can do this better than Pablo Jiménez, no one!'

'My friend, my dear friend,' insists the lover, 'I might have done such things once upon a time, but this heart, that held sway over a thousand dazzling pairs of eyes, is but a remnant of its former self. What is there left for me now but to live like a beggar, pleading for the favours of this Jezebel, and to live out my days in the shadows of despair? No, my friend, my pride cannot countenance such a fate, it is better that I end it all, here and now!'

And so it goes, until the disconsolate lover is made to feel like facing the world again. I was never able to decide how seriously these exchanges were meant to be taken, because this absurd mixture of chauvinism and melodrama struck me as deliberately inviting ridicule. But when I found myself on the inside on one occasion I was not only grateful for the support my friends gave me, I was amazed to find that all this 'corn' actually works – it is guaranteed to have you up on your feet in no time.

As my Spanish improved and I came to appreciate some of the nuances of the language, I was astonished to discover that the wit and humour of Riobamba were quite similar to that of the district where I had grown up in Bristol. There were practical jokes like the time, nearly a week in all, that Mauricio took a tiny tropical animal called a 'cuzumbo' around with him everywhere he went – to school, to the doctor's, to the 'Manabita' and to the police station to see if the police could find a mate for it. In fact he tried to get its non-existent mate listed as a 'missing cuzumbo'. And then there was the time that his younger brother Paco sat the whole day in class without saying a word to anyone wearing a pair of spectacles without the lenses. He followed this up the next day by wearing the lenses without the frames.

But it was in the repartee that the greatest similarity lay. I couldn't believe it the first time I played football and discovered that my team-mates were saying exactly the same things to each other that we used to say back home, the same terms of encouragement and disparagement, and the same threats and abuse. And naturally the poor old 'ref' got it from all sides all the time. Once you had the language, therefore, it was fairly easy to slot in. You just translated exactly what you would have said back home and it went down a treat, in fact, usually better because no one was expecting it.

'Whose side are you on today then?' you might say to a team-mate as you lined up for the kick-off.

'Depends whose side you're on,' comes back the instant reply. 'If your passing is as good as it was last week I'd be better off playing for the opposition.'

'You've got to be joking! I was the star, laid on six and scored three more, the crowd loved it!'

The essence of this type of humour is really the extent to which you can promote your own talents while demolishing everybody else's. The abuse is directed not at the individual as such but at the false ego-image that he deliberately throws up around himself so that, whereas one may appear to be ruthlessly cutting someone down to size, one is in fact merely tampering with the ego-image that he doesn't believe in anyway.

The aggression inherent in this type of humour is the same as that which underpins machismo generally, and it grows out of the brutality of the social environment. But it is a mock aggression, and one that conceals the deep affections and loyalties common to any community under siege.

CHAPTER TWELVE

EL VALENCIANO

HISPANIC MACHISMO is widely considered to reach its ultimate and most convincing expression in the bull-fighter. I had been to bullfights in Spain and, although impressed with the antiquity and the pageantry of it all, I had soon become bored with the predictability of the 'fights' themselves and had invariably come away feeling that the whole thing was a sham. The three matadors who between them dispensed with their six opponents in the course of an afternoon were always flawlessly efficient and left you convinced that the contests were so one-sided as to be pointless and cruel. The rest of the show, with all its strutting and preening, seemed little more than an exercise in self-aggrandisement. But that was before a remarkable afternoon in April 1969 when my feelings towards bullfighter and beast changed forever.

It was during Riobamba's big annual celebration, the 'Fiestas de Abril', that this particular 'corrida' took place. Bullfights are not the norm in Ecuador – perhaps no more than a couple of dozen take place in the whole country each year, and most of these are in Quito and Guayaquil, fairly lavish affairs with bullfighters flown in from Spain and Mexico for the occasion. In the provinces it is a different story, and most towns are fortunate if they get to stage a single one, and a fairly basic one at that. This was Riobamba's sole bullfight for that particular year, and it was only then I discovered Riobamba had a bull-ring at all, so inconspicuous was it.

I should have realized when I bought the ticket that it was going to be different. There was no 'sol' or 'sombra' classification as you would find in Spain, where your ticket is priced according to whether you sit in the sun (least expensive), the shade (most expensive), or the sun and the shade (moderately expensive) as the sun moves round. In Riobamba they sold only unnumbered and unrestricted tickets, which meant that you were never really sure if you were going to get a seat – the territorial struggles that took place before and during the shows were notorious.

We arrived in reasonable time, my Peace Corps friend Chet and I, and we managed to find a space on the concrete terracing where we could survey the scene. It was a small ring with a capacity of no more than 6,000, and it was close to full by the time we arrived, a good hour before the scheduled start.

The arena was more dirt than sand but it was properly marked with the conventional two white concentric circles defining the area of combat, and the barrier around the perimeter had been freshly painted an acceptable shade of brown. Everyone was in carnival mood and clearly enjoying the chance to be out in the sunshine. The same sodas and sandwiches were on sale as at the football matches and were being trotted out by the same people, along with the same jokes you heard every Sunday morning. 'Sanduches de chancho, puerco, cerdo y pernil!' they would shout. 'Sandwiches of pork, pork, pork and pork,' using the four words for 'pig' and 'pork' that exist in Ecuadorean Spanish, as they picked their way amongst the overcrowded terraces.

There was a general buzz of excitement but somehow it did not add up to the sense of expectation you would have found on a similar day in Spain. No one seemed to be talking much about bull-fights. It was almost as if they were expecting the coming spectacle to be anything but spectacular, an irrelevance even.

Our train of thought was eventually interrupted, not by a team of musicians in gold-braided uniforms blasting a fanfare through a battery of silver trumpets, but by the scratching of a 'seventy-eight' placed somewhere near a microphone. The crackling told us that the bullfight was about to begin. Instead of the customary parade of the matadors and their entourage, three young lads, no more than eighteen years old at most and dressed in sadly ageing and ill-fitting costumes like cast-offs from some local repertory company, stepped sheepishly into the arena and took up their positions at equal distances around the barrier. They were the *banderilleros*, whose job it is to plant the darts into the bull's neck so as to provoke its wrath and make sure that the matador has a fight on his hands. Their appearance met with instant, ecstatic applause.

There was a second crackled fanfare of trumpets, and a gate in the barrier opened. The afternoon's anti-hero, the bull, emerged, creating a spectacle impossible to forget. No sleek, silky black power-house of a beast, the sort of semi-mythical creature that thunders into the ring in Spain drawing gasps of amazement from the crowd – but a scrawny, light-brown animal with horns as wide as a pair of motorcycle handlebars, which seemed to stumble into the ring as if by mistake, looking decidedly bewildered, and not a little abashed at being the centre of so much attention.

'Parece vaca!' yelled a voice near me. 'Looks like a cow!'

The audience participation had begun and they were clearly loving it. 'It's going to be a brave fellow who comes out to face this lot,' I said to myself.

One of the *banderilleros* took off at high speed in the direction of the bull with his two darts poised elegantly in the air like a conductor's baton, and plunged them decisively towards the animal's neck, jinking as he did so to one side of the enormously elongated horn.

'Olé!' cried the crowd, as the two darts completely missed their target and fell harmlessly to the ground, leaving the bull indifferently statuesque in the middle and blinking vacantly in the sunlight. The crowd loved it. It couldn't have been worse.

Banderillero number two took off, breaking into a colossal sprint and repeating the performance of his colleague, only this time one of the darts stuck.

'Bravo!' cried the crowd. 'Ése sí sabe algo!' – 'This fellow knows a thing or two alright!'

Number three was next to go and he aimed himself at the bull in similarly splendid fashion, racing towards it head-on with great speed and determination. Unfortunately, the animal, in delayed reaction to the previous assault, decided to turn and inspect the damage at precisely the moment the young lad was taking off, thereby causing him to change his mind in mid-leap, pirouette magically in the air, and collapse in a crumpled heap in the dirt, darts still in hand.

'Olé!' cried the crowd. 'Now this is what you call a bullfight!'

Few people have the ability to laugh at themselves like the Ecuadoreans. It was sumptuous self-parody of the highest order, confirming all the worst suspicions they had ever had about themselves. The poor *banderillero* pulled himself to his feet, dusted himself off, straightened his shoulders, and prepared to try again.

Off he went at an enormous gallop towards the hapless animal, and with admirable sense of purpose he leaped high into the air, determined to salvage his reputation. His nerve must have suffered somewhat at the first attempt, however, because he seriously mistimed his run and landed a couple of feet short of his mark, then watched as the darts bounced harmlessly off the boniest part of the bull's head and dropped limply down into the dirt. The crowd went wild. It was too good for words.

'Give him a hand,' someone cried, 'he's doing his best,' and a sympathetic ripple of applause broke out.

The record player crackled back to life with a blast of trumpet noise setting the scene for the entrance of the picadors, the men on heavily quilted horses who wield the lances that pierce and weaken the bull's neck muscles so that the head drops and the matador has a better chance of delivering the fatal thrust of the sword down into the bull's heart. At least, this was what I thought was going to happen. In the event the picadors must have been deemed an unnecessary luxury because the next person to emerge was the matador himself, who appeared looking surprisingly dapper in an eminently respectable 'suit of lights'.

A hushed silence fell over the crowd, no one daring to think about what might come next. The tall, lithe, light-skinned figure – a young man in his mid-twenties with a mop of hair the same colour as the bull – strode powerfully out into the middle of the ring and bowed, cap in hand, in the direction of the box where the local dignitaries were seated.

'Well, he certainly looks the part,' I said to myself, but El Valenciano, as the matador was called, now had the immediate problem of goading the docile beast into action. He picked up two of the darts that were lying on the ground, aligned himself squarely in the bull's vision, arched his back like a ballet dancer, then eased himself forward into the gentlest of trots and thrust both darts deep into the lower neck of the immobile animal. He made it look simple.

A ripple of surprise ran through the crowd. The man was obviously a professional. The bull snorted indignantly and shook its head madly in an effort to rid itself of the darts, but they remained rooted, hanging down either side. It had been badly stung, and was now committed to a fight. Its docile look was gone and the mood of the afternoon had changed.

The matador called for another two darts from one of the helpers stationed behind the barrier, held them aloft for a second as if in dedication to some ancient god of war, then moved confidently forward, his pace barely rising above a brisk walk. With arms outstretched to their fullest extent, he arched his back once more and lunged forward, leaving both darts dangling from the animal's neck and skipping neatly around the tip of the horn.

He must have been quite pleased with his performance thus far for, with his back to the beast in a gesture of open scorn and with his head held high, he strutted off in the direction of the box and bowed, cap in hand, towards the occupants; then he pivoted deftly on his heels, and with a sweep of the arm that embraced God, the universe and the watching public, accepted the rising acclaim.

The bull was not so impressed and, no longer prepared to remain a standing target, decided to take the battle to the man. It turned towards its antagonist and charged. The screams of the crowd alerted El Valenciano to the danger. He had neither cape nor sword to hand but he stood his ground and, a split second before contact, stepped smartly to one side, allowing the bull to thunder past and crash resoundingly against the barrier — but not before it had done something that sent a shiver through the crowd. It had missed El Valenciano alright, but as it passed him it had hooked wildly with those enormous horns. The bull was obviously a maverick and unpredictable, which was something that even the best bullfighters in Spain seldom had to contend with — the thoroughbreds they faced, though differing in temperament, varied only within certain limits. This creature was in another category altogether. Suddenly it had become a much more interesting afternoon.

El Valenciano took his sword and cape and strode purposefully out into the middle, his firmness of step indicating that he understood this was going to be no ordinary contest. He took up his position in classic matador fashion, body side-on but face turned directly and defiantly towards the animal, which was now snorting and hoofing dirt. He shook his cape to invite the charge and the bull responded.

He stood like a statue, in perfect readiness for the first pass, but the animal did not go for the cape as it should have done but straight for the matador, scooping him up with its head and tossing him like a feather high into the air and down into the dirt. The spectators screamed and the three young *banderilleros* sprinted frantically forward, flapping their capes wildly in an effort to distract the bull from its helpless victim. One by one they were chased from the arena, giving El Valenciano time to get to his feet, pick up his cape and sword, and regain his composure.

A second time he took up his stance and invited the bull to charge, and again he stood his ground as the raging beast came towards him; and again the flaying head of the bull caught him and hurled him skywards, bending him like a rag doll and depositing him heavily in the dirt.

'Jesus Christ!' said Chet. 'Did you see that?' He was watching the action through the lens of his Pentax, getting shots of El Valenciano in mid-air. 'I've never seen anything like it!'

El Valenciano was thrown nine times, and every time he picked himself up, brushed himself off and started all over again. The tenth time he didn't. Those lethal horns that had been cutting through the air like a scythe had hitherto miraculously passed either side of his body, but on the tenth attempt one of them connected. It struck the inside of his thigh, lifted him high into the air and held him there for a second, like a piece of skewered meat, then tossed him casually to the ground.

The crowd gasped, the *banderilleros* ran, and the stretcher-bearers came in through the gate but couldn't get near the prone figure – the bull was charging and hooking at everything that moved. The *banderilleros* stuck valiantly to their task and tried to turn the bull, circling round and round and offering their capes in quick succession in an effort to make it dizzy, and for a moment it worked, but then the beast straightened up and headed for one of the stretcher-bearers. The portly, balding figure ran for his life and dived over the five-foot barrier, while the bull leaped high after him, straddling the wooden rail. The crowd shrieked as the animal see-sawed for a second then dropped down into the outer circle where the helpers were standing and started to rampage. Panic-stricken bodies hurled themselves one after the other over the barrier back into the arena and for a moment the bull was harmlessly trapped between the two fences, allowing the stretcher-bearers to get to El Valenciano and carry him off to the infirmary.

There ensued a great hubbub. What should be done? The matador who was due on next made it clear that he wanted nothing to do with the psychotic beast, so who was going to deal with it? Great consternation arose at the prospect of the collective humiliation that would result if no one could be found with the wherewithal to dispose of it. 'Bring in the army and shoot the son of a bitch!' suggested someone.

A gate in the barrier was opened inwards, blocking the channel, and the bull was guided back into the now empty arena. It stood there alone, unmoving, perhaps confused at being ignored after so much attention. No one seemed to know what to do. Then one of the *banderilleros*, the young lad who had flown through the air with the greatest of ease, took up El Valenciano's cape and sword and ran out into the middle, in an act of either astonishing courage or mental unbalance.

He called to the bull, admonishing it and waving the cape in imitation of its owner, but looking more like a scarecrow flapping in the breeze. The bull for the moment was recovering from its exertions and declined the invitation. The young *banderillero* persisted and moved forward, taunting continuously, until eventually the animal stirred and took up the challenge, charging at him murderously. The lad had clearly decided to dispense with ceremony and was going for the kill. He held the sword high above his head and launched himself forward between the thrashing horns.

He drove the sword straight, but the sharp tip bounced off the animal's back-bone and the lad was thrown high into the air and down into the dirt, just as El Valenciano had been — but at least he was not gored. His fellow *banderilleros* ran to his aid and managed with some energetic cape-work to distract the marauding beast just long enough for him to make his escape over the barrier to safety.

The great debate resumed among the officials as they sought desperately for a face-saving way of extricating themselves from the situation. With the minutes ticking embarrassingly away, the crowd growing more restless and abusive by the second, and still no indication from the officials that they were any closer to finding a solution, a lone figure hobbled in through the gate at the far end of the arena. It was El Valenciano, his thigh heavily strapped in bandages, returning to his place in the middle, sword and cape in hand.

'He's coming back for more!' exclaimed Chet in amazement. 'He's crazy! I've already got shots of him flying through the air ten times. I don't think I can stand any more.'

El Valenciano was indeed back for more, and the crowd that had been ready to laugh itself to hysteria only forty-five minutes earlier was now trying hard not to notice the lump in its throat. The man was back and he was standing there in the middle, straight as a ramrod, sword in hand, ready to finish the job he had begun.

For the eleventh time he baited the beast, flaunting his cape and calling to it in open invitation to go for the kill, and for the eleventh time the beast responded, charging straight for the man with the aim of dispatching him unceremoniously into the next world.

El Valenciano once again stood his ground, but this time he made no pretence at cape-work. He levelled his sword and thrust straight between those fearful horns, the full weight of his body behind the blade. He struck home, and the sword went right to the hilt; but the bull, driven on by hate and its own momentum, lifted the matador high into the air and sent him crashing once more to the ground. The battle, however, was over. The animal staggered for a second, searching wildly for its tormentor, then gave up the fight, sank weakly to its knees and keeled over, bright red blood gushing from its open mouth onto the dark brown earth.

The crowd erupted. People poured into the ring from all sides, lifted El Valenciano shoulder high and paraded him around jubilantly until he collapsed, and had to be taken back to the infirmary. Chet and I looked at each other. 'I think I've seen enough for one day, buddy; what about you?' he asked.

'Yep, let's call it a day,' I replied, and we left the arena.

I never bothered to ask how the rest of it went. Anything after that was bound to be an anticlimax, and anyway, I had seen just about as much as I could take for one day. The sight of the bull's valiant corpse being dragged out – not by a team of jangling horses but by a dirty old tractor – did nothing to persuade me otherwise. I just wanted to get away, to be able to think it all through.

That evening we talked it over, recalling with unbelieving admiration, both for our own benefit and for a few others who had not been present, the spectacle of El Valenciano, half-crippled, standing there like Theseus against the Minotaur.

'Man, I can't wait to see these prints!' said Chet as he wound back his film. 'Just wait till my old man sees this – it'll blow his mind!' And he wound and he wound and he wound, finally looking up at me with a lunatic grin on his face.

'Something wrong here, fella!' he said apprehensively as he opened the back of the camera. 'I knew it! Son-of-a-bitch didn't wind on! Can you believe it? Not a single one! Not a single goddam one!'

'Hey, that's a real shame,' I said, trying hard to conceal my indifference.

The Riobamba bullfight set me thinking about the relationship between man and beast, and helped me to appreciate another remarkable incident that took place in December of the same year, during the Quito Festival.

Manuel Benítez, El Cordobés, the most famous and highly paid bullfighter in the world at the time, had been invited over and his promised appearance was generating a great deal of excitement. According to the experts he lacked the technical excellence of some of the other all-time greats, but everyone agreed that he had style.

On this occasion everything was more or less as it should be and, thank goodness, the spectacle bore no resemblance to the rodeo I had seen in Riobamba. The Quito Plaza de Toros is a fairly grand affair with a 20,000 capacity, and the seating, although lacking any cover and therefore the 'sol/sombra' distinction, was at least numbered and graded, which meant that you had to pay more the closer you were to the action, but you were assured of a seat. I went in the company of a young priest, a teacher from the University who happened to be an *aficionado* of the sport and who had offered months in advance to come with me to explain some of the finer points. We chose to take the more expensive seats near the front so as to get a good look at the man so many people were talking about.

El Cordobés was the last of the three matadors to perform. From the moment he took up his position behind the barrier to observe how the bull was responding to the provocations of the *banderilleros* and the picadors, I had the binoculars on him. He was a lean,

sinewy, energy-packed man in his early thirties, good looking with
a flow of jet black hair. As he stood there pushing and pulling
against the barrier in an exercise designed to sharpen both muscles
and wits, I sensed creative tension and quick reflexes. The first
impression was positive; the second, which took thirty seconds to
create, was to last a lifetime.

The bull had been flown in from Mexico for the occasion, and
was 'purpose-built' – gleaming black, front heavy, and snorting with
destructive energy. It was a truly magnificent animal and the crowd
responded to it with excited applause. By the time El Cordobés
came on, the scene was set for high drama.

Things happened so quickly that six hours later I was still asking
myself whether I had dreamed it. I still have only scant understanding of the dynamics of it all. What happened, to the best of my rec-
ollection, was that El Cordobés entered the ring in a relatively
unflamboyant fashion and waited a moment for the bull to acknowledge his presence. Nothing happened and so he attracted its
attention in the usual manner by closing in a few feet, entering
directly into its line of vision and shaking his cape, and this
produced the desired response with the bull engaging in a full-
blooded, say-goodbye-to-your-mother charge.

El Cordobés then threw his sword to one side, his cape to the
other, and dropped down onto his knees directly in the path of the
charging animal. The bull – rather like in a cartoon – reversed
thrust in mid-assault and skidded to a halt, stopping about a foot
short of the kneeling figure. It then stood there pawing the dirt like
a young colt, whereupon El Cordobés butted it on the head
between the horns, rose gracefully to his feet like Nureyev, and
walked away, his back turned contemptuously on the bemused
animal.

The crowd was so astonished that this act was greeted with
virtual silence. The priest and I, bewildered, did no more than
exchange glances, and never made mention of the incident. It was
as if everyone in the vicinity had been plunged into a state of
numbness.

The rest of the corrida was carried off with customary precision and did not interest me a great deal, but that one incident remained, and still remains with me today as an unsolved mystery. I came a little closer to unravelling it a couple of months later in Riobamba.

I was at a friend's house and we were chatting about one thing and another when there came a knock at the door and in walked a couple of young fellows, in their mid-twenties like ourselves. They were acquaintances of the friend I was visiting. One of them I thought I recognized but couldn't place; it was a strange feeling, as if I knew the man fairly well, and we had shared something in common, but at the same time I was quite sure we had never met.

We exchanged greetings and information about ourselves in the usual way, and the man told me that he worked as a lorry driver for a local soft drinks company. 'Perhaps I saw him at a dance somewhere, or played football against him in the park sometime,' I speculated to myself. 'Being tall and fair he would certainly stand out from the crowd.'

'Es torero también,' chipped in one of the others cheerfully. 'He also fights bulls.'

I joined in with the mild laughter that followed, thinking a joke had been made – but then did a double-take. That was where I had seen him before, in the bullring, of course! It was El Valenciano!

'I know you!' I blurted out. 'You're El Valenciano – the bull-fighter! I saw you perform last year at the festival.' I leaped to my feet and shook his hand.

'You're a very brave man,' I said. 'It is an honour to meet you.'

'Thank you,' he replied modestly. 'Yes, it was a bit of a rough day, that.'

'What are you doing here in Riobamba? Back for another bullfight?' I asked eagerly, assuming that he had come from further afield, from Quito, or even Mexico or Spain.

'No, I live here,' he said; 'just down the road, in fact.'

'But where did you learn to fight bulls? I thought you had to go to a special school and train for years to do that?'

'Oh no,' he replied bashfully, 'just practised a bit with the bulls on my uncle's farm, and thought I'd like to give it a try one day; that's really how it started. But there's not much demand for it around here, you know – just once or twice a year if you're lucky.'

The nonchalant way he spoke about his brushes with death left me speechless; the only way I could relieve my sense of shock – once I had found my tongue – was to keep on asking questions, until we found ourselves deep in a discussion of the art of bullfighting.

It soon became apparent that, for all his reticence, the man was really quite an authority on the subject, although most of his knowledge had been gleaned from books for he had only been to about half-a-dozen bullfights in his life – probably less than I had. I brought up the question that had been nagging me for weeks, of El Cordobés and what I had seen him do in Quito, and I asked El Valenciano what his own impression had been.

'Unfortunately I couldn't get off work that day, so I didn't see it, which was a pity,' he replied, to my amazement, but then he went on to explain: 'It's what they call the "don de mando" – it's a special power certain gifted people have over the animal. They say that some of the all-time greats could paralyse a bull on the spot just by looking at it. Yes, I heard that El Cordobés has it.' Then he added with a laugh, 'Wish I did; could have saved myself a lot of trouble!'

'Any idea what the life expectancy of a bullfighter is?' I asked.

'No,' he replied, with just a touch of irritation, presumably the result of having been asked the same question a hundred times before. Then he turned the question pointedly back on me.

'And what about you? I hear you're playing football for Liga. How do you feel about having eleven hired assassins try to break your leg for ninety minutes every week – that's if the crowd doesn't break your skull with a beer-bottle first? No thanks! Now the bull,' he continued, his eyes lighting up, 'the bull is just a poor dumb animal obeying the laws of nature; it doesn't know any better; it was born to fight and only in fighting does it fulfil its life's purpose. But *people* are different; they have choice but do not exercise it. We always end up being so much less than we could be. Now that is reprehensible; that is evil.'

He paused, as if moved by his own words, then continued: 'I find it curious in the extreme that so many people claim to feel sorry for the bull and condemn the art of bullfighting, when the bull is one of the few domesticated animals allowed to die with dignity. How much better to die fighting out in the open than to die panic-stricken and helpless in a slaughterhouse! The bull has nobility, and courage — it never flinches and it never fails, and it dies with dignity as few human beings ever do. Can you imagine the incredible rush of excitement you get when this magnificent animal comes hurtling towards you? I tell you there is nothing in the world like it — nothing! No, give me the bull any day; the bull is a noble creature!'

I searched for something meaningful to say.

'Oh, football's not that bad,' I replied eventually. 'It's probably not as violent as you think, and anyway I seem to be spending a lot of time in the reserves these days, and there they only try to knock your teeth out.' This was a reference to a blow in the face I had received a few days earlier that was still evident.

'That's precisely what I'm talking about!' he said indignantly. 'Now, if I were you I'd pack it in. It's just not worth it, my friend — believe me. You'll get yourself hurt one of these days!'

CHAPTER THIRTEEN

TOMASINA

SHE ALWAYS SWORE she was not the one who phoned me that day in the restaurant, but I knew all the same that she was. 'Tomasina' is just too uncommon a name, and the store where she worked was just around the corner. We eventually met quite by chance, or so it seemed at the time. Looking back, I am not entirely sure.

Adelfonso, a young mestizo boy from the poorest of Riobamba families, with a talent for befriending gringos and a gift for languages, asked me one day 'if I would like to do something positive'. I replied that I would. And so we agreed to meet later that day to do whatever it was he thought I ought to be doing.

The family occupied a corner house, some nine blocks up the hill from the main square towards the dusty edge of town. It was one of the older parts where the houses had been built in the traditional style, with shuttered windows and thick, white-washed walls enclosing a simple cobbled yard.

Most of the early settlers in the Americas had been from southern Spain, the part that had fallen directly under the influence of the Moors, and their distinctive values and customs soon became the norms of the New World. Evidence of this is still there today in the universality of southern Spanish pronunciation; in the surrender of individual will to 'fate'; in the haughty disdain that many bosses have for their employees and most shopkeepers have for their customers; in the use of construction techniques that owed more to northern Africa than southern Europe; and in the suffocating control of women that still goes on in some of the more conservative towns.

For the Moors, whose concern with privacy – especially where women were concerned – was paramount, the house was a veritable fortress, and the courtyard an inner sanctum. This was reinforced among some of the more well-to-do by the introduction of fountains and flower gardens in their courtyards. The architects of Spanish America, instinctively seeking to reproduce what was proper and best in Spain, often made the courtyard the focal point of a building, be it for private, public or religious use.

Somewhat unusually, this house had two entrances to it. There was a wide guest entrance at the corner opening onto an immaculately kept, sparsely furnished parlour. Corner houses were invariably built this way so that the room could be turned into a small shop if desired. There was also a single entrance at the side for family and friends. I always felt privileged when, later on, I was expected to use the latter.

I might have met any or all of the five attractive sisters that same evening when Adelfonso took me to the house, and conceivably struck up a friendship with any one of them; but I didn't, I met Tomasina, and that is why I am wondering now if it really was the chance encounter I had imagined it to be.

From the first, our relationship was so agreeable and effortless that I didn't trust it. I kept expecting it to go wrong, forever on the look-out for the upper-cut and the right-cross I had come to expect from girl-friends I had had back home, usually just when I was thinking things had never been better. But the blows were never thrown, and it took me a while to realize that they never would be.

Although mestiza, Tomasina was more Indian than Spanish in many ways. She was a kind, patient soul, dark-eyed and dark-skinned, attractive, with prominent cheek-bones and slightly aquiline features, and there was a wistfulness about her that sometimes had me wondering if she was listening to what I was saying, yet suspecting that she knew my thoughts even before I spoke them. In all the time I knew her she asked for nothing and gave everything, in the hope that she would somehow be appreciated. It was a new and confusing experience for me. Her friendship and kindness, of a simplicity and in a measure I had never known, stirred emotions inside me that I did not recognize, but which gave me energy and purpose; somehow I knew even then that whatever the outcome, moments we shared were destined not to fade from memory.

The three brothers had not spoken to her since the night she walked to the hospital to give birth. Incredible as it may seem for a family of ten living in a small house, the women had managed to keep the pregnancy a secret. Tomasina would come home from work each day and go straight to the girls' room feigning fatigue, and the sisters would bring in her supper. 'It was', she told me, 'just a small pregnancy.'

The eldest sister broke the news to the men, about the time Felipe was being born. Concerned with the 'family honour' in the traditional manner, they might well have inflicted some damage on Tomasina had she been around – but by the time she emerged from hospital a couple of days later with the baby in her arms, they had cooled down. They went through the necessary motions of outrage and rejection – as much to appease the neighbours as anything – but melted on contact with the baby and allowed mother and child back into the home.

It was not all plain-sailing, however, and the brothers were still not speaking to her, although the child was nearly three by the time I arrived on the scene. My relationship with the brothers, which rarely stretched beyond the bounds of 'football' talk, had only ever been friendly and courteous on both sides. I became instantly indignant on Tomasina's behalf, however, and wanted to confront them then and there; but she made me promise never to mention it, hinting that I didn't understand the situation properly and that I would only make matters worse. I outwardly conceded but wasn't convinced, and I silently reserved to myself the right to bring the matter up with them at a suitable moment.

It came one night when we were out drinking at the 'Manabita'. I hadn't gone there with the intention of looking for trouble, but I found it all the same. I hadn't wanted to go there at all on this particular occasion and so I wasn't feeling kindly disposed towards my companions. It was during the 'gringo-baiting' stage of the evening, which I only ever managed to endure with considerable difficulty, that I decided to hit back and take them to task for the way they had treated their sister; but it was a mistake of the highest order and one I came to regret.

These macho games have rules every bit as binding as the law of gravity, and one of them is that you don't talk about the female family members of present company – family honour is at stake and the subject is too sensitive to touch. And besides, the bonds of male friendship are supposed to be above such matters as women, whatever the issue. I'm not sure what moved me to do it because I already had a good idea of what the outcome would be, and I sensed that the moment was completely wrong, but still I said my piece.

Suddenly, the booze-filled air seemed to freeze over with shock and anger; there was silence, for if mention of the subject was taboo, so was reacting to it – at least in public. In fact the subject was never mentioned again, not even by Tomasina, but I subsequently learned from a sister that there had been reprisals. I wanted to apologize but it was not easy when I had been so well warned in the first place, and when nothing had 'officially' happened, in the second. It became something that I had to learn to live with – and a valuable lesson for a Brit who thought he could change the ways of the world.

The child's father was a mining engineer from New Mexico. He had been seeing Tomasina for nearly three years before she became pregnant, and the moment he found out, he got himself transferred 200 miles further south to Cuenca. He had never mentioned that he had a wife and family back home, and he subsequently never contributed a penny to the boy's upkeep. I went with her to see a lawyer once to find out if there was some way she might obtain compensation – still fondly believing that a sense of justice existed, as it did back home. But the lawyer procrastinated and lied at every turn, assuring her that he had secured an order for the man's arrest, that the bailiffs had been sent in to remove his possessions and that her financial worries would soon be over. In fact he did nothing, except bleed her for the few sucres she had and leave her practically penniless and broken in spirit.

It was a common enough story, and one along with many others that aided me on the road to discovery, for it is only through contrasts of this kind that one gets to learn about the merits or demerits of one's own country. It also provided ammunition of sorts for those tedious tussles I was forever getting into with left-wing revolutionaries who, incensed by my newly acquired belief that moral standards were every bit as important to a nation's development as dialectical materialism, would condescendingly point out that 'We have corruption in Britain, too, you know'. To which I would reply, 'My friend, you have no idea – no idea!'

I got to know the family fairly well, and once my prejudices had subsided I learned to recognize and appreciate a whole host of traits I had been blind to at first. There developed an affection and an estimation on my part that has never wavered.

The mother was the rock on which the family was built – a diminutive lady, stubborn as a mule when she chose to be, permanently awake to what everyone – especially the boys – was up to, untiringly hard-working, reticent to a fault and religious to the bones. To have raised eight children as successfully as she did under such harsh conditions as theirs was every bit as impressive as the work of her virtuoso husband.

The father was a composer-musician of some renown, although the family only really became aware of the extent of his fame after he passed away, when his music was played non-stop on the radio, and when the funeral was attended by several thousand mourners, many of whom had travelled from the furthest corners of the country. Appreciation of his talent had stretched far and wide, but in characteristic fashion he had never made a song and dance about it. He also had a remarkable knack for making people feel special. Each of the five daughters confided to me in turn that 'she was her father's favourite', and each one probably was.

As I observed the richness of the family's experience and the closeness of the bonds that held them together – albeit with the usual squabbles – I could feel stirrings of envy inside me and I found myself remembering my parents' (mostly failed) attempts to communicate to me what life had been like for them, brought up as they were between the wars in large families and in poverty. I began to question in earnest for the first time something I had been told all my life to question – the notion of wealth as we in Europe perceive it. In fact, when I think of it now, it is amazing how many times that tired old nag must have come round before I finally decided to sit up and take notice.

The dream that so many of us seem destined to pursue, I noted with admirable insight, with its planned families, modern comforts, comprehensive medical cover and universal higher education, seemed suddenly and all too clearly to be missing the point – that material wealth is only useful if it satisfies want; that comprehensive medical cover only means anything if it takes away the fear of sickness; that universal higher education only has value if it contributes to the common good; and that all of these things only matter if they create more happiness.

It does not take a genius to appreciate that this has not happened. In fact, it is almost as if the opposite has happened – the greater the wealth, the greater the want; the more comprehensive the medical cover, the greater the hypochondria; the higher and more accessible the education, the more selfish and elitist the educated ones; and the more there is of everything, the less happy everyone is. I suspect most of us are well aware we are missing the point, but don't quite know what to do about it.

Material progress, unless accompanied by a counterbalancing expansion of the spirit, will defeat its own purpose, and hardship is the best teacher. I believe we know this deep down and feel guilty

about our lack of exposure to it, in a way perhaps that makes it one
of the great complexes of our time, which is why so many of us are
prone to exaggerate the deprivations of our childhood.

The question that has to be honestly asked is whether we have
been any more ready to handle our wealth than we have our
weaponry, and the answer is an obvious 'no'. We have been given,
for the first time in history, just enough rope to hang ourselves –
and we are making a pretty good job of it. The final judgement
depends on us.

The night that Tomasina 'accepted me' – which is the phrase
Ecuadoreans use to describe the moment when two people agree to
start 'going out together' – was New Year's Eve, and it happened at a
party that Adelfonso and I had organized at my apartment for the
occasion. Adelfonso must have done most of the organizing because
throwing parties was something I truly detested. In fact, the only
reason I even contemplated it in the first place was that 1 January
also happened to be Tomasina's birthday and I decided that some
sort of monumental sacrifice on my part might be in order.

We invited crowds of people – all the volunteers and their
Ecuadorean friends and acquaintances – but had planned little in
the way of 'cuisine'. In fact, apart from a birthday cake for
Tomasina, our fare consisted merely of an enormous bowl into
which I threw a few pieces of orange and then poured virtually
every kind of drink I could lay my hands on. The result quickly
assumed a deserved place in local folklore.

The evening could hardly have failed because the whole of
Riobamba pulsated with parties from one end to the other, most of
them spilling out onto the streets and into other houses so that you
were never really sure whose party you were at until you were asked
to leave. The centre-piece of the New Year's celebration was the
torching of the 'años viejos' – effigies representing those individuals
who had figured most prominently in the news during the previous
twelve months. They were ceremoniously burned on bonfires at
midnight, and since 1968 had been the year of Jackie Kennedy and

Aristotle Onassis, their grotesquely inflated but clearly recognizable images went up in flames on every street corner.

The party went well, and not without a little drama to help it along. Adelfonso had invited a doctor friend from the local hospital and he happened to be 'on call' that evening. He had warned us beforehand that he might have to leave at some point because a birth was imminent, but that we shouldn't worry because he would be back just as soon as he could. And sure enough, shortly before midnight, a breathless messenger-boy arrived, and off ran the doctor as fast as his still-sober legs could carry him. Naturally everybody knew the mother-to-be and we awaited the doctor's return with a good deal of excitement, or at least, with as much as the festivities would allow. When he reappeared a couple of hours later with the news that she had given birth to a healthy boy and that 'she had decided not to call him Aristotle after all', he set the place alight.

It was not just one mestiza girl who caused me to re-examine my view of human nature – the whole of Ecuadorean society set me thinking for one reason or another, and the party was yet another occasion when I found myself reflecting at length on things I had taken for granted back home. At gatherings such as these everybody dances – all evening. There is no division between the ages, no self-consciousness and no respite. It is a function that is as natural as breathing, and it embraces everyone – even babies are brought along.

I have seen something very similar in Africa and the Caribbean, which makes me wonder what went wrong with Northern Europe. When and why did this division between music, dancing and living take place in our society? And how? For music and dance are so obviously bound up together in the celebration of life. Is it a by-product of our materialist ways? Was it the Puritans? Did our concentration on literacy have anything to do with it? Is climate a factor?

The many circles of standing stones in Britain clearly testify that they were the places where religion, fertility, healing, music, and dance came together. But today we no longer have this fusion. There are so many barriers to break down before we can take to the dance-floor, and so much introspection when we do. Most Northern Europeans dance as if they are looking at themselves in the mirror.

In Latin America, Africa and the Caribbean, on the other hand, even the smallest children are irresistibly drawn to music, and they take to dancing as easily as to walking. People do not compartmentalize as we do, so that you are conscious of either dancing or not dancing — there is no break in continuity. In the Caribbean, for example, you might see a young person alone on the street — waiting for a bus, perhaps — listening to music through headphones and moving easily to the rhythm, quite oblivious as to who might be watching. It is the most natural and proper thing in the world. Evidently somewhere along the line there has been a dislocation of some magnitude in our social behaviour, separating us from much that is vital and good. I see it as an ailment for which we are in urgent need of a cure.

There was a powerful old-world charm about any dance you went to in the Sierra, such that the most notorious lout would become the personification of courtesy the moment he entered the room. At the very first chord, the gentlemen would spring to their feet — as if afraid that the merest delay on their part might be interpreted as a lack of eagerness — walk briskly over, and politely ask if the lady would like to dance, which, of course, she always did. And when the music stopped, the partners would smilingly thank each other and return to their seats.

There was no skulking in corners or eyeing up 'talent' through a haze of tobacco and alcohol fumes, and no groping around in the darkness. No one was ever rejected on the grounds that he or she was too ugly, too fat, or too old, and as a consequence no one was ever humiliated and made to feel unwelcome. The formality grew out of a respect for people's feelings and an appreciation of where true happiness lies. The kind of free-for-all that goes on in Europe is not freedom at all, nor is it the behaviour of liberated people. It is rather a type of bondage, for both men and women are condemned to live in fear of rejection and humiliation, and they carry the signs

of their captivity around with them everywhere they go. Discipline
of the right sort, as just about every culture on earth understands,
ensures freedom, and without it the law of the jungle slowly but
surely encroaches, the stakes rising higher and the instincts sinking
lower all the time.

The music most in request on these occasions was the *cumbia*,
the classic Colombian rhythm that is virtually impossible to resist.
There were a number of Ecuadorean dances of Spanish and Indian
origin, but none as popular as the *cumbia*, which not only had a
vibrant Caribbean beat to it, it also had a clever lyric that was
sometimes topical, often risqué, and always good-humoured.

At times, just to please the gringos, someone would put on a
Beatles or a Rolling Stones record, but somehow it always seemed
to jar. It was not just a question of different rhythms, it was more
that the self-absorption of records like *Sergeant Pepper* and the sado-
narcissism of others were so hopelessly out of step with the spirit of
the occasion. It made us feel uncomfortable – the gringos, that is –
and although we undoubtedly felt it more than the Ecuadoreans
who did not understand the words, we sensed that this might
influence the proceedings as a whole and so we would thank them
for the gesture and kindly ask them to take it off, affirming that we
preferred the *cumbia*.

Shortly after midnight, when we had toasted in the New Year
and embraced each other, I slipped out into the kitchen to put the
finishing touches to Tomasina's cake. I wish I could say that I had
baked it myself, but I hadn't. I had ordered it in town and then
carefully implanted the twenty-two extra-long candles that I spent
half a day tracking down. I was in the midst of lighting it with a
hand made unsteady by the punch, when who should walk in but
Tomasina, who had been wondering where I had got to.

'Salga de aquí de inmediato!' I shouted in panic. 'Get out of here
at once!' and frog-marched her back into the room.

The poor girl who, as ever, had nothing but the kindest of
thoughts in mind, was quite abashed. She turned her head towards
me with an uncomprehending, crestfallen look, but I pointed an

imperious finger in the opposite direction and off she went, probably wondering if the New Year might not possibly turn out to be even worse than the old.

Afterwards I realized what I had done and what a shock it must have been, because she had no idea that I knew it was her birthday and Ecuadoreans didn't go in for birthday cakes very much anyway, so she can hardly have suspected what I was up to. It became a source of shared mirth in due course, but for a brief moment it cast a shadow over the evening. A few minutes later, however, I emerged from the kitchen carrying a large brown cake gloriously ablaze with the light of twenty-two king-size candles.

Few latinos can resist an opportunity to subject their fellow countrymen to a long, boring and pompous speech, and I was catching on fast to this endearing habit.

'Ladies and gentlemen,' I began, clearing my throat and struggling to recall my best Castilian Spanish, 'this evening I have the priceless honour of receiving you all into my home, the humbleness of which I sincerely hope you will all excuse. And I would like to thank you all, with absolute sincerity and from the very bottom of my heart, for allowing me the indescribable privilege of sharing this historic occasion of the celebration of the New Year of one thousand, nine hundred and sixty-nine with you. It is something I shall never forget for as long as I live, for an indelible mark has been made upon my soul.'

'Hey Rick – give us a break!' complained Chuck, one of the Americans. I decided to ignore him.

'Furthermore, my esteemed companions, moments such as this are treasures to be passed down to our children, and our grandchildren, as small but indisputable evidence of the profound cordiality that rightfully exists between the wonderfully diverse peoples that inhabit the scattered corners of our planet – conclusive proof, that is, of the brotherhood that needs must prevail, eternally, amongst a caring humanity.'

'Jesus Christ! I can't believe this!' groaned Chuck. 'I think I'm going to throw up.'

'And I trust that in the days to come,' I continued, undaunted, 'that must surely pass as fleetingly as the smoke from our Old Year's bonfires,' as Chuck ran for the bathroom, 'we shall recall and cherish the inestimable friendship that has been born and nurtured here this evening; for in the words of the great German poet, Goethe – forgive me if the translation is lacking, my German is a little rusty – "Love concedes more in a second than honest labour can earn in a lifetime." My dear friends, today, the first of January, nineteen hundred and sixty-nine, also happens to be the birthday of our dear sister, Tomasina, and I would like to ask you all to join with me now in celebrating this wonderful occasion by partaking of a piece of this most humble cake, which is so unworthy of the person in whose honour it was baked.'

There followed the most thunderous applause. 'Bravo, Ricardo, te pasaste, viejo! Te has hecho latino!' shouted Adelfonso. 'Well done, Ricardo, old man, you've excelled yourself! You've become a latino!'

The flicker of understanding that had crossed Tomasina's face as I emerged from the kitchen behind a wall of flame had now become a broad, bashful and relieved smile. She had obviously been touched by my dazzling oratory – or my nerve – and appeared to be on the verge of tears.

'Sorry, Tomi,' I said, offering her my handkerchief, 'but you came in at the wrong moment.'

'Indio bravo!' she replied quietly. 'Bad tempered native,' and blew her nose.

We all then joined in with a chorus of 'Happy Bird-day to Joo', which the Ecuadoreans know, as does the whole world, in English.

The door of the bathroom opened and a pallid Chuck emerged. 'Is it safe to come out now?' he asked. And then, turning to me, added, 'I just hope, for the sake of your grandchildren and a caring humanity, you lose the recipe for that goddam punch.'

The party came to an end at about four o'clock, and I walked back with Tomasina and her brothers and sisters to their house, then left them at the door and retraced my steps the twelve blocks to my apartment. As I breathed in the cool night air, I realized that I was feeling good – better than I had felt in years. Not only, to my absolute amazement, had I managed to host a successful party, I realized too that I had been in the company of people who mattered to me, and I felt that they had accepted me into their lives. It was the fulfilment of a hope that had been too deeply buried to acknowledge before then but which I now realized had been with me since the day at Heathrow when I boarded the plane.

I let myself back into the apartment and surveyed an already nostalgic debris of glasses and cigarette ends, and then sank down in a chair and listened to the Loving Spoonful. I could not bring myself to break the spell and climb into bed, so I let the dawning of the new day break it for me.

If we had ever had any intention of keeping our relationship secret, the whole thing would have been blown apart one evening the following week, when I had been visiting Tomasina at her house. I had set off home at a leisurely, meandering pace at about 10.30, and had just reached my apartment when I realized I didn't have my door-key. Assuming that it was at Tomasina's, and that I had dropped it on the parlour sofa, I turned straight round and headed back to the house, scanning the cobbles all the while just in case it had fallen out of my pocket somewhere along the way.

When I arrived back at the house, some forty-five minutes later, I found, not surprisingly, that all the lights were out and that everybody was asleep. In classic fashion I selected a small pebble from the dust in the street and lobbed it in the direction of Tomasina's window, the top two panes of which were just visible above the wall. She must have been soundly asleep because, a handful of pebbles later, each one bigger than the last, there was still no sign of life. Not so some of the neighbours, unfortunately, whose lights clicked on with embarrassing brightness, silhouetting curious heads against the glass.

'I'm awfully sorry,' I mouthed apologetically in the direction of an opening window. 'I'm afraid I've lost my key. I think I left it inside when I was visiting Tomasina.' Not one person in her house had heard me, yet I had woken up half the street.

The neighbours were clearly not amused; and their humour didn't improve as I continued hurling ever bigger and louder pebbles over the wall, peppering the house at random. The night air was suddenly shattered by an ear-splitting shout: 'For God's sake, Tomasina, give the gringo his key!'

Instantly the window flew open and Tomasina's face appeared. At the same time half a dozen more lights came on in the street.

'Sorry,' I called to anyone and everyone. 'It's OK. No trouble. It's my key. It's alright now – thanks – sorry to trouble you.'

I lied in desperate anticipation of a solution to my problem. 'Hey, Tomi!' I called in a loud whisper. 'I can't find my key. Did I leave it inside?'

'Oh no!' she groaned. 'I told you to check before you left!' and hurried off to look.

'Fancy that!' said an indignant voice from out of the darkness. 'And she told him to check before he left!'

Tomasina returned in a flash and threw down the key, which I failed to catch and then picked up from the dirt.

'Sorry folks!' I called out in the direction of a score of closing windows, and hurried off into the night, leaving Tomasina to sort out the mess in the morning.

Our relationship continued to progress at a steady, gentle pace and I soon found myself learning to appreciate the simpler things in life – the visits to the Post Office on a Thursday evening when half the town turned out to see if the overseas mail had come down from Quito; the short bus trips that we made into the *campo* with little Felipe, not with any specific objective in mind but simply to go and come back; the Sunday morning strolls to the small reed-filled lake that lay just twenty minutes dusty walk from the house, out beyond the edge of town; and the occasional Sunday afternoon when one of the brothers would turn up with a friend's pick-up and we would all pile in the back and tour the streets looking for people to wave at, and trying to remember to duck whenever we reached some low-hanging telegraph wire. And finally, best of all, stretching out on a rush mat on the roof, feeling the gentle warmth of the sun and gazing up at the sky and the mountains above us and listening to the sounds of the street below — the tooting of the car horns, the greetings of the people, and the bleating of the sheep and the goats.

She agonized with me all through the Radiofónicas debacle, and provided genuine comfort whenever I returned worn and dispirited from the long round of rejection at the hands of the Quito and Guayaquil businessmen, but urged me all the while to try harder to make it work. She begged me to ask God for help, assuring me that if I did I would find sponsors, both in Ecuador and outside. But I didn't listen. I was from a country and a culture that thought it knew all the answers, and I rejected her counsel as superstition. After all, I reasoned to myself, if Ecuadoreans are so smart, how come their country is in such a mess? I know better now, of course, and recognize that had I paid the least attention to her advice things would have worked out differently, and my life would have taken a turn for the better much sooner than it did.

As it was, I parted company with Radiofónicas and did what I could to find something else that would allow me to stay in Riobamba, but without success; and when we finally saw that a move to Quito was inevitable for me, we both knew it was not going to be easy for us to continue to see each other. The teaching post that the British Consul had found for me at the Catholic University occasionally had me working on Saturday mornings, and the football team I had joined was now in hot pursuit of the championship and occupied the whole of Sunday. A four-hour bus journey either way, therefore, became increasingly out of the question for me, and the prospect of Tomasina travelling to Quito was remote, unless she managed to combine it with a visit to a relative and travelled with one of the family.

Something else was working against us too, something that was every bit as obstructive and harmful as my own prejudices had been

at the start, which was that Tomasina, as an Ecuadorean woman
long accustomed to a tradition of deception and abandonment, had
always been expecting me to take off and leave at some point, and
despite dreading this moment she had long since planned her
escape and was ready to move whenever she saw the writing on the
wall.

It has been said that the Middle Ages in Europe were responsible for
two deadly inventions – romantic love and gunpowder – and the
more one travels the more one begins to suspect that the connection between the two was not entirely fortuitous. It does not take
very long, for example, to realize that the romantic 'love' we so
fondly celebrate in our songs is not the universal human truth we
like to believe, but an invention that, like any other, depends for its
survival upon our consent. In fact, it is not 'love' at all so much as an
emotional conflagration which, unless replaced by the real thing, is
destined to flare up and quickly die, leaving an awful lot of debris in
its wake, as our miserable divorce rate clearly shows.

The indigenous peoples of the world have not invented either
romantic love or gunpowder. Latin America, on the other hand, is
full of both, and the reverberations, both amorous and incendiary,
are audible from one end of the continent to the other. Reference to
the 'treachery and betrayal' and the 'fire and destruction' of love are
constant themes in their lives; and their songs and literature are full
of pledges to blow one's brains out, leap off bridges or drink oneself
to death; or, as a milder alternative, to sail off into the sunset.

The imminent move to Quito, therefore, produced a predictable
impression on Tomasina, and she took my inability to meet her
regularly as a decision not to, despite my protestations to the
contrary. Protestations never amounted to much in this situation,
given that denial was all part and parcel of the same explosive
package. One day, therefore, from out of the blue, she told me she
was going to the United States permanently.

The practical aspect to this was that her father had undertaken
to have a house built, just a block away from the old one, and had

run into financial difficulty. The children had rallied instantly to his assistance and five of them had decided to make the uncertain trek north to see if they could earn some quick cash. Tomasina was one of them – although she no doubt had an eye to Felipe's future at the same time. I was truly shocked, for I had in no way interpreted the changes in my circumstances as Tomasina had done.

'But why?' I asked with disbelief. 'Why? And why didn't you even mention that you were thinking about going? You could have said something. I mean, don't I have a say in the matter as well?'

'I know one day you will leave without me,' she replied deliberately, as someone who had thought the whole thing through in great detail. 'And I want to go before you do. I couldn't bear to be abandoned – not again.'

An enormous crowd was there at the airport to see her and a sister off – all the family from Riobamba, lots of friends, and countless relatives from Quito. The 'boys' had even brought along a guitar and composed a song for the occasion. We all did our best to feign an atmosphere of gaiety and good humour, but the undercurrent of sadness was unmistakable. It was misery for me – partly because I still did not really understand why she was going.

It was far from the first time that I had been to the airport to see off someone I cared deeply about and did not expect to see again, and every time I felt as if I had lost something; but this time it was different. Afterwards, as I climbed into a taxi and sank into the cold plastic seat, I felt plunged into the depths of loneliness. The world seemed suddenly hostile and dangerous, and I was swept along in a deluge of thoughts and feelings I did not understand and could not control. What made matters worse was that I knew, deep down, that I could have prevented her going with a single word, and yet I didn't. I suddenly understood, in a way that unnerved me totally, that she had been right – I was not ready for responsibility and I would, despite all the tears and the heartbreak, have eventually left the country without her.

I sensed that I was going seriously wrong somewhere. I thought of friends back home, many of whom were now married and settled, and seemed to know exactly where they were going and how they were going to get there. I couldn't for the life of me work out how they did it. I had no particular desire to follow in their footsteps, but the distance between us bothered me. I saw the world stretching out before me, immense, fascinating and irresistible, and I felt as if my life had not even begun. How could I take on lifelong commitments, I reasoned, when I didn't even know what life was all about? How could I organize my living if I didn't know the purpose of it all? How could I plan the journey unless I knew where I was going? My curiosity was insatiable and I knew I would not rest until I had found some answers.

I was beset by feelings of inadequacy and alienation, and it disturbed me profoundly; but I also knew that the condition was not terminal and, like a good many other things I was not prepared to deal with at the time, I somehow managed to push it to the back of my mind with a note to myself to 'review some time in the future'.

Twenty years were to pass before I was to see Tomasina again; when I did, she was living in Ohio in a large house in the country, happily married to an American industrial engineer with two more fine children. Felipe was now a handsome man in his early twenties – a carpenter with a construction company – and Tomasina was a supervisor in the quality control unit of a tennis ball factory.

It was a happy reunion, especially for me, to see Tomasina so well settled and contented, and the good home she had made for Felipe after so much hardship and uncertainty. But there was nostalgia too, as there must be for many Latin Americans, millions of whom took part in the great diaspora of the sixties and seventies.

'The sun is not the same here, you know, Ricardo,' she said to me one sultry Sunday afternoon, somewhat distractedly.

'How do you mean?' I asked.

'Well, you recall those times when we would sit on the roof and look out at the mountains, when the wind would come sweeping along the streets, throwing great clouds of dust up into the air?'

'Yes, I do,' I replied quietly.

'Well, in those moments I could feel myself float upwards – up towards the sun – and I could look down on the house, and the whole of Riobamba, and it felt good.'

'Tomi!' I said, half-startled, but recalling how at times, like the Indians in the *campo*, she would fall strangely silent and become distant, as if lost in a dream.

'I never told anyone,' she said calmly. 'But it doesn't happen now, not since I came to the United States. The sun is somehow different here.'

PART
IV

PARADISE
LOST

Chapter Fourteen

CITY LIFE

PEOPLE OF ALL AGES apply to do voluntary service, and they do so for many reasons. One always hopes that among these reasons there is a genuine sense of service. The desire for travel and adventure figures prominently of course, but you will also find reasons such as loneliness, longings for self-discovery, the 'Foreign Legion factor' (seeking a cure for a broken heart), and also the desire to suffer. Still today, a good many feel that suffering is somehow bound up with life's purpose – 'I suffer, therefore I am', wrote Graham Greene of the nuns in the leper colony in *A Burnt-Out Case*. But there is general unanimity on one aspect, and that is the desire to experience a different life from the one you have known. It is because your native country cannot fulfil all your needs that you are getting on the plane in the first place. If it could, there would be no reason to leave.

As a general rule, therefore, the more the country of posting differs in culture, geography and economy from the country of origin, the happier the volunteer is likely to be. For this reason I always felt sorry for those volunteers (and Peace Corps sent quite a few) who were posted to capital cities. Big cities are pretty much the same wherever you go – anonymous places that sap your energy and leave you feeling restless. In the midst of plenty you find yourself lacking something, and surrounded by people you can feel very much alone. It has been truthfully said that 'the city is the home of the body and the country is the home of the soul'.

I had done everything I could to stay in Riobamba and it hadn't worked out, and now I was heading for the capital city I had spent so long reviling and trying to avoid. In a sense, it was the end of my term as a volunteer. Teaching at a university in the capital city and living just a couple of blocks from an ice-cream parlour and a supermarket was not what I had had in mind when I applied to go overseas. Quito would no doubt provide attractions of its own, but I doubted that they would appeal to me. There was a finality about my move and a sense of anticlimax, therefore. It felt like the end of an era that had given me everything I had hoped for. I had seen the exotic and the simple, the beautiful and the tranquil; for me, it had been life fully experienced for the first time, a chance to discover where we had all come from and why, and it had filled me with passion and purpose. All this was now gone.

'Quito is beautiful,' everyone kept telling me, and indeed I knew it was — a spectacular, white, shining city, surrounded by green mountains and dazzling blue skies, with two giant, snowy peaks dominating the skyline; not to mention its history — its renowned 'Quito School of Art' and its architectural masterpieces from colonial times. But it was like telling someone to look for a new girl-friend while still smitten with the old — everyone and everything seemed to pale in comparison with what I had known in Riobamba.

I had indeed become enamoured, at one and the same time, with Riobamba and one of her daughters, and I sensed that if my condition had a cure at all it was time that would do the healing. This was the best I could hope for, because I was no hero when it came to affairs of the heart. Broken bones, dysentery and hepatitis I could just about handle, but the heart was another matter; its control commanded reserves of strength I knew I didn't have.

My arrival in Quito in the summer of 1969, therefore, was marked by sadness and regret, but at the same time there was a certain amount of determination on my part to see out the two years I had undertaken to stay in Ecuador. And underneath it all, there was still the hope that something would happen to make sense of all the upheaval, that there was a purpose for my being where I was, unlikely though it seemed at the time.

It was only natural that I would use my Peace Corps contacts to help me get settled when I arrived in Quito. The house I would share with three other volunteers, and which we referred to as 'the Mansion', was situated a few blocks from the Catholic University on Valladolid Street. It was a squarish, two-storey structure, built in the neo-colonial style popular with middle-class Ecuadoreans at the turn of the century. By the time we moved in it had become something of a white elephant – over-sized, badly maintained and shoddily furnished; the fact that it was also decrepit and dark seemed oddly in keeping with the characteristics of the three ageing spinsters who owned it.

The three of them would descend upon us periodically like angels of death, stony-faced and draped in black, and cackle with self-righteous scorn over the condition in which they found their property. Most of the chairs were lame, or had arms missing, and my bed, I recall only too well, was splitting apart and exposing the straw in which the fleas had long since made their home. I sprayed it incessantly and even soaked it completely once in kerosene, causing a stench that made sleep difficult, but the fleas came back. One of the abiding memories I have of that time is waking up in the morning and seeing dozens of fleas hopping from my reddened body onto the blankets and disappearing into the fibres.

The furnishings, in so far as they existed, were pretty much as they had been when we moved in but nothing would convince the old girls that we were not inflicting damage, and in the end we gave up trying. We let them carry out their impromptu inspections without comment and suffered their threats of eviction in silence. And when the time eventually came for us to move out, we gave them the necessary notice and braced ourselves for their last nit-picking descent upon the dump.

The battle was, as we expected, without quarter. The Inquisition had nothing on these three old crows. They threatened and accused, wailed and lamented, and then produced a list of alleged damage as long as your arm, adding up to several months' rent. I can't recall how much we paid them in the end, but it was far more than they had any right to expect. We figured, in the way that hindsight can convert weakness into wisdom, that the blame was ours for believing them when they said that 'inventories were unnecessary among honourable people'. We reckoned 'gullible' was a better word.

Country Joe just turned up on the doorstep one day and uttered those magic words that ensured admission anywhere in the late sixties: 'Need a place to crash, man.' And he did just that. He crossed over the threshold, rolled out his sleeping-bag and stayed for two months.

The Mansion was soon to become a fixture on the hippie circuit, a landmark on the California-to-Cusco trail, and as the hippies met on the road and swapped wisdom and addresses, so the knocks on our door increased. I can recall going down to breakfast one morning and having to step over half a dozen bodies soundly sleeping on the kitchen floor before I could get to the sink. In the end it all became too much and the four of us decided to surrender.

The crunch came one day when one of the 'guests', mistaking his Peace Corps host Ben for a fellow itinerant, said, 'I don't care where you are, you can always find saps like this to live off'. And so we moved out, leaving whoever came after us with the unenviable task of turning away scores of impecunious nomads.

But when Country Joe arrived, or C.J. as he was affectionately known, we had not yet reached the point of desperation and we welcomed him in with the casual camaraderie of the young and disaffected at that time. Not that C.J. was young. He must have been forty if he was a day, and to us that seemed pretty old, but there was, all the same, a certain agelessness about him. He told us once that he had served in the Marines, but we never actually found out when or where it was because he always seemed to have trouble concentrating long enough to come up with an answer; and in fact, we never found out very much about him at all. The conversation always seemed to get side-tracked somewhere along the way.

'Hey, C.J., tell us about the Marines,' we would sometimes urge.

'Hell man, the Marines – now that was some trip! Some trip, I tell you! Say, have you read Velikovsky's *Worlds In Collision*? Man, that book is far out! I mean f-a-r o-u-t!' And so it would go.

Half the time he spoke in riddles, although it didn't seem so at first. In fact, the first impression was usually that he had said something terribly profound – until you stopped and thought about it, and found it didn't add up to much.

'Say Rick, what you doin'?' he asked me once.

'Oh, nothing much,' I answered vaguely, as I flicked through a magazine.

'Is that *nothing*?' he continued. 'Or is that *no thing*?'

'Well, let me think now,' I replied cautiously. 'I suppose I really mean *no thing*.'

'That's what I reckoned!' he came back triumphantly. 'You need to be clear about these things.'

But the fellow was harmless and we enjoyed his company, even if we couldn't understand what he was saying half the time. In fact all round he was something of an asset. He was a gangling streak of Americana, tall and thin and held together by a thick leather belt that sagged heavily under the weight of his life-support system – the inevitable leather pouch. His long, straight black hair was pulled together at the back in a pony tail, and his lean, sallow face sprouted a cobweb of unvarying growth. His grey tee-shirt had once been black, his jeans were more patches than denim, and his leather sandals were worn without respite, and without socks. I never saw him in any other outfit, and judging by the odour I would say he had been wearing that one for some time. Perhaps he didn't believe in washing, because I never saw any evidence of it, or perhaps it was just something that had slipped his mind – like his past – and become a non-issue.

His perpetual good humour was like a tonic to us and we found ourselves habitually asking about him, seeking his company, and bringing him into our conversations. When he wasn't bamboozling us with semantics he could be extremely entertaining, especially when his thoughts started to run riot, and this alone was enough to earn him his floor-space. You always had the feeling that he was about to say something 'mind-blowing', or that he just had but you didn't quite catch it. It was no good asking *him* what he had just said because he could never remember. He would just laugh, and say, 'Did I say that? Did I really say that? Man, that is far out! F-a-r o-u-t! Man, I must really be tuning into something!'

He had read widely of everything non-mainstream, the more freaky and bizarre the better; and his experiments, needless to say, had not stopped at literature. It was not long after the time of Timothy Leary and his 'acid farm' in Mexico, when he had invited everyone to 'turn on, tune in and drop out', and C.J. had done just that, with whatever he could lay his hands on – hash, marijuana, acid, cocaine, magic mushrooms, peyote and opium, and I long suspected that this was where he had left his past.

When he came into our lives he had been wandering around for a month living on nothing but wild honey. He had read somewhere that Christ, alone in the wilderness, had hallucinated about the devil doing just that, and it sounded to him like a pretty good trip. I suspect, though, that it didn't work out too well, because he didn't like to talk about it much.

It was Ben who decided to call him Country Joe, partly because he didn't tell us what his real name was, and partly because he supposedly bore a passing resemblance to the protest singer of that name. Whether or not our C.J. did resemble the singer, or whether Ben just plucked the name out of the air, I can't say, but C.J. didn't seem to mind. In fact, he positively seemed to like it – but then, given that he seemed positively to like just about everything, that might not be saying too much.

It was also Ben who showed him the poem 'Magic Psalm' by that dubious poet-guru of the sixties, Allen Ginsberg, which describes

the effect of ayahuasca – a hallucinogenic vine that grows down in
the Ecuadorean Amazon and which certain of the Indians use for
the purposes of initiation and divination.

The effect of the poem on C.J. was instantaneous and profound.
He reacted like a herd of dying cattle at the scent of rain. He
grabbed his small army pack, in which he kept all his worldly possessions, and headed straight for the jungle.

It was no mean journey that he was undertaking. It was tarmac
as far as Ambato, of course, but after that the road to Puyo, and
then on to Tena, turned into a narrow, precipitous track clinging to
the mountainside.

The drop was always there, just a foot or two away, and like the
threat of war when it is imminent, it remained unacknowledged in
heavy silence. With a single cloudburst the track could turn into a
skating rink, and then occasionally buses would skid and plunge to
their destruction in the depths below. I almost took the plunge once
myself while travelling in a car that braked suddenly and slid ago-
nizingly towards the edge. We came to a halt with one wheel
poised freakily over the void.

At other times the heavy rain would cause landslides, blocking
the narrow way and bringing buses to a halt. Then the passengers
would be forced into what the Ecuadoreans call a 'trasbordo', clam-
bering across the rubble, luggage in hand, to meet a bus from the
opposite direction. It is a curious and harrowing spectacle to see
two files of heavily laden people moving in opposite directions
across the slope and struggling to avoid sliding down into the abyss.
The bus drivers then had to reverse along this knife-edge of a track
until they could find space wide enough to turn round – this could
be anything up to a quarter of a mile.

The bus drivers were brave men, and good drivers too. No one
has the right to expect such heroism from mere mortals every day,
for nine, ten, eleven, twelve hours at a stretch; and yet, sure
enough, there it was for all to see, every single day. Only when the
conditions worked seriously against them – mechanical failures,
landslides, rainstorms – did they make mistakes, and these were few

and far between. Perhaps one day some poet of stature will come
along and record their exploits – the genuine courage of ordinary
and unprepossessing men who put their lives on the line every day.
And perhaps, at the same time, this poet might tell of the countless
other millions whose daily heroism under the Sisyphean rock of
underdevelopment also goes unnoticed, except by the few.

C.J. arrived in one gangling piece and it didn't take him long, once
he got to Tena, to track down the 'sacred vine'. He simply asked the
first Peace Corps Volunteer he came across, then found someone
who was willing to go with him and trotted off into the rain forest in
the right direction. Most people seemed to know where you could
get hold of the stuff even if they didn't actually indulge themselves.

For most Amazonian Indians, ayahuasca is still a genuinely
'sacred' plant, very much part of their belief system and their
ceremony. They refer to it as the 'drug of death' because it has the
potential to transport those who know how to use its power both
into the future and into the land of departed souls where they are
able to converse with their ancestors. They are completely familiar
with its effects, are judicious in its use, and hold it in great esteem.

Country Joe, on the other hand, did not have such a sense of
reverence. He arrived back at the Mansion, his pack bulging with
dark brown creepers, and immediately set about brewing up his
concoction in one of our larger saucepans.

It was still only just light when he began, as the bus had reached
Quito in the hours of darkness, but he was so totally absorbed in his
experiment that I doubt very much if he could have told you what
time it was. I happened to be up and about, and I watched as he
meticulously washed the twisted shapes, cut them into small pieces
and dropped them, one by one, into the simmering water. He
seemed to be guided by some sort of instinct, mixing quantities
with great assurance as if he had studied the subject all his life.

It was a Sunday morning and I had risen early because I was
going off to play football some short distance outside Quito. I had
my bag in my hand as I stood there in the kitchen watching him.

'Say, where you heading?' asked C.J., looking up from the saucepan.

'Playing soccer,' I replied.

'Far out!' said C.J. 'Now, is that to *play* soccer, or to play *soccer?*'

'No, mate, this is the real thing. I'm going to play *soccer*,' I replied.

'I knew it!' he said confidently; and then added, 'Say, you not gonna try some of C.J.'s magic brew? I tell you man, this stuff is gonna blow your tiny mind!' And he gave a whoop.

'No thanks,' I said. 'You know us jocks — strict diet and all that. But take care, man.' I trotted out the lingo to conceal a vague feeling of unease stirring inside me.

Ben and the others, hearing the conversation, had come down to see what was going on and were peering into the saucepan at the dark brown liquid.

'Has to be nearly black,' asserted C.J., like some guardian of the ancient wisdom, and the others, humbled by his confidence, nodded in assent, apparently persuaded that here was a master at work.

I returned some five hours later to find mayhem. It was as if someone had tossed a hand-grenade through the window and run away. Writhing, groaning, vomiting bodies were strewn all over the place. My three house-mates, C.J., and a couple of others who happened to be 'crashing' at the time, were convulsed on the floor as if in the throes of some painful death. It had crossed my mind on the way home that they might have something interesting to relate, but I hadn't anticipated being called upon to administer the last rites.

One of my house-mates, Gerry, had a glimmer of light in his eyes. Through clenched teeth and painful gasps he managed to speak.

'No wonder they call this stuff the drug of death. Man, I tell you, I've been there and back. Never again. Never again!'

Bit by bit Gerry revealed to me the whole revolting story. After I had left that morning, C.J. had masterminded his concoction for an hour or two longer until the liquid was thick and black as treacle. Then he had poured it into cups – one cup per person. They had downed their draughts, and for a good fifteen minutes nothing happened, so C.J. decided it probably hadn't been strong enough and what they needed was another cup – each. All of them except Gerry, who was already having second thoughts about taking it at all, drank a second draught of the brew.

We learned later on that one of the early symptoms of having overdosed is the feeling that you could probably do with a drop more. They had, therefore, doubly overdosed on the sickly stuff.

The question now was whether to get them to hospital and, perhaps because we all shared a deep distrust of Ecuadorean hospitals, we opted in favour of Gerry's surmise that they would probably 'come down' in a couple of hours. I was pretty worried. I couldn't help speculating on why, exactly, the Indians called it 'the drug of death' – whether its transporting of people into the next world was temporary or permanent. I feared there might be a fine line between the two, and hence the Indians' respect for its powers – maybe if you were not careful you might end up joining the ranks of the ancestors yourself, ahead of time.

Anyhow, we decided to sit it out and sure enough, after a couple of hours they started to come round, one at a time – all of them groaning and retching, and vowing 'never again'. All of them except C.J., that is, who, though stricken with the same spasms, never uttered a word of complaint. In fact, he didn't speak at all until right out of the blue, like some prince gently awakened by the kiss of a beautiful princess, he exclaimed, 'Man, that was some trip! S-o-m-e t-r-i-p!'

Later that same day, when things had calmed down a bit and everyone was more or less back on track, we decided to go out to the Chinese restaurant for a meal. Their minds were still buzzing with excitement, and they were all gabbling away nineteen-to-the-dozen about where they had been and what they had seen. But beneath it all there ran a clear undercurrent of relief and a resolve 'never to go back'.

One of them, an artist, later expressed his experience in paint, and depicted himself inside his coffin, very much alone, his face pale and drawn, floating up through space towards a serpent-infested Land of the Dead. I sensed that in his particular case the experience went much deeper – it was as if he had come face to face with something he had hoped never to see and it had left him with a terrible sense of foreboding.

For the moment, though, the mood was one of joyous relief at having escaped the jaws of death and the food, good though it was, was no match for the delicious sensation of being back in the land of the living in the company of friends. It was a splendid evening and one that vibrated with humour and *joie de vivre*.

Then, just as we were leaving, feeling thoroughly convinced that life could not possibly be better, C.J. caught a protruding toe in the edge of the big square rug and went sprawling, headlong, out of the door, down the steps and into the bushes; then he sat there for a moment in silence, his head bowed, contemplating the miracle of his escape – his second within hours. I didn't have the heart to ask him if he had had a good trip.

'Hey man, did you see that?' he exclaimed at length, exhibiting the same bemused delight that he showed in everything. 'Man, that was far out! I mean – just too much!'

'Are you all right, C.J.?' I asked, but wished I hadn't, the second the words were out.

'If you mean, am I all *right* – I guess so; but if you mean am I *all* right, I ain't so sure.'

And he sat there for a while just shaking his head at the mind-blowing unpredictability of it all.

Life went back to normal after a while – at least as normal as it ever could be with C.J. around – until one day he upped and left without a word, in a way that matched his sudden and unheralded arrival. I was making my way down to breakfast one day, intending to grab some tea and run in my usual hasty fashion, when I caught myself stepping over a non-existent bed-roll and realized that something was not quite right.

'Hey, where's C.J.?' I asked Ben, who was sitting there sipping coffee and staring into space.

'Oh, he split. Moved out while it was still dark,' he replied from inside his cup.

'You mean he's gone – for good – without even saying good-bye?' I asked incredulously.

'Sure did. In fact, I was lucky to catch sight of him myself. Said he threw the I-Ching last night and it told him to move before the cock crowed. So he did. Hauled it real fast. And man, I mean *fast*! You'd have thought his life depended on it!'

CHAPTER FIFTEEN

FOOTBALL
FAILURE & FANTASY

THROUGH A CASUAL conversation and a link between one of my less able pupils at the Catholic University and the president of the first division football club, Liga Deportiva Universitaria, I was invited along to the stadium one Monday morning in June 1969 for a trial. I'm not sure what it was that inclined the president to think a complete stranger was worthy of a trial with a prestigious club, but I suspect it might have had something to do with the fact that England were world champions at the time, so that he may have thought all Brits had the potential to produce the footballing skills of Bobby Charlton. He cannot have seen the two games I had played in Riobamba for the second division side Olmedo which, because of my lack of fitness and the debilitating effects of altitude, turned out to be the most disastrous performances of my life and convinced me, under a hail of derision, to hang up my boots.

On this occasion, however, I made sure that I was both fit and fully adapted to the conditions, which also meant being familiar with the rapid movement of the ball through the thin air. The Liga pitch proved to be a little too hard for my liking but there was plenty of grass on it and it allowed me to play something like my normal game. The trial went reasonably well, with the result that I was offered a one-year contract immediately afterwards.

The manager of Liga was a Brazilian named Gomez Nogueira. He was tall, black and commanding. Five years before, when he had first been with Liga, all three teams – the first, the reserve and the youth – had run away with their respective titles, but the club directors had been so disturbed by Nogueira's colourful language and his general 'lack of culture' that his contract had not been renewed. Now in 1969, with Liga having spent the intervening years in the doldrums, he was back with all three teams firmly in his uncultured grasp. By the end of the season, all three teams would once again have walked off with their titles; Nogueira, despite being a Brazilian, would have been appointed manager of the Ecuadorean national side for the World Cup qualifying rounds; and his contract would not have been renewed.

My arrival at Liga coincided with Nogueira's return and also with the blossoming of a Uruguayan of phenomenal talent by the name of Francisco Bertocchi. Bertocchi had been a member of the Uruguay squad that travelled to England for the World Cup in 1966, but had never really settled in his home country and had seldom produced the type of performance he was to produce that season in Ecuador.

Liga had a history of glamour and ready cash behind them and were backed by a number of prosperous businessmen. In Ecuador, and Latin America generally, many professional clubs do not own their stadiums and would normally spend the week training in a local park somewhere, and then turn out in municipal stadiums – the standards of which vary enormously – on Sundays. Liga, however, had permanent access to the well-planned and well-equipped University stadium for training, while playing their home games in the monumentally impressive Atahualpa stadium that I had seen the morning of my arrival in the country.

Uniquely for Ecuador, there was a doctor, a professional masseur, and an assistant who ensured that you always had clean kit to wear – right down to your boots. Also unusual was the fact that salary payments were punctual, with no suspicion of under-the-table dealings, and there was certainly never any suggestion of drug abuse. In most ways, therefore, they were a prestigious outfit and the only criticism that could be levelled at them was that they were not a team of 'the people', but rather of the upper classes, which bothered me a little and also goes some way to explaining Nogueira's unpopularity, despite his runaway success.

The star of the team and of that 1969 season was the Uruguayan Francisco Bertocchi, whose talent was clearly extraordinary. Bertocchi was tallish and burly, and scored a phenomenal number of goals; however, he was not a striker but an inside-forward with excellent ball-skills. One salient feature of his otherwise impressive physique was his bandy legs, and his colleagues had imported into Quito the corresponding nickname 'Chueco'. This was how he was affectionately referred to more often than not.

Whatever it was that kept him from performing to the best of his ability in Uruguay proved to be Ecuador's good fortune. Some of his performances during that season were among the finest I have ever seen anywhere in the world. And when I returned to Ecuador some twenty years later I found that people were still talking about that '69 season as if it were some Golden Age, not just in the fortunes of Liga Deportiva Universitaria, but of football in the Sierra generally. Reference was still being commonly made both to Bertocchi's brilliance and the nine goals that he scored in one par-ticular game. Golden days indeed they were, and days that were destined not to return; neither, of course, was Nogueira.

I never stopped to ask how it was that Bertocchi came to Liga when he might easily have gone to any number of more wealthy clubs in Latin America, until I was in Mexico three years later, and perusing the sports pages of the newspaper one day I saw a reference to an exciting new signing by the club Monterrey. As I read on I discovered that the signing in question was a certain Uruguayan by the name of Francisco Bertocchi. Further down the page I discovered that the manager who had clinched the deal and who was himself new to Monterrey, was none other than a Brazilian by the name of Gomez Nogueira. The two, it seemed, had entered into some sort of partnership and were hawking their not inconsid-erable skills around the football circuit of Latin America, in much the same way that a prize-fighter and his manager might have done around the boxing booths of North America.

I don't know how or where Bertocchi's playing days came to an end but I do know that he was back in Ecuador for a while, as manager of a local team, and doing moderately well. Of Nogueira, I know nothing, but I imagine that he withdrew into prosperous retirement. I dearly hope so, not simply because he deserved it, but also because I developed quite a liking for the fellow.

One day at Liga he asked me if I would teach him some English, so keen was he to acquire 'culture', and I managed to find time for a couple of lessons, but I could see that it was going to be hard work. He realized this too and laughed it off, saying that his academic prowess was what you would expect from someone descended from a long line of slaves and brought up in the slums of Rio. But what an impressive figure he cut for someone who could barely read and write. He was a belligerent, articulate, kind-hearted giant of a man, with a magnetic personality and a string of outstanding achievements to his credit, who could speak to crowds with ease and without a single page of notes, but who was forever haunted by his lack of education.

I had to wait for my playing permit to come through, and although the procedure was rendered fairly straightforward by the fact that I had not played professionally before, it still took an agonizing few weeks. Eventually, Nogueira came striding into the dressing room one day waving a piece of paper at me, and declared, 'Here it is — you're ready to go!'

Indeed I was. I had been straining at the leash, and it would be no exaggeration to say that this moment was the fulfilment of a lifetime's ambition, a dream about to come true.

The game that Sunday was an away fixture against one of the better sides in the division, a team called Emelec with a long, impressive record in both national and South American football. Because of the tropical heat, games on the coast were usually scheduled to be played in the evening under floodlights, most often in the municipal stadium of Guayaquil, which was how it was on this occasion.

It was far from certain that I would be selected to play. The first team was on a winning streak and was looking fairly settled, and the best I could hope for was to be brought on as substitute at some stage. It was a nervous business — and not just for myself. The rivalry between the Sierra and the coast was deeply entrenched and not always healthy, and the games had a habit of ending in violence. There was also the question of climate — we were descending to sea-level, and the heat, despite the evening schedule, had a habit of sapping your strength in much the same way as the altitude.

Luck was with me and I was named among the substitutes. I duly took my place on the bench and did my best to gauge the pace of the game and the level of physical contact, so as to be 'psyched up' in case I was called on at a moment's notice. But it was no easy task under the artificial glare of the floodlights, which lent an air of unreality to the players' movements, and with a large, partisan crowd behind me whose roars contradicted my own impulses.

Things went badly for us. With twenty minutes remaining and the score at three–one in Emelec's favour, Nogueira signalled me on to cover the midfield. Within seconds I went for a 'fifty-fifty' ball and felt the studs of an opponent's boot rip into my knee. He had gone over the top, viciously, but the referee did not respond. I saw and felt it happen but, astonishingly, felt no pain. It was almost as if I was watching someone else.

The ball ran outside and I went to take the throw, retrieving it from the foot of the wall of wire mesh that separated the crowd from the pitch. My approach was met with a chorus of 'gringo, son of a whore', and a shower of saliva that covered me from head to foot. A plastic bag filled with urine, descending from a great height, burst on the ground behind me soaking the backs of my legs. I continued with the throw and put the ball back into play, pretending not to notice.

In the remaining minutes we succeeded in pulling a goal back, and I personally managed to supply a couple of fairly long and accurate passes that brought praise from my team-mates, so I left the pitch feeling reasonably satisfied. Inside the dressing room Nogueira reiterated the congratulations of my colleagues and gave me the reassurance I needed.

The blow to the knee was clearly more serious than I thought and the joint had blown up like a balloon, although the cuts left by the studs were fortunately superficial and did not need stitching. The doctor came over to disinfect and dress the wound, but his attentions were superfluous. The adrenalin was pumping fast and I was feeling good – on top of the world, in fact – and the injury meant precious little.

When we had all showered and changed, we moved out *en masse* with the police opening a channel for us through the crowd to our bus. I climbed inside and took a seat next to the window, being careful to keep my leg straight and out of harm's way. The windows on these coastal buses have no glass to them and I instantly found myself in conversation with a young Emelec supporter who had attracted my attention from outside.

'Hey, Richard, get down!' yelled a team-mate, and I turned to see the rest of the team flattened as if by a bomb, some to their seats, others to the floor. I did as I was told.

As we pulled away the bus was pelted with missiles – bricks, bottles, stones, anything that came to hand – some of which thundered against the side of the vehicle, while others came in through the open windows but fortunately failed to make contact. After a minute or two we were out of range and able to get up and breathe again normally. I felt the warm Guayaquil air blow over me and it felt sweet. My baptism in Guayaquil was over, and I had reason to believe, at long last, that the future might well have something good in store.

Violence is never far from the surface in Latin America. It is a culture of violence and has been ever since the Spaniards arrived, and, in some cases, well before. It is said that the Aztecs of Mexico, who were unassailably strong at the time of the Conquest, were so locked into human sacrifice that they dispensed with anything up to

10,000 of their fellow countrymen in a single session, which goes some way to explaining how the bearded strangers found allies the moment they stepped off the boat. In South America, on the other hand, the ascendant tribe, the Incas, were not given to such practices – at least, not on anything like the same scale. Theirs, in the main, was an orderly and constructive society, and the culture of random violence that you find in South America today was largely imported from Spain.

Small wonder, then, that something as emotive and partisan as football should be the focus and the occasion of so much violence; what is scary about it, from a European perspective, is that it takes only the merest spark to set it off and thereafter the conflagration can rage for hours. In England it is extremely rare for a dispute between players to involve more than two people at any one time, and these would normally only square up to each other after a fairly long preamble of provocation and threat. The second a punch is thrown team-mates are quick to intervene and break it up. It is all part of the sporting tradition.

It is not the same in Latin America. When a fist-fight breaks out between two players – often without warning – the other twenty usually join in. Each one lashes out at the opponent nearest him with fists or boots in an attempt to floor his adversary before he gets floored himself. Fear is at the root of it all, of course, and the result is pandemonium. The police then move in, swinging their batons at everyone in sight, and this is usually enough to calm it down, although I have seen instances where the players stand and slug it out with the police as well. It is not unusual either for the substitutes and managers, and even the press, to rush out and throw themselves into the fray, the photographers wielding their cameras. Indeed no one seems to be immune and even the most respectable, level-headed family man can be transformed in a trice into a fiend who won't quit until all the enemy have been razed to the ground. The first time it happens you can't believe your eyes, but you soon get used to it and after a while you begin to sense when the thing is about to break.

Violence on the terraces and outside the stadiums can also occur but is much less likely than in England. The past twenty years have seen mayhem in and around English football grounds and it is scarcely an exaggeration to say that just about everyone has heard of it. In fact, the word 'hooligan' has entered the vocabulary of even the most remote villages. My feeling is that it is something that afflicts materialistic societies generally, and happens wherever and whenever money is considered to be more important than people. We like to believe that the root of the problem is a complex sociological matter that involves deprivation and hardship, but that argument doesn't really carry much weight among people who are infinitely more deprived than we are and don't have the same problem.

Football violence in England has become an ugly reality and a source of great shame and regret to all of us who love the game and its traditions. English violence differs from the Latin American version in that it is organized and premeditated, which undoubtedly makes it all the more sinister. On the other hand, since it is a recent phenomenon, and one that is fairly localized and has its roots in social change rather than cultural idiosyncrasy, there must be grounds for believing that its eventual eradication will not be beyond us. In Latin America, on the other hand, even such modest levels of optimism would appear to be unfounded.

In May 1970 the England team visited Ecuador. The party was on its way to Mexico to defend the World Cup and it was considered that a couple of warm-up games in the highlands of Colombia and Ecuador would help the players acclimatize for the lower, but still problematical altitude of Mexico City. It was directly following this visit, incidentally, when the plane touched down in Bogotá, that the England captain, Bobby Moore, was arrested on suspicion of having stolen an emerald bracelet from the hotel in which the team had been staying.

Being familiar with the underhand way that things often operate in Latin America, especially Colombia, I felt deeply sorry for Bobby Moore. That he handled the affair with so much dignity, and then went on to produce some of the finest displays of defensive football ever seen in the World Cup, is testimony to the man's greatness. That the England party should have been unprepared for such eventualities was symptomatic of a general ineptitude on the part of the organizers that was to cost us the world championship.

The 1970 World Cup was a disaster for England and in fact has to be seen as a watershed in the nation's footballing fortunes. The Bogotá affair; the Mexican mariachis playing outside the hotel all night long; the controversy that raged over the fact that the England party reputedly took its own drinking water to Mexico, when any sensible person would have done the same; the strange 'illness' that overtook the world's number one goalkeeper, Gordon Banks, on the eve of the decisive game against West Germany; the lunatic decision to take off the genial Bobby Charlton with twenty minutes remaining, thereby allowing Franz Beckenbauer to run riot and turn the course of the game – all of this conspired to bring down an impenetrably dark curtain on English football from which it has yet to emerge.

It was agony for those of us who believed in England's world class quality and their rightful claim to be champions. And it had been all the more important that they should prove it in Latin America, in the eyes of a footballing public who see every World Cup tournament as a war between Latin America and Europe, and who sincerely believed that, not just one Russian linesman in the final, but a whole series of other senior officials had been bribed to ensure England's triumph in 1966.

England's failure had as much to do with incidents off the field as on it, and I was able to see for myself the sorry state of their unpreparedness when I was invited, along with other members of the British community living in Quito, to meet the players and officials at a reception held at the Ambassador's residence.

We, the British expatriates, assembled early; partly, I think, on account of our excitement and the desire not to miss anything of the big occasion, but also to make sure that we were there to greet the party and make them feel welcome the moment they arrived. I consider it doubtful that we succeeded in this because I can still see now the look of dread on some of the players' faces as they rounded the corner of the residence and caught sight of us standing there on the lawn, glasses in hand, ready to pounce. In that moment I realized just how far out of their depth many of them were — not merely in this neo-colonial setting, which was an ordeal for many of us, but in Latin America generally, and just how much they were in need of guidance, protection, and a public relations expert.

I asked some of the first-team players how the altitude had affected them in their game in Bogotá, and they replied, echoing the conventional wisdom of the day, that they were now, after two weeks, virtually acclimatized and that it was just a question of taking a little longer to regain their breath. Gordon Banks displayed a better grip on reality when he spoke of the ball coming through the air faster at him, but for the most part it was clear that they still had no idea — an impression that was confirmed a couple of days later when they played the Ecuadorean national side, scored two goals in the first few minutes, and then spent the rest of the game dragging themselves painfully about the pitch in a mediocre performance against a depleted, inhibited and only partially fit opposition.

If the players realized then that the altitude was more of a problem than they had originally thought, they also knew that it was too late to do anything about it. It takes, in fact, several months of living and training there — perhaps as many as five — before you can honestly say you are acclimatized and no longer feel the effects.

But altitude was only one chink in their armour. There was also the psychological element and the team's unpreparedness for the general hostility that had been smouldering ever since in 1966 the England team manager Alf Ramsey referred to the Argentines as 'animals'. Many Latin Americans, given the way the battle-lines were drawn, took this as a reference to the continent as a whole. Neither were they prepared for the personal attacks of the press and its bent for muck-raking and invention, the allegations of drunkenness and womanizing in particular; nor for the antics of the 'dirty tricks' departments of Colombia and Mexico.

I wished then, and have wished ever since, that I had asked for just a few minutes to talk to the players or officials about such everyday occurrences and to bring to their attention the fact that they were walking though a minefield. But it never occurred to me that a mission as important as this could possibly be anything other than perfectly organized. Now, I am not even sure there was a Spanish-speaker in the whole party. If there was, I never met him, and I myself was asked by several members of the press to act as interpreter for their interviews with local footballing authorities.

Of course I don't believe for one moment that any intervention on my part would have made the slightest difference to the outcome. I suspect, in any case, that whole party were at saturation point by the time I met them, and past the point of listening; but still I think it would have been worth a try. And even if it didn't change the course of this particular piece of history, it might at least have planted a seed for the future which in itself could have been useful.

My debut against Emelec, instead of being the stepping-stone to a brighter future as I had hoped, proved to be my downfall. My appearance from out of nowhere had caused a certain amount of speculation and the press – never ones to let the facts spoil a good story – had wasted no time in producing the appropriate commentary. They quoted me as saying, among other things, that 'I had played for several of England's top clubs' (and thereby implied that I was not the 'amateur' I had made myself out to be) and that 'I knew Wembley like the back of my hand' (which I probably did – from the terraces). As a result, my playing permit was instantly revoked and I spent the next three months in the reserves, while letters of enquiry reputedly went back and forth between the English and Ecuadorean Football Associations – although, needless to say, I never believed a word of it.

Eventually the matter was cleared up – I suspect, as ever, by some piece of bureaucratic chicanery – and my permit was revalidated, but by this time Liga were way out ahead in the championship, the team was virtually selecting itself every week, and my only hope of getting back into it lay in someone breaking a leg or being pole-axed by a beer-bottle. The sum total of my first-team appearances, therefore, amounted to no more than those twenty saliva-soaked minutes against Emelec and a couple of easy victories against bottom-of-the-table clubs towards the end of the season, with the championship already won. My only game in the Atahualpa was as a member of a winning cup-final team, but with the reserves.

The pay kept coming in, however, including the winners' bonuses that were part of the original contract, and I left the country a relatively wealthy man, but this was no compensation for all my inactivity. In fact, it only made matters worse, for it merely served to underline all that I had not been doing and made me feel like an impostor.

Today, buried somewhere between nostalgia and self-parody, I feel fortunate to have spent those days with Liga despite the overwhelming disappointment they brought. I still believe I could have joined a lesser club in the same division and held down a regular first-team place, but I'm glad I didn't. It was good to share the euphoria of success, even from the bench, and to have trained and played alongside a genius like Bertocchi – also, to have been allowed some insight into what he must have felt at not being recognized as such by the world at large, an injustice that he bore with patience and good humour. It turned out to be my last season when I might have expected another five or six – a bout of hepatitis that pre-dated the arrival of the England party by a couple of weeks robbed me of the chance of playing for Liga against the England B side, and proved to be sufficiently debilitating to lay waste any lingering ambitions I might have had.

And yet, at the end of it all, usually in one of those moments of mellowness brought by the passage of time, the question from a schoolboy's dream returns – could I really have held down a regular place in that championship-winning side if everything had gone right?

My first answer has to be 'no', principally because I have always had doubts about my ability to rise to the big occasion; but perhaps it is a myth that temperament is innate, and it is always possible I might have acquired it, given time. Then again, I have always felt that you need to be 'hungry' to get to the top, and whereas most of my colleagues were 'starving', I personally was barely peckish; I was lucky enough to have other options open to me, and that tends to dilute one's resolve. So I have had to concede, once and for all, that the answer really is 'no'. But I can't help wondering – just a little – about what might have been . . .

Chapter Sixteen

CHOTA

ONE OF MY COLLEAGUES in the Liga reserves – the goalkeeper – was a Black by the name of Nelson. He was from Chota Valley, a small but remarkable collection of black communities situated in the Sierra of northern Ecuador. Local history tells that Ecuador's black population came originally from Angola, the Congo and Nigeria, and reached South America by way of Spanish slave vessels and the Caribbean port of Cartagena, from where they were transported further south for sale along the coastal plains of New Granada (Colombia) and Peru, of which Ecuador was a part. Nelson's forefathers were purchased by Jesuit priests in what is now Colombia and taken to Chota in the early seventeenth century, and there they remained for the next 350 years in a state of economic and cultural limbo, an isolated and shunned ethnic minority.

Nelson was a quiet type, or so I believed for some good while, and it was only when I came to see him in his home environment, extrovert and at ease, that I realized his reticence was not a natural trait but the product of centuries of racial abuse. He first came to my notice when, while leaving the stadium after a game, an irate spectator – for no reason that I could fathom except, perhaps, that his team had just lost – had called him 'a black son of a whore'. Nelson's response, which was characteristically brief and to the point, had been to leave his antagonist prostrate on the pavement following a short right jab to the nose.

Contrary to appearances, Nelson and I had something important in common in that we both belonged to despised racial minorities – he being from a race that was black and supposedly inferior, and me from a race that was white and supposedly superior. Our isolation threw us together and made us friends.

We would usually sit next to each other on the bus taking us to our matches and this extended to occupying adjacent pegs in the changing rooms. Afro-American history meant nothing to me in those days – the dimension of the thing was far too vast for me to grasp – but all the same I felt an instinctive warmth towards Nelson and his people, and I soon found myself asking questions that led me step by step into his personal life, and then into Chota. One day he asked me if I would like to go with him to visit his village – one weekend during the close-season in early 1970 when he was going home – and I gladly accepted.

Chota Valley is at the relatively low altitude of 4,000 feet above sea-level, and as a consequence it has a fairly hot climate, hot enough to grow grapes and sugar-cane; this is why the Jesuits took the Blacks there in the first place, to do all the hard work entailed in the cultivation of these two crops.

The slaves were taken not to one valley but to two, the valley of the River Chota and the neighbouring valley of the River Mira, both of which today, along with the village, are often lumped together under the generic name of 'Chota'.

The village lay a good eight hours from Quito. It was not far as the crow flies – less than 150 miles in fact – but the bus had to thread its interminable way along a rough dirt track that traced the million twisting contours of the mountains. You could always see the brown ribbon way ahead of you in the distance cut half-way up the mountainside, although sometimes it would double back on itself in a criss-cross so that you weren't always sure if you were looking at where you were going or where you had come from. Occasionally on this roller-coaster ride you would find yourself way up above the cloud, great banks of it that drifted through the valleys below.

At one point I looked out across the valley to see what was in store for us and noticed, way over on the other side, a bus that seemed to be parked at an odd angle. I assumed that it had broken down and that the driver, in the usual fashion, had chocked up the wheels with stones and then strewn the road with branches as a warning to approaching vehicles. Such practices, incidentally, had a habit of back-firing because not infrequently the driver – his vehicle fixed – would take off in haste, forgetting to remove the stones and branches, and causing a hazard to the very vehicles he had been at pains to forewarn.

When we reached the spot some ten minutes later, what we found was enough to make your hair stand on end. The bus had certainly come to a halt, but not as the result of any mechanical failure. It was perched with its two front wheels hovering over a 1,000-foot void. All the luggage was still intact, both inside and on the roof, but there was no one to be seen. We never learned the full story but we deduced that the driver had misjudged a bend and run out of road, and then just managed to pull his careening vehicle to a halt before it took the plunge. The passengers, we reckoned, had exited through the rear window and probably made for the nearest church.

Our bus deposited us some short distance from the village – the track being too narrow to go right in – and we covered the half-mile or so on foot, scuffing up the ridges of loose dirt and circumventing the sleeping dogs and the herds of marauding pigs as we went. It was early afternoon and the sun was beating fiercely down from a clear blue sky, baking everything and everybody in sight.

The houses were randomly arranged and all of the same construction – oblong in shape with mud and wattle walls and thatched roofs – with some of them perched precariously on the slope that rose up steeply from the river on one side. In the old days they had been round, Nelson told me, as had those of the Indians, the Pastos, who lived there before, but as the years went by they had adopted the shape of European houses.

There was no electricity or piped water, just a spring that served for drinking and the river that ran noisily around the edge of the village and served for washing. A couple of ample women were ambling from the river towards the houses, too weary to converse, bowls of clean clothing balanced gracefully on their heads. Small clusters of men sat somnolently in doorways, heads bowed, not noticing our approach. From window-sills young children, wide-eyed, innocent and deadly serious, stared at us over folded arms. There wasn't a White, or a mestizo, or an Indian in sight. It didn't feel like Ecuador at all.

Quite unexpectedly I felt a jolt of excitement run through me. My pulse and my breathing quickened noticeably and I felt myself overtaken by an urgent need to know more, to see everything there was to see, then and there. Nelson's village, I had just realized, was quite magnificent.

Everyone knew Nelson, of course, and he acknowledged them all in turn as we passed, but it was a casual kind of recognition on both sides that revealed nothing of the strength of the bonds between them. There were no expressions of surprise or welcome as such, and there were no young kids flocking around him as I thought there might have been to greet this local boy who had made it in the 'big city' as a professional footballer. It was almost as if such displays of emotion were somehow beneath them, a form of address they had long since learned to do without.

Nelson's house, situated in its own small compound on a flat some fifty yards from the river, was neither bigger nor smaller than the rest. It had the customary two rooms, one of which was the bedroom and the other the cooking/living/eating room with its beaten earth floor partially covered with a rush mat, and an assortment of furnishings. It seemed cool and dark inside.

A low wooden table stood in the middle and a collection of stools and chairs lined the two longer walls. In one corner near the doorway was the 'tulpa', the traditional three stones on which a large round cooking pot rested over a small pile of wood ashes. And at the far end, high up on a wall, half a dozen neatly framed black and white photographs, their subjects formally dressed and unsmiling, stared authoritatively down. Directly beneath was a cabinet loaded with trophies. I asked about them.

'Sports mostly,' replied Nelson. 'Some are mine; some belong to my sisters – one's a sprinter and the other throws the javelin. And the rest are my kid brothers' – both of them are boxers. That one there' – he pointed to a chromium-plated model of a guitar – 'is my father's. He's a musician.'

He introduced me to the family members, who had emerged from the other room and lined up. I shook hands with them all; the parents first – fine, straight people, who welcomed me with genuine warmth; then the sisters, tall, lithe and giggly – something told me that their awards had come fairly easily; and finally, the two brothers, powerful, serious and still growing. As I stretched out my hand towards them I playfully sparred for a second to lighten the occasion and to indicate that I already knew something about them. They smiled pleasantly back but did not respond. Little did I suspect then that within a few years both of them would be contending the World Lightweight title, one in New York and the other in Tokyo.

That weekend was Chota's annual festival, and this was the reason for Nelson's visit. The highlight of the occasion was the dance that was to be held at the local primary school that same evening, and everyone in the village was expected to be there. I had long since learned to enjoy dances – it was one of the many great things that Ecuador had taught me – and I was looking forward to it, although, like the village itself, it turned out to be more than I had bargained for.

The traditional music of the valley is known as the 'bomba', after the goatskin drum that provides the beat. Other instruments of Spanish origin, like the guitar and the flute, have found their way into the ensemble, but virtually anything that can hold a note is liable to turn up – machetes, dinner-plates and a donkey's jaw-bone included, and also the *hoja*, which is the leaf of the male orange tree and produces an eerie whining sound when blown across. A 'good' leaf, I was told, will last a performance.

But it is the *bomba* that has given the music its name and its
character and has come to symbolize Chota's African connection,
providing an essential link with the mother culture. The significance of the drum to African music and African culture generally
cannot be overemphasized, and cannot be properly understood
from the outside. It is the heartbeat of the continent, the spiritual
and psychic pulse that moves all things. It has even been suggested
by one authority on African affairs that drums 'speak' not so much
through their rhythms in a type of Morse code, as by raising consciousness and encouraging the transmission of thought over vast
distances. Anyone who has spent much time in African villages, and
kept his ear to the ground, will have realized that there is a system
of communication at work that we know nothing about.

The British sensed and feared this affinity between drums and
cultural survival, which is why they banned their use in the
Caribbean and why steel bands grew up in their stead. The goatskin
may have been replaced by steel, but the rhythm remained, eventually to be exported back to Africa in West Indian guise where it
took root instantly. You can hardly go to a village anywhere in
Africa these days without hearing the music of Bob Marley and
other reggae artists being played constantly – villages that for the
most part have never heard of Elvis Presley, The Beatles, Mozart
and Beethoven. The heart is still beating and the thread that links
the two continents is still intact – after 300 years.

Somehow Afro-Americans, despite the humiliations they have
had to endure, have managed to preserve within themselves a part
that is forever Africa – a spiritual reserve that neither time nor circumstance can reach – in a way that the Indians of the Sierra have
generally not managed to do, for the latter have been crushed in
spirit, their self-esteem is in tatters and their culture is up for sale.
But African culture is alive and kicking and you see it clearly, not
just in the music, but in the laughter and the gestures, the ties of the
extended family, and in the continuing thirst for the spiritual.

Black, anti-White racism is a recent phenomenon and is
practised today by people who have less reason to be prejudiced

than their forebears. The old folks somehow learned to dig deep inside themselves and to allow the injustices of the world to flow over them; and then to emerge with precious little rancour, and with eyes that radiated kindness. When it comes to values the Afro-American has emerged victorious. In surrendering one world they gained another and established a pre-eminence that no one can match – spirit intact, head unbowed and drum still beating. It would be sad if subsequent generations, not understanding the feats and insights of their forebears, were to debase this glorious spiritual heritage.

The musicians who were to perform that night were from Chota village and they dropped by Nelson's house during the early evening for a drink and a chat before the show. As ever they started messing around with their instruments – and not just the musicians in fact, but anyone who felt like playing, and the evening started to take off. The *bomba* was pounding, the *hoja* was whining, the jaw-bone (teeth and all) was clacking, the guitars were plucking, everybody started to dance, and always the laughter was bubbling to overflow. There was no build-up to it, no alcohol, no 'breaking the ice' – it just happened.

As I listened to the conversations that were going on around me I began to sense something of the gulf that separated us; the European from the African, that is, and by extension the European from the Indian, for in many ways the Blacks and the Indians are spiritual brothers, as all the indigenous peoples of the world must be. It was something I should have been sensitive to before, especially with the Indians, but had not been; and, in fact, it was only much later in Africa that the full implication of what was taking place that evening became apparent.

Sometimes when you are listening to humorous exchanges between Africans, or Indians, what they are saying may not make a great deal of sense. There often appears to be no thread of logic to their repartee and no intelligible basis to the humour that has everybody in stitches. There is no wit, no word-play, no innuendo and none of the elements a European would normally consider essential for making somebody laugh. It often leaves us feeling confused and left out, and sometimes even indignant.

That a European should fail to understand a foreign culture is nothing new, of course; the British have been doing it for centuries all over the world. One example is the gulf between what we, the Europeans, perceive as gratitude on the one hand, and what constitutes social responsibility in traditional African society on the other.

In any African community it is both the duty and the instinct of every member to help whenever someone has a problem. It would be unthinkable to do otherwise. This being the case, the need to express gratitude openly, to say 'thank you', becomes redundant. To use the term at all would be to imply that some kind act is out of the ordinary and unexpected, and would be tantamount to an insult, as if to say 'Good God, what's the matter with you? You've actually done me a good turn for once!' The word, therefore, becomes unnecessary, but the reality is quite the opposite of what many Europeans think, which is that Africans are never grateful for anything — a judgement based purely on the fact that they do not happen to say 'thank you' every five minutes the way we have been taught to do.

A second example relates to the astonishing capacity Africans have for enduring hardship and pain — their stoicism. Within traditional African society it is considered unacceptable to make an open display of weakness and suffering. Children, for example, are trained from their earliest days to accept adversity with patience and courage, and without tears. Part of the mechanism for handling adversity is the ability to laugh, both individually and collectively, at whatever life chooses to throw at you. I see laughter now, in fact, as central to the survival and well-being of African society.

When someone meets with an accident that falls short of death, it is the immediate responsibility of his fellows to raise his spirits so that he can see his problem in perspective and deal with it. This they do by laughing and getting him to laugh along with them. As a therapy it works quite well. Contrary to what many Europeans think, therefore, such laughter does not represent callousness on the part of the African, but rather an expression of deepest concern and solidarity.

Who among us expatriates can honestly say he has not been disturbed when, on a visit to the cinema in Nairobi or Kampala or Lagos the local people have roared with laughter at some heart-rendingly tragic incident, at the most crucial and poignant moment of the film? But what we Europeans seldom see is the African sobbing his heart out in private on the way home.

Such misconceptions are common between the two cultures, but what I thought I glimpsed on this occasion in Chota was different because it did not relate to a single identifiable trait so much as an entire relationship. The mistake I had been making, I realized, was in trying to follow what was being *said* in these humorous exchanges rather than what was being *felt*, because the essence of the communication in such instances is not so much intellectual as emotional. What is taking place is primarily a sharing of being, of friendship, of joy, and of love, and this takes precedence over the spoken word.

If this seems unreasonable then try turning it round for a second and imagining how our *emotional* exchanges (that we are always at great pains to hide from each other) would appear to someone who is super-sensitive to such things – when we strive to reach ever new heights of brilliance with our wit and our logic, and trample over everyone else's feelings in the process. Our emotional responses would surely seem every bit as fragmented and meaningless to them as their verbal responses do to us. There is a fundamental difference in the way we perceive our relationships, therefore – they are more concerned with sharing feeling, whereas we, if we are sharing anything at all, are more concerned with thought.

This difference is seen even more clearly when it comes to telling jokes, virtually all of which will probably strike the European as being far from original and exceedingly dull; but again we are missing the point. For an African a joke does not necessarily have to be original to make him laugh. If his principal concern is that of sharing joyous experience with others, then the important thing is to know that something is funny enough to have made people laugh once, and from then on it is guaranteed to have the same effect every time. If something is funny, it does not cease to be funny simply because you have heard it before.

Compare this with our concern for originality in Europe. We even preface our jokes by asking 'have you heard the one about . . .?' And the quickest way to cut someone dead is to respond to the intro with – 'heard it!' Such a remark would be unthinkable to Africans. Why would they, in any case, want to stop somebody from trying to make them feel happy? The nearest that we in Europe get to this is when we are listening as a family or a group of friends to a well-loved humorous classic, and we wait for and laugh together at what we know is going to come. But perhaps the key word here is 'loved', for I suspect that what we have lost relates somehow to our capacity for sharing.

The dance that evening was really a continuation of what had begun at Nelson's house, so I cannot actually recall 'going to a dance' as such. Music seemed to be emanating from just about everywhere and people of all ages were responding to it wherever they happened to be – on the streets and in the houses as well as in the school, together or alone. It didn't seem to make a great deal of difference where anyone was or who they were with.

About half-way through the proceedings we were treated to a couple of local dances with *bomba* accompaniment that totally captivated me, and the like of which I was not to see again until many years later in East Africa. The first was the 'bottle dance' in which a team of dazzling young girls with head-scarves, white blouses and long swirling skirts danced in front of their male partners with a full bottle of trago balanced on their heads. Needless to say, despite all the rapid movement, the intricate footwork and the repartee, not a single drop was spilt. The second was a 'fire dance' in which young kids, boys and girls no more than twelve years old at most, energetically went through their paces wielding flaming torches spectacularly against the night, and without the slightest suspicion of a false step or a singed eyebrow.

I saw that – some minor innovation apart – I was watching a performance that had its roots deep in history, and I could readily appreciate its power to weld those present into a single euphoric family. The whole community was at one; it was a perfect circle that left no one unembraced. I felt the miracle of it all, and at the same time I was weighed down with considerable sorrow.

I felt I had to leave the school for a while and walk alone down by the river. As I stood there beneath a sky heavy with stars, and listened to the sugar-cane creaking in the wind, I began to wonder what I had done with my time and how I could have lived a third of my life without knowing that such feelings were possible. I felt sad for my fellow countrymen and women, that they should have been deprived of such an experience, for it was a wealth that we in England could not imagine. I wished that all the people I knew and loved could have been there at that moment to see and feel for themselves. It was we who lived in poverty, did we but know it, for in our obsessive concern with the material we had lost contact with each other and become content to do no more than go through the motions of living – walking and talking, laughing and joking mechanically, without purpose.

The music, the stars, the sugar-cane, and the overwhelming power of human fellowship all conspired in that moment to inspire in me a love for Africa, born that evening in Ecuador, that was to stay with me for a long time.

It was only in the Caribbean many years later, after some half a dozen years in Africa, that I finally came to understand the barrage of emotion that had assailed me that evening in Chota. In the Caribbean, having come full circle from Chota and Africa, the pieces finally began to fit together and I was able to gain some sort of hold on what it meant. One evening in Barbados during that sacred hour between day and night, I had parked my car next to a cane-field with the ocean in view, just to be alone and to listen to the creaking of the cane in the wind. I saw an old couple sitting silently in wooden chairs on the veranda of their chattel house, gazing steadfastly out to sea in a posture I knew had been handed down from father to son, from mother to daughter, over the long years of exile. It was an act of faith in the purpose of being, in the reason that must one day make sense of all things. I saw in that moment what it is that characterizes these old folks of the Caribbean and elsewhere in the Americas.

Despite all the justification in the world, there was no anger in their eyes, no bitterness or hatred, no mission to right a wrong that even the Abolition and Civil Rights movements could never hope to erase. The old folk simply bore their cross with patience and forbearance. What unites them now is a sense of loss, of something so long forgotten that it is perhaps no more than an extra furrow on the brow and a gaze out over the ocean in the direction of a land where the sun now only ever rises.

In the newly independent Caribbean states of today, barely a word of their African languages survives, from times that date back little more than a hundred years. Every trace died on contact as if the air was poisonous to the tongue. What was it that drove the plantation owners to seek to crush their culture out of existence, to give them European names, European beliefs and European ideas? Was it fear that one day they might remember? Was it guilt and the need to destroy the evidence? Could they possibly have believed what the Spaniards had believed a century and a half before, as they baptized and butchered countless thousands of Indians, that God was on their side?

All that could be hoped for with the passing of time was the repentance of the one and the forgiveness of the other. The long years of slavery are the story of a people singled out to exemplify all the courage and forgiveness of which the human race was capable. It is a history too recent, too great and too central to our future for any response to be appropriate, other than veneration of its survivors.

As previously arranged, Nelson's brothers gave up their bed to me and I gratefully accepted it around four o'clock in the morning. I slumped down and slept soundly with dreams too deep to recall until about ten o'clock when some demented cockerel broke through with news of the new day. In the other room people were already moving about and there were hushed voices, clinking cups and brewing coffee.

Breakfast was an enamel mug in one hand and a piece of bread in the other in the company of those of the family whose heads allowed them to be mobile, and others who had spent the night on the floor and were shamed into rising. Nelson was doing fine. He was plucking away on somebody's guitar, earnestly trying to work out the chords to one of the *bombas* we had been dancing to a few hours before.

We sat talking for a while and then went for a walk down by the river; all the while I was hoping to catch sight of the girl I had been dancing with for most of the evening, but without any luck. I was too shy to mention it to Nelson. But it was he who had suggested I dance with her in the first place, without mentioning, of course, that the pretty young lady happened to be his cousin.

We got back to the house a little after midday, just in time for lunch – a liberal serving of the rice and chicken the womenfolk had been preparing since early morning for the many family and friends. Mindful of our long journey back to Quito, we took our leave fairly soon afterwards and headed for the Panamericana, accompanied by a dozen well-wishers who wanted to see us off.

When we reached Quito eight hours later it was pitch black and cold; it felt like another world. We lived at opposite ends of the town and so the bus station was the obvious place for us to part company. I offered to hire a taxi and make a round-trip of it but Nelson declined, affirming, unconvincingly, that his normal bus would have him home in no time.

'Nelson,' I said, knowing full well that my words would sound empty almost to the point of futility, 'it's been a fantastic trip. I feel privileged to have had the chance to know your family and your people. It was something I'll never forget. I really don't know how to thank you.'

'Glad you enjoyed it,' he said simply. And we shook hands and went our separate ways.

Today Chota is dying. The Panamericana, now a fast tarmac road, runs through the middle of the village and a few years ago a flood took away thirty-seven of its houses, Nelson's included. None of the old-style houses remain. Concrete blocks and tiles, and more recently zinc sheeting, have become the norm in construction.

But town-planners and acts of God are only some of Chota's problems. With the coming of electricity has come television and the cassette-player, and now even its music is under sentence of death. A couple of groups from the valley have successfully brought the music of the *bomba* to the attention of the nation and the neighbouring countries, but in the villages it is more often the music of The Jackson Five that is heard, and the traditional instruments and the skills that kept them alive have for the most part been discarded.

With population ever on the increase and no prospect of work locally, many of Chota's youth have taken to trafficking contraband across the Colombian border. Others have drifted to the town in search of better things. Some of them join the army and the police, but with reluctance, and knowing that their colour will bar them from any rank above sergeant. Others find jobs as caretakers or messengers, but on salaries well below the legal minimum of $40 a month, and without the social security payments that the law prescribes. They also know full well that dismissal will come the second the boss feels inclined to employ a relative or a friend in their stead.

Many of the women take up employment as domestic servants in the homes of the wealthy, only to find themselves with alarming regularity the victims of sexual abuse, both verbal and physical – a fate that seems to follow black women around. And the few who dare to speak out against their harassment usually find themselves quickly accused of theft and back out on the street.

A few will enter the Central University, where there are no entrance exams and no education fees, but most will drop out along the way for want of the money to support themselves, their prospective careers left dangling with the vague hope that one day, if things get better, they will be able to pick up again where they left off.

Others, weary of the endless round of job-application and rejection in a society that operates exclusively on nepotism and bribery, avail themselves of the extended family and move in with relatives. Some end up hanging around the markets in the hope of casual employment as labourers, an easy target for prejudice and for the temptation to antisocial behaviour.

The old folk are concerned about the abandonment of positive values and the passing of an age. Their oral traditions and their handicrafts, many of which travelled with them from Africa, are fast disappearing; knowledge of local plants and their medicinal properties is becoming a thing of the past; and the customs – the festivals and the celebrations, the everyday courtesies and greetings – are all on the wane. It is the concern of old folks the world over, but more so. To have kept it alive for so many years, in the face of so much hostility, and then to lose it just when things are beginning to look as if they might get better would be an irony too sad to contemplate.

But if life in the villages appears to be in decline, the impact of the valley people on the nation as a whole is growing out of all proportion to their numbers. I subsequently discovered that it was not just Nelson's family who had a cabinet full of trophies – half the valley, it seemed, had awards of one sort or another stashed away. Almost every family seemed to have its star – an athlete, a footballer, a basketball player, a boxer, a volleyball player, a musician, a singer, a dancer – the winners of countless awards.

As time goes by and prejudice starts to subside, we should expect to see many more equally gifted people emerging from this extraordinary place and making their mark in a number of other fields – science and medicine no doubt, and business; and who knows, perhaps even one day in politics. It is truly remarkable that so much talent has been concentrated in a few dozen impoverished and neglected communities scattered through two river valleys which, from time immemorial, have only ever been known for massacres, exploitation and disease.

One can but hope that one day the sons and daughters of Chota will be allowed the opportunity they deserve, not just for the sake of the individuals themselves who, in spite of everything, are surprisingly patriotic, but also for the country as a whole, because heaven knows Ecuador needs all the help it can get.

CHAPTER SEVENTEEN

SIMÓN BOLÍVAR & THE
TAXI DRIVER

'**W**HAT DO YOU THINK of our country?' a taxi driver had asked me one day early on when I was visiting the capital. It was a common enough question and I had the answer off pat.

'Great!' I replied. 'Terrific! Spectacular scenery, decent people, safe to walk around anywhere, any time. In fact, I don't know how you manage it, sandwiched as you are between Peruvian politics and crazy Colombians.' The response had become automatic over the months, and I churned it out without thinking.

'It stinks!' he replied abruptly, cutting through my patronizing waffle like a knife. 'It's a mess!' He used the word 'porquería' – 'a pig's mess'.

I was taken aback by the brutal frankness of his reply and did not know how to tune back into the conversation, being unaccustomed to speaking plainly in such situations; so I remained silent, waiting to hear what might come next.

'The whole continent is rotten, from Mexico to Argentina. Rotten. Just one *porquería* of lies and corruption from one end to the other. I lived in Newark for ten years – drove a taxi there too. I got to see a lot of things, so I know what I'm talking about. There they leave you alone; they give you a chance. They don't step on you just because you're poor; the police don't squeeze you for every cent you've got to fill their pockets. No, they leave you alone and give you a chance to make an honest buck. If you're prepared to work, you can make it.'

'Why did you come back?' I asked with growing curiosity.

'Family reasons, mainly. You know, parents getting old, the wife getting homesick. It is home after all, I suppose – you can't deny that, in spite of it all.'

'What do you think is the cause of Latin America's problems?' I ventured after a moment, feeling a little more confident about the way the conversation was likely to go.

'It's all in the minds of the people. You shouldn't take any notice of what the students and the like say – they know nothing. All this stuff about "yankee imperialism", that's just politicians looking for scapegoats to disguise their own incompetence and their graft – and they've brainwashed half the population into believing it. No, it's all in the minds of the people. I tell you this, if you moved all the people from South America up north to the United States tomorrow, and let them take over all the wealth and all the resources that the gringos have got right now, and then you brought all the gringos down here and let them take over Latin America, exactly as it stands at present – I tell you, within thirty years, less even, the United States would be in the same poverty-stricken mess that we are in today, in fact it would no longer be a 'united' anything, and Latin America would be sending rockets to the moon. It's all in the minds of the people, I tell you. We are the ones to blame and no one else, and we haven't got the courage to admit it. We blame everyone on earth except ourselves – everyone – the CIA, the multinationals, the World Bank, the Mafia, you name it! Anyone and everyone except ourselves.'

I was more than a little surprised by his belligerent tone, coming as it did the moment I got into the taxi. He seemed to be in a state of anguish and in need of someone to talk to, but what he had to say was interesting because I had never heard a Latin American talk like that before.

For several years I had been wrestling with a sense of guilt over the way that Europe and the United States were manipulating the world between them, and particularly our negative role in the field of development. Before my arrival in Ecuador, I had more or less

accepted the standard explanations for Third World poverty –
political conspiracy, cultural imperialism, multinational exploitation,
and economic and technological dependency – but now, faced with
the reality of the Third World for the first time, I was no longer sure.
The whole thing seemed so much more complex, and I suspected
that the 'victims' were also somehow involved in shaping their own
destiny. I knew I would have to draw my conclusions on the basis of
my own experience and no one else's, and that the opinions of
neither Latin American nor European intellectuals, who between
them had assumed a monopoly of development theory, could be
trusted – they both had a vested interest, the former in saving face,
and the latter in making the evidence fit the capitalist crime.

As the weeks and months went by and I became more involved
with the problems of the *campesinos* and the urban poor, I began to
see what the world looked like from their perspective, and it was
not a pretty sight. The country was – and still is, in fact, for little
has changed – divided into two clearly defined groups, those with
authority and those without, and the former instinctively abuse the
latter. To deal with bureaucracy in any form, anywhere in Latin
America, is to undergo an object lesson in humiliation.

Everyone in authority, from the president down to the man who
sells stamps in the Post Office, carries himself with a haughty
disdain and squeezes the last drop of advantage from his position,
using rules and regulations to vaunt his power at every turn. And
when this isn't enough or he is feeling particularly despotic, he will
invent rules as he goes along. Legitimate queries and claims are
dismissed with callous disregard; in government offices they feed
you the wrong information deliberately, and then insult you for
bringing the wrong papers and wasting their precious time. Then
they instruct you to come back the next day knowing full well that
the office will be closed. I have personally seen peasants who have
travelled for twelve hours to get to Quito being sent away in
seconds by some clerk who couldn't be bothered to deal with them.

It is ego gone mad, and for the first time in my life I had some
inkling of what it must be like to be a minority in a racist society.

Here the phenomenon isn't localized – it can strike anybody, anywhere, any time, depending on where you happen to stand in the hierarchy. It is capricious, mean and unnerving, and all of it has to be borne with a smile because to raise your voice is to lose all hope of attaining your goal. The tyrant behind the counter can only be appeased, he cannot be reasoned with, much less challenged.

In daily life, lies circulate endlessly like flies – big, fat, ugly and droning. As with greetings cards, there are lies for every occasion – why I was late; why I left my job; why it couldn't have been me who got your daughter pregnant and why my sudden departure to the United States had nothing to do with it; why I didn't hand over the gifts that your son gave me to bring back from New York; why the peasant leader was never seen again after he was held in police custody; why $3 million is missing from the Treasury, and so on.

The instinct is always to invent, even when the truth is simpler and more palatable. It is even reflected in the language, from the servant's 'el plato se me cayó' – 'the plate dropped itself from me', or 'el cambio se me perdió' – 'the change lost itself from me', to the pompous circumlocutions that disguise simple facts, like the former vice-president who wrote a book condemning the criminal conduct of his former president, but rejects the suggestion that he be put on trial despite the alleged existence of irrefutable evidence: 'Well, we have to take fully into consideration the fact that human nature is very complex, and that a human being, at any given time, is subject to a whole series of pressures of varying descriptions, and that sometimes what might appear on the surface to imply a degree of culpability could, seen from another perspective, be interpreted as the product of a different motivation entirely' – and so it goes, on and on.

Bombast abounds; hyperbole too. The word replaces the fact and the act. Shelves sag under the weight of tomes of legislation, elegantly written, beautifully bound, and signed and sealed by all and sundry, but the spirit is dead and nothing changes. The precious few who are insane enough to dream out loud silently disappear from circulation like old banknotes – university lecturers, peasant leaders,

trade-union officials, students, humble clergymen – and life goes on.
No one objects, and no one speaks out, for to speak out is to become
one of them – another unrecorded statistic – and mention is seldom
made of 'the one who had the courage to . . .'. The memory soon
dies and lies buried beneath a conspiracy of silence.

The currency of cash, like the currency of words, has no basis in
solid value. The same conspiracy of silence that allows words their
face value gives the useless currency its apparent worth, but no one
outside the country's borders buys in to the myth – the foreigner
recognizes it as merely paper. The relationship between integrity
and strength is not fortuitous, and the value of sterling, the
almighty dollar or the rising yen is a reflection of the worth of the
people – their energy, their organization, their technology, and
their sense of purpose. As the heart and soul of a nation start to
decline, so the currency declines along with it – as the people of
Britain are only too aware.

The only escape for those who seek salvation is to leave –
knowing that every effort is pointless and that more words will only
add to the inflationary mess. So they go in their millions, all
heading north to the United States, with a handful making it to
Western Europe and Australia as second best. No one goes to Cuba,
or Russia, or China, or Albania, or the Arab world, except perhaps a
desperate student who can't make it anywhere else, or a fanatic who
prefers hijacking a plane in a blaze of publicity to working his
passage. No, it is to the United States that they go, many fording
rivers and riding cattle-cars at the risk of life and limb in their desperation to get there, the calumnies on their big, bad neighbour to
the north long forgotten in the headlong rush. Forever in the
vanguard of the movement are the greatest gringo-haters of them
all, the Mexicans.

How does this pattern of falsehood become established in the
first place and how does it retain its hold thereafter? To answer such
questions one has to go back to the early days of the Conquest.

The Conquistadors and those who were to follow in their
footsteps were by general consent the dregs of sixteenth-century

Spain. They were powered by a single motive – ambition, whether material or ecclesiastical – and they had the military expertise, the technology and the confidence commensurate with the most powerful nation of the day to back it up. It was a lethal combination. Imagine a land colonized by Chicago gangsters and Iranian mullahs, with a handful of English football hooligans thrown in for good measure, and then ask yourself what odds you would give for the survival of the previous inhabitants and for the emergence of a harmonious, peaceful, compassionate and just society.

Spain passed laws for the protection of the Indians, and later of the slaves who were brought from the Caribbean, but such legislation was invariably disregarded by the colonists and precious few were ever held to account. Running through this chaotic assault on an ancient and civilized way of life was the famous Spanish 'pundonor' – the Code of Honour – a disfigured form of chivalry by which a man's reputation was all-important, regardless of his moral conduct. The barbaric behaviour of the Conquistadors and the early settlers had somehow to be reconciled with a Christian image, and this accounts for both the wretched moral standards and the wholesale hypocrisy prevalent in Latin America today.

Such norms were established soon after the Spaniards and Portuguese arrived, and there followed a crystallization of prevailing values in the formative years of the hybrid culture when not only the social structure, the customs and the language took shape, but also standards of integrity and sincerity. Once all this has been formulated it takes all the powers of heaven and earth to change it. The disparate elements of the new society soon assumed an equilibrium, with the hand of injustice holding the balance.

The decades immediately following the Conquest set the pattern for the values of today and nothing has happened in the five intervening centuries to threaten it. The accumulation of years has added to the sense of hopelessness – 'this is the way it always was; this is the way it always will be'. To remain aloof from such conditions becomes the prerogative of the handful of saints, both religious and secular, who miraculously appear from time to time.

Still today no one of any standing is ever held to account for his actions – politicians plunder, police brutalize, employers abuse their employees, especially the women; and anyone with any influence to hawk is routinely bribed. Property, health, education and justice all go to the highest bidder, while government contracts go, not to the lowest bidder, but to the minister's nephew. The sense of hopelessness that results from living in a society where there is no semblance of justice is hard to describe to anyone who has not experienced it.

One of the first things that President Carlos Menem of Argentina did on assuming power was to grant an amnesty to all those members of the police and military who had committed atrocities during the so-called 'Dirty War' against terrorism. All those who had tortured and murdered tens of thousands of their fellow citizens, including, presumably, those who pierced a small boy's eyes with steel needles to make his father 'talk', and the officers of the Argentine Air Force who pushed people out of helicopters into the River Plate – all such model citizens are now free to go about their normal lives.

The same President Menem, who himself had been imprisoned for five years and tortured, later declared that 'the whole question of development is a complete and utter mystery'. It might be so for someone who is accustomed to blaming everyone on earth for his problems except himself – even to the point of explaining away the disappearance of 16,000 Argentines. But how can any society progress when there is hardly a public, police or trade-union official who does not abuse his authority from day one and who cannot be bought off at a moment's notice? When every legitimate expression of protest leads to imprisonment, torture or death? When the rich plunder at will, the politicians lie with impunity, and the owners of the means of production only produce enough to satisfy their own immediate needs?

At present, the world is in danger of being held hostage by the Brazilian government over the question of exploitation of the Amazonian rain forest. The politicians defend their inertia and their myopia by retorting to the United States and Europe, 'you destroyed your own forests and now you try to tell us what to do with ours!' — as if the fact that the Amazon is still largely intact were due to some moral superiority on their part, when everyone knows the only reason it wasn't cut down long ago, along with the Indians and everything else that got in their way, was that the Portuguese, like the Spaniards, would not contemplate the honest labour that such exploitation would have demanded. It was always far easier to force Indians down mines or keep them as serfs, and to bring in Blacks to replace them when they died off, than to go trekking into some steamy, disease-ridden jungle. There was easier money to be made.

But no one is allowed to say such things, for such accusations are taboo. The only crime that never goes unpunished in Latin America is that of speaking the truth — this demands and gets the maximum penalty every time. Everything else, murder, rape, torture, fraud, or larceny, can be accommodated within the status quo. 'Justice' is whatever keeps the rich and powerful happy, and 'injustice' is whatever makes them unhappy. The tyranny of self-interest, fear and nepotism instituted five centuries ago is so deeply rooted in the continental psyche today that few people can imagine things otherwise.

Culture shock is insidious. At first you don't realize it is taking hold. There is the common, everyday stuff, like people refusing to queue, and forging on buses before the departing passengers can get off; men urinating in public; soiled toilet papers released from refuse bags by scavenging dogs, wafting around the streets; and being called 'gringo' fifty times a day. Such things, irritating though they are, can normally be assimilated into the pattern of your expanding awareness. But there is another type of culture shock that hits you on a different level, and changes you forever. You might get used to it on a conscious level, but underneath something remains and continues eating away at you. I will give a few examples of what I mean.

Swimming in the sea at the coastal resort of Atacames, the guidebook tells you, is dangerous. I only spent three days in Atacames, and two people, a married couple from Colombia, drowned while I was there. If I hadn't read the guidebook I would never have known that the sea is dangerous. No one tells you, and there are no signs to warn you. When yet another corpse is dragged up onto the beach, the locals say, 'Qué pena!' – 'How sad! It happens all the time.' But no one thinks to put up a sign. How does one arrive at an understanding of such inconsequential behaviour? And from people whose livelihood depends on tourism? Here, I believe, we are coming close to the real explanation for the mess in which Ecuador and the rest of Latin America finds itself. There is no compassion, at least of the sort that moves mountains to help and to heal, just a dewy-eyed sentimentality of the sort that the Church calls 'loving your neighbour' and which involves occasionally holding out pennies to the lame and the destitute.

In the early evening a man is riding without lights through the outskirts of town on an ancient, extremely noisy two-stroke motorcycle that is hopelessly underpowered and belching out clouds of blue smoke everywhere. He has an infant perched on the tank in front of him and two other children sitting behind him. The one at the rear – a boy of seven or eight years old – has his satchel sandwiched between himself and his younger sister, so that he is sitting half on the seat and half over the back wheel, and holding onto nothing. Meanwhile the father endeavours to negotiate the inevitable pot-holes and stones as best he can.

Behind him, at the wheel of a big new Toyota, is a solid member of the establishment, his face contorted in anger and frustration at his inability to overtake, repeatedly blasting his horn as he tries to get the man and his family to pull over. All the while the motorcyclist's face is fixed in an embarrassed, humiliated grin as he wrestles to control the jolting vehicle.

In the old part of Quito in mid-afternoon I pull up at the traffic lights, I am the first in the queue. I notice an old woman standing by the roadside. She is grey and wizened and bent, not just with age but with the weight of a heavy gas cylinder that she carries on her shoulders. I judge from her resigned stance that she has been there for some time so I get down from the car and go across to help her. At this precise moment the lights change. I can still see the face of the woman driver of the car behind, full of fury and hatred, mouthing obscenities at me for making her wait – for a peasant.

Such incidents provoke culture shock of the kind that leaves scars. In twenty years I have not got used to it – neither do I want to.

Looking at the behaviour of traffic gives a good indication of a nation's capacity to organize and of the importance it attaches to human life. The chaos and the slaughter are one thing, but there is also the mentality of the car owner, for in his own mind he is worth more than anyone without a car. The pedestrian has no rights whatsoever, and he takes his life in his hands every time he ventures out onto the road. Pedestrian crossings exist but they mean nothing, except that if you put your faith in one you are more likely to die there than anywhere else. Most drivers have no insurance. There is a hierarchy dictating that the bigger and more expensive a car is, the greater is the personal worth of its owner, and everyone must acknowledge this – police included – and toe the line.

And the traffic police? They are at their most spectacular in Lima and Mexico City, where they perch like vultures on stationary motorcycles at road junctions, waiting for some hapless creature to commit the merest infraction so they can pounce. Their concern is not so much safeguarding human life as lining their own pockets, which they do with dazzling efficiency, their polished leather boots and their impenetrable sunglasses gleaming like Aztec obsidian. At the first hint of an infringement, perhaps a front wheel that has crossed the yellow line by a foot, they will blow their whistles and move in on their prey, strutting about in a preposterous display of self-importance, their faces contorted with anger and indignation. They then demand to see the all-important 'papers'.

Seeing these police swoops always reminded me of the way I obtained my first driving licence. I had gone to the traffic police to enquire about the necessary documentation and was told that I should bring my current British licence; a certificate from a doctor to say that I was fit to drive; a statement from Scotland Yard confirming that I did not have a criminal record; four photographs full-face; four photographs from the side; US$50; and an application form properly filled out.

I eventually got all they asked for, except the police report which, for reasons obvious to me, I was unable to obtain ('just tell them we don't do such things in Britain,' the Embassy told me). But when I got back to the Traffic Department I found that they had run out of application forms and would not be getting any for at least a month.

'Can I drive the car in the meantime?' I asked innocently.

'Could you drive a car in your own country without a licence?' barked the official, and without waiting for my reply, added, 'Well, you don't do it here either!'

'What's the answer then?' I ventured, realizing that I was probably taking my life in my hands.

'Not my problem,' he said barely audibly, and stared vacantly into space.

'There must be *something* I can do, for heaven's sake?' I protested.

'Could get a temporary licence,' he offered after a moment, with an undisguised yawn.

'OK,' I said, 'what documents do I need? How much is it? How long does it last?'

'You need all the papers you've brought, the photographs, and fifty dollars, and it lasts a month.'

'What!' I exclaimed. 'The same price as a full five-year licence?' But then, seeing the hopelessness of my situation, I immediately added, 'OK. Give me a temporary licence – *please.*'

I must have ruined his day; it was as much as he could do to get up from his seat, move across to the typewriter and put the blue piece of card into the carriage.

'Passport!' he snapped.

'Passport? You didn't say anything about a passport when I came in the first time and asked what papers I needed.'

'No passport, no licence,' he said matter of factly, and turned away.

So, off I went, and returned an hour later with the passport. He was still sitting at the counter in the same position, slumped over the typewriter, with no one else in sight. He took the passport without comment, and started typing. He clacked away for a couple of minutes and then handed me the blue card. It was in the name, I noticed, of 'Richard Great Britain'. I thanked him for his kind assistance and got out as fast as I could.

As the month-end deadline approached, I mentioned to a friend the problem I was having with the licence, and he offered to take charge of it for me.

'Just give me fifty dollars for the licence, and a couple more for the official, and I'll have it for you in no time,' he predicted confidently.

'What about the police statement and all the rest of the stuff they told me I needed?' I asked.

'You don't need all that!' he replied derisively, and off he went. A couple of hours later he was back with a full five-year licence made out in my correct name, having presented no documentation of any kind.

Such occurrences are common in Latin America, everybody knows it and everybody does it, and given that most people don't have the time to spend whole days running around on a paper chase, they have very little choice. The system is especially designed this way, of course, to frustrate your good intentions and get you to play into the hands of the officials. And if you were rash enough to point out to the man behind the counter that in selling licences in this fashion he was directly contributing to the wholesale slaughter that takes place daily on the roads, he would think you were crazy.

So what does all the huffing and puffing on the part of the traffic police add up to? They are simply finding out whether or not you have paid the bribe for obtaining a licence – nothing more nor less. The whole ridiculous performance has no more substance to it than this, and the chance to bully some pathetic non-Mercedes driver into handing over a few more of his hard-earned sucres.

Confronted with this depressing reality day after day, I eventually came to the conclusion that a whole generation of development activity has been wasted because we have been dealing with issues that are not central to the problem. We have been concerning ourselves with politics instead of ethics, and if ethics has figured in our deliberations at all it has only been in relation to the countries of the North. It has never been a consideration with those of the South.

The blame for this, I feel sure, has to lie squarely with those political and social scientists of Western Europe who have been far more interested in promoting their own personal ideologies than in examining reality. Consciously and systematically they have diverted attention away from what is happening inside Third World countries to politics on an international level, and thereby circumvented the primary issues that must be resolved before we can bring about sustained social and economic development.

When I look back, in all the countless articles and papers I must have read on the subject of Third World development over the years, I can hardly recall a single reference to the importance of morality. My own experience has led me to conclude that the arguments most commonly put forward to explain underdevelopment are not actually central to the debate – such matters as unfair trading relationships between North and South, the conditions laid down by the International Monetary Fund, the iniquitous practices of certain multinational corporations, the machinations of the CIA, and the dumping of both second-rate machinery and outdated and harmful drugs and chemicals. Important though such things may well have been in the past, and unquestionably still are in some instances, the notion that any or all of these could possibly be more prejudicial to a country's development than the exploitation, deception, plunder, and systematic abuse of its own people by those in a position of power, I now find perfectly ridiculous. The arguments of those who would have us believe that this is the case, however, have held sway in the development forum for thirty years.

There are several reasons why this question of Third World morality has been ignored: first, any criticism along such lines is liable to smack of racism, and racism, quite rightly, is taboo in the modern world; secondly, corruption, almost by its nature, defies documentation, and this inhibits empirical analysis; and thirdly, most importantly, it has never been in anybody's interest to address it. Foreign governments are not going to touch it because it is far too sensitive; the majority of European non-government agencies are not interested in it either because it jars with their theories of class domination and multinational or capitalist exploitation; the lecturers in our university departments of political and social science are not interested for the same reason; and Latin Americans themselves, apart from the astonishing handful of dedicated religious and human rights activists who have had the courage to speak out against injustice, are not interested because candid self-analysis has never been part of their repertoire.

There has certainly been a conspiracy going on, but it has not been the conspiracy of the advanced capitalist nations to keep underdeveloped nations in a state of impoverished dependency, it has been the conspiracy of silence between duplicitous Latin American politicians and gullible European intellectuals. The end result of this has been that we have had the same tired old clichés being churned out year after year, and the same tired old prescriptions being tried time after time − albeit under different names − with miserably unimpressive results. We have done no more than tinker with the problems of underdevelopment, and as a consequence three decades of development opportunity have been practically wasted.

A primary impediment to social and economic change, as I have remarked above, lies in the cultural priorities of the people, and this whole area has been generally overlooked by those who are working in the field. Matters essentially ethical in character can be equally obstructive. These two issues − culture and ethics − are key pieces in the development puzzle and they have to be addressed from the very outset, for otherwise we merely squander precious time and resources.

We can look at the examples of Japan and Germany and consider their progress since the end of World War II. By 1945 both countries were in a state of economic ruin – in fact they were in far worse shape than any country in Latin America at that time. But the cultural priorities of the people were not significantly affected by the devastation of war, and when conditions became favourable and creative impulses were again allowed to flow, a new society began to stir among the ashes, and eventually rise up and flourish.

What did these cultural priorities consist of? A wholehearted commitment to science and technology; a fiercely entrenched work ethic; a preparedness to recognize a general purpose higher than the individual self; and an appreciation of the need to mobilize energies on a national scale. What had derailed these two countries in the first place was a perverted sense of nationalism, and what kept them on track later was the moral re-orientation they underwent as a result of defeat in World War II.

It is hardly a coincidence that two nations on the losing side are among the foremost economic powers in the world today. The importance of the Marshall Plan, enlightened and humane though it was, was secondary to the cultural and moral component. This view, however, has gained little favour with the nations that have been left behind, Britain in particular, who have steadfastly believed that the reasons for their stagnation are purely economic.

The Japan/Germany example contains the important lesson that when cultural priorities are compatible with development, and when the social and moral climate is favourable, wonders can be achieved in the course of a generation. Latin America, on the other hand, teaches us that when the cultural priorities are *not* developmentally compatible, as in the case of the Indians, and when the social and moral climate is *not* favourable, as in the case of blanco/mestizo society, then you achieve practically nothing in the course of a generation.

For a culture to be developmentally compatible it must believe in its right to impose its will on circumstances through the application of cause-and-effect analysis, science and technology. In the case of Latin American blanco/mestizo society we may assume this to be the case since it is essentially a European culture. There must also be an adequate resource-base and an economy of a viable scale. Given these conditions, the edifice of sustained social and economic development rests upon four pillars, each of which is spiritual in origin: justice, humility, energy and purpose. Without justice there is no opportunity; without humility there is no learning or stability; without energy there is no effort or production; and without a sense of purpose there is no cohesion or direction.

These four pillars, or attributes, do not occur naturally among humankind in the measure required to alter the course of history. They can be generated to a certain extent by political ideology, but their duration in such instances is short-lived. The twentieth century is littered with the debris of political ideologies that at one time swept all before them. It is to that other source of mass inspiration that one must turn, to religion, if one is to get to grips with the inner dynamic of development, for it is in the divinely revealed religions of the world that these attributes have their origin. All these religions are indivisible in essence and form part of the same unfolding process, each one confirming and complementing the message of its predecessor with the aim of advancing civilization.

In each case, the pattern has been the same – a fragmented, antagonistic people are taught, albeit at great sacrifice, how to settle their differences and arrive at a higher state of consciousness; only then can a true society form and flourish. The truly great civilizations invariably rise up on the wings of the spirit, and on each occasion the ripples stretch further afield so as to embrace ever larger social units. Since the very beginning we have been moving imperceptibly towards a world community – the 'one shepherd, one fold' that the founder of Christianity spoke of.

As dogma and doctrine take over and the creative spirit starts to wane, things begin to fall apart until the society finally reverts to something like its former condition. A certain amount of the structure and some of the concepts will remain, albeit more often as ideals than realities. Occurrences such as moves towards regional independence are typical of the pattern of disintegration that necessarily overtakes any society once the divine spirit is gone; and politicians, needless to say, are powerless to stop it, despite all their avowals to the contrary.

Human history only makes sense in terms of this rise and fall of the human spirit, and the impulse that promotes change occurs on two levels – first the Prophet who appears at different points on the horizon every one thousand years or so and infuses new life into the planet; and then his followers, who provide inputs of varying degrees of purity. The Prophet's teachings transform the values and potential of the primary recipients. Perhaps the best example is Islam and the miraculous change that overtook the Arab nation following the appearance of the Prophet Muhammad – a decadent, degenerate and cruel people became world leaders in the sciences, arts and humanities in the space of little more than a hundred years.

Even those who do not come directly into contact with the Prophet and his teachings are influenced by advances in human potential; unknowingly, they become subject to a new set of parameters. For example, the revolutionary appreciation of the worth of the individual, regardless of his social origins, that coincided with the advent of Christ appears to have received fairly general recognition, if not implementation, since that time; and the emergence of nation states went far beyond the homelands of the Prophet Muhammad, 'Builder of Nations'. We may also include here the major technological advances that have appeared independently at more or less the same point in history and transformed our collective existence, and the world vision of Karl Marx, which was undeniably the product of a new global awareness that has since overtaken the whole planet. This burgeoning global consciousness, with its attendant technological innovation and human rights awareness, dates from the first half of the nineteenth century. This is a phenomenon that I never found a satisfactory explanation for until, much later, I encountered the

Bahá'í Faith. The Bahá'ís' Prophet-Founder, Bahá'u'lláh, sees this growing sense of global identity as a central aspect of the evolving spiritual destiny of humankind.

Archaeologists and historians have tended to neglect the spiritual determinants that underpin social evolution. They have concerned themselves with symptoms rather than causes, and prefer to ask, for example, why a certain civilization disappeared rather than questioning why, or how, it arose in the first place; and they settle for explanations such as soil erosion, famine, pestilence and warfare, none of which is necessarily relevant. The key factor, more often than not, is that the society was already in a state of spiritual decline and that practically anything was capable of giving it the *coup de grâce*. It is unlikely that a spiritually healthy society would succumb comprehensively to any such eventuality.

It is possible to assess the performance of any nation in terms of these four primary attributes. Japan and Germany are very strong on energy and purpose, for example, and improving, but still suspect, on justice and humility; the Soviet Union was strong on all four originally but – its impetus being predominantly political and ephemeral – one after the other they began to fail until it finally came to a halt. Britain is still strong on justice but failing badly on humility, energy and purpose; and the United States is still strong on justice, fairly strong on humility – contrary to popular belief, perhaps; very strong on energy; but presently misfiring on purpose.

In Latin America none of these four basic attributes exists to any significant degree and it is within this context that its failure to progress should be examined. Progress is a spiritual phenomenon rather than an intellectual endeavour as we in the West tend to believe – the intellect is in play, of course, but it is not the primary creative force. The major discoveries of recent history have seldom if ever been the conclusion of a reasoning process, but either a moment of illumination that follows exhaustive research, or a matter of pure chance. It is persistence rather than perception that is rewarded.

This being the case, one cannot divorce scientific and technological advancement from the prevailing moral and spiritual climate.

They are not separate issues and never should be regarded as such. Is it any coincidence that the great scientific discoveries of the past 150 years, which have so transformed our world – photography, electricity, radio, television, the internal combustion engine, the jet engine, computers and the many discoveries in medical science – have coincided with the clamour for individual freedoms and human rights? One might legitimately ask how many of these discoveries and movements that are now so central to our well-being originated in Latin America. The answer, of course, is none, and the explanation for this is, quite simply, that a dead tree does not produce fruit.

Arguments of this kind incense a good many people, not least the political and social scientists of Western Europe, most of whom prefer to deal in large impersonal issues such as the North–South dialogue and the external debt – both of which are, after all, extremely important. My answer is that even if North–South trading relationships are rendered more equitable, as they must be, and even if the external debt of each nation is written off, as it well might be, such measures will have minimal effect if the moral and spiritual climate in these countries does not change. In just a few years they would be back in the same hole, asking to be pulled out, and blaming the rest of the world for their predicament.

It is the relationship between morality and solvency that is at issue and has to be taken seriously, and social justice in particular – or rather its absence – which should be seen as a vital missing link in the continent's performance. That it has not been taken seriously until now is curious, particularly when one considers that statistics on human rights abuse and debt default coincide far too frequently for chance. Perhaps Amnesty International and the International Monetary Fund should get together and compare notes – they may find they have more in common than they think.

Wherever the Indian has survived in reasonable numbers, he has tended to have a tempering effect on colonial barbarism. The Andean countries of Ecuador, Peru and Bolivia, inefficient and corrupt as they are, and brutal as they can be, have generally been spared the sinister excesses that have characterized the regimes of Chile, Argentina, Brazil and the rest. But this influence has always cost Indians dearly, and has invariably endangered their way of life, their families, and often their very existence, as we are seeing at present in Guatemala.

The degradation of the Indians is unbearable to see – infant children of three or four years old, out on the freezing streets of La Paz at ten o'clock at night, try desperately to sell a couple of shrivelled mangoes that nobody wants; men sit until the early hours on remote street corners where scarcely anyone passes, wrapped in some thin rag against the biting cold, beside a tray of oddments whose total value can be no more than a couple of dollars, in the hope that some stumbling drunk will want to buy a single cigarette. Tiny children stand alone by the side of the dirt roads of the *altiplano*, hands outstretched for anything – a crust of bread, a biscuit, a piece of fruit. And they say 'thank you' as if you have given them the earth. You ask yourself, 'where do they come from?', for there isn't a village to be seen for miles around. Yet each of these countries possesses vast reserves of wealth, and the few flaunt their disproportionate affluence with shameless ostentation.

A century and a half ago, Simón Bolívar, the great liberator of South America – the man who led the fight for independence from Spain – reflected on his failed dream of a United States of South America, declaring that 'he had ploughed the sea'. I suspect he saw in this moment of illumination that a golden society cannot be built by a people with leaden instincts. Individuals have to change first, and until they do, society never will; this has been the story of Latin America. The revolution has to start within, it has to be self-directed and spiritual, for only this can make the difference – political and economic change will only scratch the surface.

This, I believe, is the essence of Latin America's failure to progress, and I find myself in sympathy with both Simón Bolívar and the taxi driver – it is all in the hearts and minds of the people. With a good hundred years' start over the United States, and with every imaginable resource at their disposal, they are at least a hundred years behind in virtually every way you can think of, and the gap is getting wider all the time. My own personal explanation for this state of affairs, in a single sentence, is that the United States was settled and colonized by men and women with a higher code of ethics. Simplistic? Of course – but nearer the mark than all the theories of capitalist conspiracy, cultural imperialism, multinational exploitation, CIA destabilization, and Peace Corps 'spying' put together.

Somehow individual Latin Americans have to find within them-selves the conscience and the courage to stand up and be counted – to tell the liars and the parasites, the thieves and the brutalizers, that 500 years is enough and that things have got to change; to let them know that their problems are 'made in Latin America', and nowhere else. The world is now in a state of upheaval, and perhaps for the first time in human history there are genuine reasons for believing that things will get better. There are great forces of unity and brotherhood at work everywhere, and a new awareness of our interdependence, both as a species and as a planet. The long-term outlook therefore, whatever our immediate problems, is hopeful.

CHAPTER EIGHTEEN

PARADISE
REGAINED?

WHEN THE TIME CAME for my departure from
Ecuador, I was still unsure about the kind of help the
country needed, either from volunteers like myself or
from the international community in the form of aid, in order to
transform it into a paradise of prosperity and stability. But the basic
issues had taken shape in my mind.

Aid to the Third World can be divided into what is known as
'relief aid', which is essentially the response to a temporary crisis – a
call for food, water and shelter – and is, or should be, only short-
term; and 'development aid', which seeks to improve the social and
economic conditions of a people, a longer and more continuous
process. Development aid is about the creation and control of
resources, helping the poor to help themselves rather than the
giving of hand-outs, and all development strategy should be
designed with this ultimate purpose in mind. In practice, however,
the distinction between the two is not always as clear as one might
wish – especially when politics enters into the equation – and the
questions of where to work, whom to work with and what methods
to apply are not easily resolved. Development aid has somehow to
establish a scale of priorities and decide, in the interests of satisfy-
ing want and within the terms of its overall purpose, how best to
target its scant resources so as to gain maximum effect.

On the surface, the matter would appear to be relatively
straightforward in that the prime candidates for social and

economic development should surely be those in most need – 'the poorest of the poor', as they are generally termed. In reality, however, such people will almost certainly live beyond the reach of any government services, and will lack the basic infrastructure necessary to assimilate the assistance the development agencies have to offer, whether financial or technical. In effect, this means they have yet to form an association that will serve their collective needs. Individual farmers and workers can achieve little by themselves, but by banding together they not only benefit by pooling their meagre resources but render themselves eligible for funding and technical assistance from outside, and at the same time gain the necessary legal authority for the purchase of land or the setting up of community enterprises.

There is, therefore, a strong argument to be made that aid is better directed towards a slightly higher level where a viable organizational structure already exists – and perhaps more importantly, there is evidence of a determination to progress – with which the agencies can work. This is not to imply, of course, that those in most need should be written off as a lost cause, but it is to recognize that most development agencies, especially those in the private or non-government sector, only have limited resources and that these should be targeted so as to maximize their impact. The poorest of the poor need, at the very least, to assume some kind of organizational identity before they can be reached, and this is more a question of a modest amount of awareness and desire than the application of any material or technical resource. In fact, the mere observation of a successful model is usually sufficient to prompt, if not its exact replication, then its sincere imitation.

One has to be careful when considering the targeting of aid not to think of society as composed of separate strata that key into each other at strategic points, much less should these 'strata' be seen in dialectical terms as fundamentally antagonistic, with one living at the expense of another. Any social grouping is a living organism whose component parts depend for their well-being both on each other and on the whole. Just as in the human body we recognize both the individual worth and the mutual dependence of its different parts, so that the head, heart, eyes, hands and feet are not in competition with each other but assume their rightful place in the order of things, so must the social body also recognize the intrinsic value and mutual dependence of its constituent parts. Any notion of conflict must be abolished, and this implies especially that the interdependence of capital and labour has to be fully acknowledged. This being the case it becomes apparent that aid of any kind, in theory at least, has a beneficial effect on society at large – what benefits the individual also benefits the whole, and vice versa. Furthermore, what holds good for society on a national level also holds good for humanity on a global level.

That the world is not currently running along such lines, of course, has nothing to do with any lack of or misapplication of aid – nor is it the result of any perverse political strategy. It is purely a question of human nature and the fact that, as a species, we do not care to operate in such a generous fashion. But sooner or later, I believe, the organic unity of the human race will have to be accepted by the world at large, for it is becoming plainer with each passing day that to function in this way is our ultimate destiny.

Issues such as North–South trading relations and the external debt provoke long and involved arguments, but it is still the financial centres of the North that determine the price of raw materials deriving from the South, and the manufacturers of the North who determine at what price finished products will appear on the world market. Such a state of affairs has to be unjust, and must be corrected urgently. The fate of the many cannot be allowed to depend indefinitely on the caprices of the 'free market', which is a pretty ruthless and cynical system of manipulation, heavily loaded in favour of the rich and the powerful.

The former President of Tanzania, Julius Nyerere, who was never lost for something to say on this subject, was fond of pointing out that at one time his country could purchase a truck with the hard currency equivalent of five tons of sisal, but that some time later this had become twenty tons. 'What', he asked, 'happened to the fifteen tons of sisal, and into whose pocket did the proceeds go?'

Whereas it would be wrong to suggest that commodity prices should or even could remain forever fixed, or that the world should somehow adopt a 'sisal standard' to replace gold or the foreign currency markets, it is difficult not to concede that this is a pointed question. Such arguments, however, despite their frequent reiteration by the countries of the South, have yet to gain the North's attention.

Imbalances produced by current trading practices contribute in no small measure to the continuing poverty of developing nations and often impel them to seek burdensome loans on the international money markets. This is the basis for the argument of a good many developing countries that in reality it is they who are financing the development of the North, and not the other way round. And some go on from there to argue that their foreign debts should therefore be written off. What they are saying in effect is that it is not through any act of nobility that the countries of the North are 'helping' the South, but rather out of sense of moral obligation, or even guilt, since it is the North that is responsible for their continuing underdevelopment in the first place.

This is an argument that has substance to it but fails to acknowledge the two key issues that remain unresolved on the home front – those of culture and ethics, without which the picture is incomplete.

My personal view is that development aid, whether financial or technical, is practically useless if it fails to take into account these two primary issues; and especially so in Latin America where the cultural gap is so wide on the one hand, and the corruption and human rights abuse so rampant on the other. Purely financial aid – and this includes cash grants of any kind, debt write-offs, government subsidies and commodity support, as well as donations of machinery and equipment and the like – is, in the present circumstances, a bottomless pit that will go on absorbing all that is put into it and giving precious little back by way of 'development' in return. It may have its justification in political terms or as relief aid, but as a development strategy its value is practically nil.

Technical aid, which is basically the transfer of skills and information from one person to another, does at least have a chance of being effective by virtue of its training aspect and the human contact involved, but only if it leads to a change in perception; that is to say, a change in cultural perception on the part of the indigenous people, and a change in moral perception on the part of the rest of society. Without such changes, technical aid too will disappear into the same bottomless pit.

The ultimate prescription for the problems of underdevelopment must surely include all the above-mentioned issues, some that affect the South and others that affect the North, leaving none of them to one side. And the practical context in which their immediate application is worked out demands the sharing of experience at first hand by those concerned, that is to say, by those with the know-how on the one hand, and those wishing to acquire it on the other. A human bridge must be built painstakingly of friendship and trust, over which skills and knowledge can pass. It involves long hours of sacrifice working shoulder to shoulder, and the solutions that count in the end will be those that are arrived at with the poor themselves taking part every step of the way.

Neither must one forget that development can never be reduced to a table of statistics on a sheet of paper, nor is it to be contained within the pages of some learned treatise from a university of the North. Rather, it is a question of what is actually going on in the hearts and minds of the people – all people, rich and poor, North and South alike, for each and every one of us has his or her particular part to play in the great organic scheme of things. This is where the real development takes place; all else, in the final analysis, is of little consequence.

My own departure from Ecuador one Thursday afternoon in August 1970 was every bit as depressing as all my other visits to the airport to see off friends. For two years I had wondered how it would feel finally to take my leave – whether it would be a tear-jerker or a wave of euphoria that I would have to conceal – but in the event it was neither. It was more a feeling of anticlimax and emptiness, of exhaustion even; and at the same time I felt strangely conspicuous, as if I had dropped out of a marathon half-way through and was now sneaking home on the bus, still dressed in my running gear.

It all felt so horribly unfinished. So many people I had got to know and was now leaving behind, and so many causes had been espoused and left in mid-air. What had it all meant, and how could so much goodwill and commitment have led to such feelings of failure? It seemed to violate some fundamental law somehow. There was more than a note of apprehension attached too, for I had poured so much of myself into everyday living that I had scarcely spared a thought for what was to come next and now, with decisions looming, I was belatedly having doubts about the wisdom of the whole enterprise.

The send-off party comprised an Ecuadorean doctor housemate, my one Peace Corps friend still in the country and a handful of colleagues and students from the University. They had decided to play a trick on me. The doctor was friendly with one of the immigration officials and had whispered something in his ear. You could do such things in those 'pre-oil' days, when the police and the military still had a sense of humour and their salaries and their egos had yet to inflate ten-fold.

'Where is your Paternity Clearance?' the official asked sternly.

'My what?' I exclaimed incredulously, yet knowing full well that anything was possible in Ecuador.

'According to Clause Four, Sub-section 2A of the Law of Settlement,' he continued officiously, 'anyone residing for more than nine months in the country has to present evidence of the fact that he is not leaving behind any unsupported children for whom he is legally responsible.'

The ruse continued for a minute or two until my entourage gave the game away, but it almost backfired because I was on the point of saying, 'OK, I'll stay then,' which I would have done.

The ritual goodbyes were gone through, along with the usual promises to keep in touch and check out the prospects of work and scholarships in England, and I found myself climbing the steps of a Colombian Avianca jet, with a curious sense of observing myself. I felt myself wave to the group with exaggerated enthusiasm in an attempt to compensate for my lack of feeling, and then stepped inside a plane that seemed fittingly foreign and empty. I took a seat near the window, from where I could see the group and give a final wave, but they could not see me and had already turned towards the exit. I sank back down into the seat and let my thoughts turn to Lima where I was to pick up the BOAC flight for home.

Two hours later I found myself in Lima on a quiet day. I slipped through Immigration and Customs, exchanging pleasantries with the officials, then took a taxi into town and checked into a two-star hotel.

The receptionist was a British Peruvian, a stocky, handsome man in his fifties with a full head of steel-grey hair brushed straight back and steel-rimmed spectacles to match. On learning of my nationality he lit up. He had served as a pilot in World War II and was anxious to tell me about it.

'They used to call me Peruvian Charlie,' he said in a fine Scots accent. 'Always flew by the seat of my pants. Landed six times without the undercarriage.'

It was a pleasant encounter and one that lifted my spirits a little. I was touched by the man's intense longing for Britain and by his need to share his precious memories with me. And I saw how hard it must have been for him and millions like him to return to everyday living after the excitement and camaraderie of war; I also realized that he had not quite made it, and it disturbed me.

I was impressed too, by his deep religious conviction that he told me had grown stronger during the blitz, and by the fact that this same and obviously genuine faith did not inhibit the frank and unprompted disclosure that his son used to drop him off at the local brothel every Saturday night, 'regular as clockwork', then pick him up again in the early hours of Sunday morning. It was a level of openness that was unknown to me at the time, and as refreshing as it was unexpected.

Three years later I called back to the hotel to look him up, but he was no longer there and no one could tell me of his whereabouts.

The Friday I spent visiting Lima's port of Callao in the company of an American tourist, a cheerful, lanky professional golfer, who was 'at a loose end'. We got on well together and strolled around the grey harbour watching the pelicans plummet headlong into the ocean and speculating at length about the strangeness of Lima's climate, that it should be perpetually under a layer of cloud.

Saturday morning, at four o'clock, BOAC telephoned the hotel to make sure I was awake – I had left the number when I went to confirm the ticket. They used to do things like that in the old days, before airfares were decreased ten-fold. But I was up and about well before the phone rang, so apprehensive had I become about my re-entry into 'civilization'.

All the same I was looking forward to the flight home. For two years I had savoured the memory of the VC-10 take-offs, the four rear engines that hit you full in the back and thrust you straight up into the sky, and I had told practically everyone about it and how I was going home in style. It was the last trump card I held in my hand. But when I got to the airport I found myself aboard a 707 that trundled along the runway like a tea-trolley and took to the air like a Christmas turkey. The flight, which for some strange reason chose to make two of its three stops between Lima and London in Jamaica – in Montego Bay and Kingston – seemed to hit every rain-cloud and airpocket and had half the passengers reaching for their paper bags.

In New York, for some reason that I don't recall now, we had to get down and go through Immigration and I found myself standing in line behind a respectably dressed, clean-shaven young man with hair down to his shoulders. I couldn't believe my eyes. What impressed me most was that he seemed so totally unselfconscious. When I saw that he held in his hand a British passport, I told myself that this was probably the type of Brit who made it to New York – some arty type, a left-over from the Beat generation – and left it at that.

But when I stepped down off the plane in Heathrow I felt as if I had landed on Mars. As it happened that Saturday in late August 1970 was the coldest August day on record, but it was not the temperature, nor the dull-grey cloud that hung over my head that bothered me. It was the speed of it all, and the serious expression on the faces of the people. Why was everybody moving so fast? And what could possibly be their motive? Did they know something I didn't, and had some new sense of purpose overtaken the nation in my absence?

It was the start of what is today referred to as 'reverse culture shock'. The impact of returning home to a place you no longer recognize hits just about everybody for six, but in those days it was somehow assumed that you would easily slot back in where you left off and live 'happily ever after'. How wrong they were!

Even today precious little help is available, and sooner or later the volunteer-sending agencies are going to have to face up to the implications of reverse culture shock, not least because the volunteer movement is now well over thirty years old and because the effects can be debilitating, not just in the short term.

There are several reasons, I believe, why the subject has yet to be taken seriously: first, it is not an easy matter to grasp, especially for someone who has not experienced it first hand, and secondly, most voluntary agencies are overworked and understaffed and have enough to do just keeping their current programmes ticking over without concerning themselves with people who are now back home and out of sight. Returned volunteers, in other words, are not a priority. But the condition needs to be addressed because it can be serious and have broad ramifications. Twenty years of travel and enquiry have helped me to unravel and understand some of its main components, and this has made it all worthwhile, but the ride was a rough one at times.

For most volunteers, from the moment they step onto the plane that is to take them to their overseas assignment, life is never going to be the same again. In a sense they will never be able to go home again, for home, on return, will seem a vastly different place from the one they left behind. It will not be the place, of course, that will have changed so much as the individual, and what adds to the intensity and strangeness of the 'coming home' experience is that the volunteer will normally have little idea of the extent to which this has happened. He or she may not feel any different at all, in fact, and only in the attempt to slip back into the old routine will difficulties be recognized.

What is it that takes place in a person during the years away? A great many things, no doubt, but what is certain is that the former volunteer will continue for the rest of his or her life the process of acknowledging and understanding many of the insights and impressions gained during this relatively short period. All the same, I believe there is enough common ground in the experience for general conclusions to be drawn, and it usually comes down to a radical questioning of life in its every aspect that has the returned volunteer feeling unsettled, ill at ease, and anxious. The condition is disturbing because many of the questions are as yet unformed, and those that are expressed do not find answers in the home environment. The implicit trust in a 'home' that once promised a predictable and safe context has been compromised, and the returned volunteer no longer feels that he or she 'belongs' in quite the same way as before.

What the period of volunteer service does is to challenge and rearrange our concept of normality in a subtly pervasive and inconclusive way. It might be said, of course, that this is just another facet of the twentieth-century malaise of 'alienation' to which our art and our literature already pay sufficient testimony, but what has happened in the case of the volunteer is that the process has been accelerated and telescoped inward so that the effect is all the more acute. Of course, a good many young people, perhaps of a certain intellectual type, choose to go overseas precisely because they are looking to push back the frontiers of their awareness, but what usually happens is that they end up finding more than they bargained for. Expecting to undergo change, or even inviting it, does not necessarily make it any easier to handle when it comes along, because the changes will always be other than you expected; they will require explanations that your experience to date will not be able to provide; and this will be because your frame of reference is still the old one, the one you intended to leave behind. There will not yet have been time to form a new one that can accommodate the two distinct realities, and this will only ever come about gradually, for its acquisition is more a question of personal growth than intellectual effort. The dilemma is always how to reconcile two or more differing concepts of reality, and the emergent solution invariably demands compromise and adjustment. As such it belongs to that realm of learning that can only be acquired in living; intellectuals, as we know, are forever 'one revolution behind'.

All expatriates are susceptible to a similar transformation, but only to the extent that they choose to expose themselves to the host culture. Many salaried expatriates appear to be striving to create a life-style similar to the one they left behind, and their conditions of employment are normally designed so they can do just that. In contrast, the volunteer wilfully drops his guard and lays himself open to the influence of an alien environment. It is a risk worth taking, however, because if handled in the right way it can bring invaluable rewards, and this is what the 'volunteer experience' is all about.

The question of religion will illustrate this point. You can get away with saying, for example, as some Christian fundamentalists do, that 'only Christ is the answer', provided you never actually venture out and come face to face with committed believers of other religions. When you do, and you discover that they espouse many of the same principles as yourself, and even excel in the practice of some of them, and that their worship is not vastly different in essence from your own, then you are forced to examine your assumptions; for either God, in rejecting all non-Christians, has a different concept of justice to your own, or Christ is *not* the only answer. For someone who takes such concerns seriously, the effect can be devastating. And where do you go for an answer? To a Christian authority who has never set foot outside his home country? Hardly. The volunteer is left to cope with such doubts and uncertainties alone.

For other people, notions of normality are put to the test simply by coming into contact with a different way of life. A few of the more obvious examples are the variations in response to time and the concept of urgency; the way that we in Europe generally place privacy above hospitality, whereas most Third World peoples do exactly the opposite; the remarkable humility and stoicism of the poor in the face of adversity; the relevance of 'ambition' to a society where there is no opportunity for either study or employment; parental responsibility and the role of the family, particularly with regard to countries where one-parent families are the norm and the children grow up perfectly normal and healthy; our clumsy handling of death and mental illness compared with societies where both are confronted openly and accommodated easily within the status quo; our understanding of self-determination – is it realistic and fair to tell people who are without hope and energy to 'pull themselves up by their boot-straps'?

All such assumptions come under the microscope and we are forced into a crisis of sorts by a barrage of alien perceptions that the new environment is throwing at us – perceptions which, in their own context, make just as much sense as the ones we left behind, though we were often led to believe these were the non-negotiable pillars of civilization.

Disturbing though it may be, such self-analysis is not necessarily a bad thing. We are now living in a 'world community' and it is no longer sufficient blindly to accept the values of one's own society if this implies an automatic rejection of someone else's. We should, in any case, have an understanding of our cultural priorities – where do they come from and why? We should also, surely, have an appreciation of where money comes from and what determines its supply. How much of our social and industrial unrest, I wonder, has been the result of a failure to understand the basic laws of economics – ask anyone what it is that determines the supply of banknotes and see what answers you get; and how many well-intentioned plans have taken off and fallen flat on their face for want of a sense of economic realism?

We should also, I believe, feel gratitude for our social and medical services and our legal system, because they are truly remarkable achievements – especially compared with what the rest of the world has to offer. More than anything, we should feel a reverence for life in every form, for it is genuinely miraculous. We should have a purpose in life hewn from the rock of our personal experience, and not simply allow ourselves to dance to the tune of some ad-man's jingle.

There are two ways that reverse culture shock can be dealt with; one is short-term and practical, the other is long-term and immaterial.

The former consists of remaining active at all costs, and focusing the mind on specific tasks – work, studies, hobbies and the like – and screening out the encroaching paranoia until the worst of it passes, which can be anything up to a year. You can even go overseas again if you like – there is nothing like movement for creating an illusion of purpose – and this helps, for each re-entry becomes progressively easier. But sooner or later you will have to face up to the questions raised by your volunteer experience, for even if they are no longer so insistent, neither have they been answered and in the long run, for your peace of mind, they have to be.

No society is fully 'permissive'. If a society is spiritually based then self-indulgence becomes its taboo, and if it is materially based, as ours is, then spirituality becomes its taboo. Today, no serious analysis of anything political, social, economic, developmental or even psychological can admit the intrusion of religion – it is quite simply a non-subject. Yet all roads lead there eventually for, at the end of it all, the great question *why* remains to be answered. If we are to address the matter of reverse culture shock fairly we have to free ourselves from such constraints and cast our net wide enough to ensure nothing escapes our attention – even religion.

What I believe has happened to the volunteer, and incidentally to a lesser extent to everyone in this rapidly changing world of ours, is that he has become detached from the culture in which his values were first formed, and now no longer belongs to any one culture. He can neither return to being the person he was, nor can he become an Ecuadorean or a Tanzanian. He simply does not belong to any *one* place on earth. The good news is that he is in the process of becoming a member of a world community – that growing band of individuals, drawn from every corner of the earth, whose primary allegiance is no longer to a single country, culture, or ideology, but to the whole human race – and as a consequence, he now has to adopt a new vision, one that embraces the entire planet.

This is easy to say, of course, and it is not difficult to pay lip-service to the notion and defend it from your armchair. To internalize it and live it, on the other hand, implies that the concept has been espoused on a level higher than the intellectual, and this inevitably means the spiritual. I personally believe that the supernatural belongs squarely in the arena of everyday affairs – political, social, economic and the rest – and that it is only a matter of time before the wheel turns full circle and this is generally recognized – as, in fact, it always has been among the majority of the earth's peoples.

It has always struck me as profoundly ironic that religious belief, which is so fundamental to Third World societies and so central to the evolution of their operational priorities, should never have been allowed a place in the development forum. That developmentalists should have chosen to ignore it seems to me to speak volumes about them and precious little about the people they are supposedly addressing.

The only complete remedies for the condition of reverse culture shock (and alienation) are to be found in the spiritual teachings of the world's major religions – all of them, in fact – for any one of them shorn of its temporality and its dogma will be found to be universal in its compass and will serve the need. All are derived from the same source and are equally effective. It is in the pages of religious literature that the ultimate prescriptions for mind and spirit are to be found.

The years from 1968 to 1970 were probably a bad time to be away because things really did change in the meanwhile, so that I could not even take comfort from the fact that it was 'all inside my head'. The country had undergone wholesale change during my absence, and the man in New York airport turned out to be much less of an oddity than I had originally supposed – half the population of Britain appeared to have gone down with the same complaint. It was not just the 'arty set' that had hair down to their shoulders, but *schoolteachers* as well, and *men over forty*! I soon learned that, at the other end of the spectrum, gangs of youths with shaven heads and shiny boots had taken to rampaging through the streets after football matches and engaging in pitched battles. A revolution had taken place, and no one had warned me. I didn't like it at all.

I kept telling myself over and over again that only twenty-four hours before I had been on the other side of the world, in the land of llamas, volcanoes and Inca ruins – the land of Alejandro, Moscabel and Los Jets – where I felt safe and knew I belonged. And now I found myself wandering around in a daze in some kind of no-man's-land, stranded somewhere between two totally different dimensions and unable to gain a foothold in either. The old world was still inside my head, but I was not there; and the new world was all around me, but still unknown.

EPILOGUE

THE OIL FINDS of the late 1960s gushed forth in quantity from the mid-seventies onwards, bringing untold wealth to the nation and the usual bag of mixed blessings.

The positive side has included the blunting of the sharp edge of Ecuador's rural poverty as *campesinos* have taken to migrating seasonally to the town and finding casual employment; the construction of roads and infrastructure; and a marked improvement in professional standards across the board as countless men and women have travelled to the United States and Europe to be trained. Standards and facilities in the medical profession have particularly improved, at least in the towns, and a certain amount of this has trickled down to the villages.

The negative side is more telling, however. Urban migration of a non-seasonal kind, population growth, and an economy now in decline have created a problem of urban homelessness on a scale hitherto unknown in Ecuador – thousands of people, young and old, mestizo and Indian are now living on the streets. Violent crime is an everyday occurrence, something that was virtually unheard of in the Sierra in the late 1960s; and this, of course, has been aggravated by the traffic in drugs which, in transit from Peru, have left their mark on the nation's youth.

Increased opportunities for nepotism, together with the purges in public staffing that traditionally accompany changes of government, have led to the creation of ever more complex and inert bureaucracies, with most of the appointees lacking either the interest or the competence properly to perform their duties; all of this takes place against the usual backdrop of systematic corruption as successive generations of officials seek to exploit their influence and plunder the nation's resources before their term in office expires.

The Indian, once again, has suffered more than most and his continued degradation is a constant cause for concern. The growth of industry generally, and the construction industry in particular, which boomed spectacularly as the middle and upper classes and the military grew rich and invested in property, has brought *campesinos* flocking to the town to seek out employment as labourers, bricklayers and the like. Their desperation has been exploited and they have invariably found themselves criminally overworked and underpaid, and at the same time their indigenous identity has been swallowed up in the economic maelstrom. Their survival is more at risk today than at any time since the initial holocaust, and you see this reflected especially in the markets, from which so much of the life and colour has drained away.

There have been even more catastrophic changes since the Oriente was divided up into blocks and the oil-drilling rights were sold off to multinational companies – without any consultation with the Indians living there. The encampments and the access roads that the oil companies built have brought scores of settlers, penetrating even the most remote and inaccessible Indian groups and turning a good many of them, in time-honoured fashion, into the dross of western society – lackeys, go-betweens, beggars and prostitutes; economic forces having achieved what military forces were never able to do, defeating the Amazonian Indian and wrecking the rain forest at the same time.

The past two decades have seen a proliferation of aid money and aid agencies in the Central Andes, with many of them setting up their regional headquarters in Quito – because Ecuador, despite its growing social problems, is still an oasis of tranquillity alongside its guerrilla-racked, drug-obsessed neighbours Peru and Colombia. It would be nice to believe that this increase in aid effort has been responsible in part for the country's economic progress, but this is unlikely. There have been projects by the thousand but few have produced anything worthy of note. Objectives are routinely revised or abandoned; project directors come and go and are seldom, if ever, held to account for their actions; and the projects themselves invariably grind to a halt the moment support is removed. Self-reliance, the watchword and yardstick of the development agencies for so long, has become little more than a myth – widely held, but a myth all the same.

Along with all this spectacular non-achievement has arisen a phenomenon of equally dubious character, that of the 'independent evaluation' which often takes the form of a silent pact in which the aid agency and the 'independent evaluator' are partners. The evaluator must seem to be independent so as to avoid accusations of partiality, and yet at the same time he knows only too well that if he oversteps the mark and says anything too damaging he is unlikely to be invited back and his company may have to fold. A conspiracy to avoid seeing what is taking place affects a good many of the agencies, therefore; and as a general rule the greater the resources and the more prestigious the agency, the greater is the collusion between evaluator and agency.

Not many people are willing to wade through tomes of jargon-filled reports – which cost a fortune to produce and lie gathering dust on forgotten shelves – and then go back to the project site to see for themselves. Certainly no one in a head office located a few thousand miles away. In the main, they are only too happy to believe in the myths that the evaluator peddles.

There is no way the massive expenditure on aid can be justified in terms of the results achieved. Its impact has only ever been small-scale and piecemeal, and usually takes a decade at least to show through, if then. Of more direct benefit to the countries concerned are the cash and the employment that the aid agencies bring to the local economy. The governments know this, of course, and one suspects that this is the reason why they accede so readily to the requests of an ever-increasing number of agencies to come and set up shop. Well motivated and sincere the majority of them may be, but ingenuous also and soon, without realizing it, most of them will be acting out the same absurd charade that has come to characterize aid everywhere.

On the human rights front the outlook is only marginally brighter, but there are grounds for limited optimism. Successive democratically elected governments, wary of the new climate of world opinion and sensitive to their financial obligations to the North, are tending to seek negotiated settlements with dissident groups instead of applying the heavy-handed tactics that were routine in the past. Even if this change is largely cosmetic, it does reflect a certain amount of new self-awareness and opens the door to the possibility of pressure from international human rights groups.

In Ecuador, the abduction in 1988 of two adolescent boys, the Restrepo brothers, on false drug-trafficking charges, and their subsequent torture, murder and dumping in a lake near Latacunga by members of the provincial Criminal Investigation Department, have for once not been allowed to remain 'hushed-up'. The courage and persistence of the parents, a middle-class couple of Colombian origin, in the face of lies, abuse and threats from the authorities – all of which have now been fully documented and made public – have won through and led to the setting up of an international commission of human rights, the arrest of those implicated and the disbandment of the Criminal Investigation Department involved. While those indicted for the murders have yet to be properly tried and sentenced (two named accessories who were supposedly under surveillance have predictably 'escaped'), and while unlawful detention, abuse and torture still goes on, there appears to be a new climate of possibility, if not yet of practice, in the country, and perhaps the continent as a whole.

The example of the Restrepo parents has inspired others who have suffered a similar fate to speak out, and many more to come forward on their behalf, creating a new climate of openness. In the arena of continental politics, the two recent failed coup attempts in Venezuela were regarded by Latin Americans generally as both anachronistic and pointless, and in fact received scant support inside Venezuela itself despite a general belief in the incompetence and corruption of the ruling Pérez régime – this in a continent where only a short while ago coups were the norm. One gets the feeling that for the first time there may well be a glimmer of light appearing at the end of the very long and very dark Latin American tunnel, and that a semblance of moderation and decency might possibly be in sight at last.

Riobamba has more than doubled in size since 1968 and a good many of the streets are now tarmacked, although the cobbles still remain in the centre. 'Monique' and the 'Botecito' have both been taken over and put to other use and a plethora of snack bars and flashy restaurants have sprung up in their stead.

Riobamba was declared a 'garrison town' in the mid 1970s, and Riobambeños were granted the dubious honour of playing host to thousands of the 'illustrious armed forces' that have never actually engaged in anything more serious than a border skirmish in the 170 years since independence. The main barracks is located on the purpose-built, and impressively named, Avenue of the Heroes of Tapi, a reference to one of the minor engagements in the struggle for independence.

The trains that once provided one of the world's great travel experiences died a slow death by poor management and lack of investment, and were finally given the *coup de grâce* by the earthquake of 1987. The railway station, located near the centre of town, no longer operates, and the bus station that stood alongside it has been moved a few blocks further away to the north. Riobamba, as a consequence, has lost its heart.

Of people, I have precious little to relate. Alejandro is still alive and well and living in his home community, though more attuned these days to the life of a venerable village elder than that of the 'action man' he once was. Of Moscabel, I know nothing of course, never having returned to the village; except that her particular part of the Amazon has so far managed to escape the spreading tentacles of the oil companies. The agreeable thought has crossed my mind on more than one occasion that she could well be a grandmother by now. And the Jets – the few that are still in the country, that is – are now enjoying portly middle age, and no doubt urging their buckish offspring to stay away from the 'Manabita', which still exists, but in different hands and a block away from the old place.

Bertocchi is back again as manager of a local team, presumably motivated, like myself, by a chance to bask a while longer in the residual glow of those golden days of the late 1960s. Nelson continued to play professional football for another fifteen years, eventually making it to the first team and winning a league championship medal. He now works for a transport company and voluntarily manages a semi-professional side in his spare time. Liga Deportiva Universitaria have won the league championship twice since 1969, the last time in 1990. Of Nogueira, I know nothing.

My Peace Corps friend Jethro spent four years in Columbe trying to raise consciousness and another three years doing the same thing in the nearby community of Troje. He is now, at long last, within sight of finishing his doctorate in anthropology at the University of Salt Lake City – his consciousness well and truly raised. He returned to Troje for a brief visit in July 1991 to find that twenty-seven of its members had died in the recent cholera epidemic. The Indians, however, had seemed more concerned about the death of a village elder freakishly killed in a tree-felling accident some weeks before, and at whose wake the other twenty-seven had become infected, their food contaminated by a mourner returning home from the coast. Cholera, it seems, was somehow easier to handle.

Bob, the Peace Corps surveyor, has recently retired and is now a man of leisure at home in New Jersey, living off his pension and – like the rest of us from that same era – his memories of what now seems like a golden age in Ecuadorean history.

GLOSSARY

Altiplano	high exposed plain (Bolivia and Peru)
Ayahuasca	hallucinogenic vine found in the Amazon
Bayeta	Indian woman's shawl, woollen wrap
Blancos	Whites – of pure European descent
Bomba	drum, traditional music of Chota Valley
Caldo de gallina	chicken broth/stew
Campesino	peasant farmer
Campo	countryside, rural areas
Canelazo	local drink made from trago and hot cinnamon water
Cargador	porter
Chagra	yokel, country bumpkin
Chicha	maize beer
Choclo	corn-on-the-cob
Cordillera	mountain range
Corrida de toros	bullfight
Cuy	baked guinea-pig
Fritada	fried pork
Gringo	North American, European, any non-Latin
Hacienda	large farm
Hoja	leaf (of orange tree used as musical instrument)
Indio	native American
Machismo	manliness, virility
Mayordomo	foreman, steward
Mestizo	of mixed race
Minga	Indian system of voluntary collective labour
Nevados	snow-clad peaks
Oriente	Ecuadorean Amazon region

Páramo	high exposed plain (Ecuador)
Patrón	boss, proprietor
Puna	high exposed plain (Bolivia and Peru)
Rondador	pan-flute
Seco de chivo	local dish of rice and goat's meat
Sierra	mountains, mountain range
Sucre	Ecuadorean currency; in 1968 US$1=18 sucres approx.
Trago	local alcoholic spirit distilled from sugar cane
Tulpa	traditional cooking stove of black communities consisting of three large stones with fire in middle
Yucca	tuber of American origin

ISLAM AND THE WEST

THE MAKING OF AN IMAGE

N o r m a n   D a n i e l

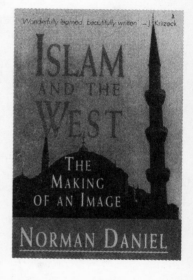

When it first appeared in 1960, Norman Daniel's study of the formation of western ideas about Islam was at once hailed as a classic. Intervening events have added urgency to its message. This scholarly and balanced work – newly revised and thoroughly updated – offers vital insights into the relationship between two of the world's greatest religions, Christianity and Islam. Tracing its development from mediaeval times to the present day, the author draws on a lifelong study of the subject as well as a lifetime's experience of cultural exchange.

The development of multicultural societies and the growing interdependence between peoples of very different – and sometimes conflicting – backgrounds makes it more important than ever that scholar and layman alike should increase mutual understanding. This book has an important contribution to make to the development of religious tolerance and appreciation so essential to our multifaith world of the 1990s and beyond.

'Wonderfully learned, beautifully written'
– J. Kritzeck

467 pages, hardcover
UK £17.95
US $33.95
ISBN 1-85168-043-8
225 x 146 (9.5 x 6)

TRANSITION TO
A GLOBAL SOCIETY

*Editors Suheil Bushrui, Iraj Ayman
& Ervin Laszlo*

What will be the structure of a united world? Can we achieve global unity in the 21st century out of the chaos of conflict we still face, and what will happen to cultural diversity as the peoples of the world become more integrated every day? The First International Dialogue on the Transition to a Global Society, hosted by the Landegg Academy in Switzerland, investigates these and many more of the vital issues of multicultural relations.

Exploring the roles and responsibilities of the public and private sectors, science and technology, culture, ethics, religion and the arts in the transition to a global society, these essays provide lively and challenging perspectives for a world in flux.

Introduced by the Director-General of UNESCO, Dr Federico Mayor, contributors represent a wide range of backgrounds and include Professor Volodymyr Vassilenko of Kiev State University; John Huddleston of the IMF; Professor Ian Angell of the LSE; Nobel Laureate, Professor Ilya Prigogine; the poet Kathleen Raine, and many more.

'Human diversity is a fact, an inescapable reality; the challenge facing humanity lies in establishing unity'

176 pages, softcover
UK £6.95
US $12.95
ISBN 1–85168–039–X
225 x 146 (9.5 x 6)

THE
MULTICULTURAL PLANET
Editor Ervin Laszlo

To commemorate the United Nations Decade for Cultural Development, a group of independent experts under the aegis of UNESCO came together to investigate our planet's multi-cultural diversity and the implications this has for humanity's future.

As well as addressing the general problem of the balance between unity and diversity, and stressing the commonality of human experience, *The Multicultural Planet* discusses each of the world's major cultures in detail, celebrates their distinctive features and considers the specific questions of cultural interrelationship that affect each of them.

Contributors to this vital study of our global community include: Professor Kishore Gandhi (India), Professor Saad Eddin Ibrahim (Egypt), Professor Richard Hoggart (UK), Associate Professor Min Jiayin (China) and Dr John E. Fobes (USA). The volume is edited by Ervin Laszlo, who is a member of the Club of Rome, Science Adviser to the Director-General of UNESCO, and consultant to the United Nations University.

'This report hopes to make a contribution to the peaceful development of humanity by focusing attention on the phenomenon of culture as the key to development and peace.'
— Ervin Laszlo

206 pages, softcover
UK £9.95
US $17.95
ISBN 1–85168–042–X
225 x 146 (9.5 x 6)

ON BEING A TEACHER

Jonathan Kozol

In this book, Jonathan Kozol, National Book Award-winning author and one of America's foremost writers on social issues, offers a critique on the role of the teacher in America's public school system and gives suggestions on how teachers can work within the system to foster positive values.

Drawn in part from his own experiences, *On Being a Teacher* offers the practical strategies every teacher can use for eradicating prejudices and helping them to become 'warriors of social change'. Available in paperback for the first time, *On Being a Teacher* is essential reading for everyone concerned with shaping the values of the next generation.

ONE OF THE FOREMOST social writers in USA, Jonathan Kozol – Harvard-educated, a Rhodes scholar, and a teacher – has written passionately on poverty, homelessness, illiteracy and education, winning numerous awards. Among his bestselling books are *Death at an Early Age*, *Illiterate America*, *Rachel and Her Children* and the New York Times bestseller *Savage Inequalities*.

'Must reading for all teachers and parents. It may be to teachers what Dr Spock's book has been to young mothers.'
— Studs Terkel

177 pages, softcover
UK £7.95
US $12.95
ISBN 1–85168–065–9
225 x 146 (9.5 x 6)

THE GARDENERS OF GOD
AN ENCOUNTER WITH FIVE MILLION BAHÁ'ÍS

*Colette   Gouvion
& Philippe   Jouvion*

In this candid and informative account, two French journalists set out to conduct an objective and unbiased study of an emerging world religion – the Bahá'í Faith. In the course of their research, they travelled to the Bahá'í World Centre in Haifa, Israel and, here and elsewhere, interviewed Bahá'ís from all over the world and from strikingly different backgrounds.

The Gardeners of God

An Encounter with Five Million Bahá'ís

COLETTE GOUVION & PHILIPPE JOUVION

What do Bahá'ís believe? How do they live? What are their hopes, their vision of the future? Through a series of frank and lively interviews, interspersed with personal observations, they offer readers the opportunity to discover for themselves the answer to the question: 'Who are the Bahá'ís?'

Colette Gouvion is a journalist and author. Philippe Jouvion is a freelance researcher, film producer and reporter.

224 pages, softcover
UK £6.95
US $12.95
ISBN 1–85168–052–7
225 x 146 (9.5 x 6)

A THEORY
OF ALMOST EVERYTHING
A RELIGIOUS AND SCIENTIFIC
QUEST FOR ULTIMATE ANSWERS

Robert Barry

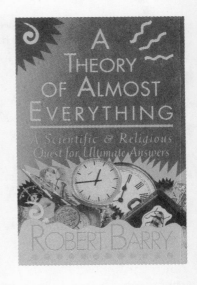

The much-vaunted grand unified theory will not be found in science alone, argues Barry, but in a synthesis of physics, psychology and religion. Searching for this 'theory of everything', Barry takes the reader on a fascinating and highly readable exploration of such complexities as the nature of reality and the purpose of life, using the insights provided by psychological theory and quantum physics to paint a new picture of the universe and our place in it.

Much more than yet another book on the new physics, *A Theory of Almost Everything* offers a radical and very broad approach to the relationship between self and reality, examines the possibility of a true 'theory of everything' that links into both scientific and religious world-views, and deftly builds a bridge from the universe of God to the universe within the human mind.

Dr Robert Barry is a statistician at the Department of Education in Northern Ireland. He holds a PhD in psychology from Queens University, and publishes widely in the fields of psychology and social research.

208 pages, hardcover
UK £9.95
US $18.95
ISBN 1–85168–045–4
225 x 146 (9.5 x 6)

ACHIEVING PEACE
BY THE YEAR 2000

John   Huddleston

In this analysis of the causes of war and barriers to peace, John Huddleston examines the psychological, moral and practical issues and puts forward a 12-point plan for establishing a lasting peace. Branded 'idealistic' on publication in 1988, it is now proving a prophetic and credible path to peace in the Post-Cold War 90s.

John Huddleston is Chief of the Budget and Planning Division of the International Monetary Fund, and previously worked for the British Ministry of Defence.

'*It puts a framework on a vision.*'
          — Bruce Kent, Campaign for Nuclear Disarmament

'*This is an interesting discussion, intelligent, far-reaching.*' — Sanity

160 pages, softcover
UK £4.95
US $7.95
ISBN 1-85168-006-3
198 x 129 (7.5 x 5)

UNDERSTANDING HUMAN NATURE

Alfred Adler

Regarded by many as a handbook of Individual Psychology, *Understanding Human Nature* offers an excellent introduction to all the main themes of Adler's work and shows the relevance for modern thinking of those issues where Adler parted company from his colleagues Freud and Jung. At the core of Adler's approach is the belief that people are decision-making beings, responsible for their own behaviour – and capable of changing it.

Here, in a detailed overview of character development, he examines the influence of our early childhood experiences on the formulation of the adult personality, explains key Adlerian terms, and shows how unrealized potential can be released for constructive change.

Alfred Adler, founder of Individual Psychology, was a contemporary and colleague of Carl Jung and Sigmund Freud. During his life he wrote over 300 books and papers on child psychology, marriage, education and the principles of Individual Psychology. These books are appearing for the first time in fresh and readable translations that make accessible to the professional and general reader alike a practical system of understanding human nature.

'. . . it offers the wisdom of Adler when the world is most in need of it.' — Dr James Hemming, Fellow of the British Psychological Society

240 pages, softcover
UK £7.95
US $13.95
ISBN 1–85168–021–7
225 x 146 (9.5 x 6)

THE INNER
LIMITS OF MANKIND

Ervin Laszlo

This is a spirited and provocative examination of contemporary values and attitudes by a leading systems scientist and philosopher. The author explores ways in which each of us can contribute to their transformation, and argues for the emergence of a new globally-oriented, environmentally-aware thinking person.

ERVIN LASZLO is a member of the Club of Rome, Science Adviser to the Director-General of UNESCO, and consultant to the United Nations University.

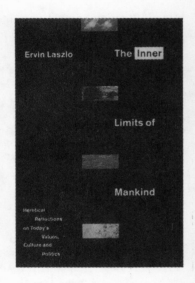

'It is a remarkably clear exposé of the problems of contemporary society and of the urgent need for a fundamental reappraisal.' — Alexander King, President of the Club of Rome

'This is a useful book appearing at the right moment. I hope it will be read by a vast public.' — Aurelio Peccei, author of *One Hundred Pages for the Future*

ISBN 1-85168-009-8 (SC)
ISBN 1-85168-015-2 (HC)
160 pages
UK £4.50 / US $7.95 (SC)
UK £8.95/ US $14.95 (HC)

CHANGE AND HABIT

THE CHALLENGE OF OUR TIME

Arnold Toynbee

Arnold Toynbee, one of this century's most respected historians, brings to this unique work both his profound knowledge of the history of the human race and his deep concern for its future.

Now that humanity acknowledges that the problems threatening to destroy it are of its own making, Toynbee's approach is particularly timely. He argues that habits, unlike instincts, *can* be changed and that faced with the inescapable choice, humanity will prefer painful changes of habit to self-destruction.

This is what is required – for the problems now confronting us can only be solved by a radical break with our deeply ingrained habits. Each of the issues facing the modern world is examined from this point of view, from the pressures of population and urbanization, the challenge of increased affluence and leisure, and religious pluralism to the question of political unification and a new world order.

256 pages, softcover
UK £8.95
US $15.95
ISBN 1-85168-044-6
225 x 146 (9.5 x 6)

THE CRISIS
OF OUR AGE
P i t i r i m   A.   S o r o k i n

Social scientist, philosopher, visionary, Pitirim A. Sorokin was sentenced to death, then exiled from the Soviet Union and later became Head of Sociology at Harvard. No mere pawn of the Cold War years, he explodes the myths of both capitalism and communism by looking beyond daily conflicts to the broader crisis of our age.

In this challenging critique, Sorokin examines the crisis of modern society as it affects art and science, philosophy and religion, ethics and law – our entire way of thought and life. To the author, the whole advancement of human history is caught in a titanic cycle of materialistic and spiritual cultures, each collapsing and being replaced by the other. Convinced that the current materialistic order is nearing exhaustion, Sorokin presents a positive vision of the transformation of our values and lifestyles to a more spiritual, global, egalitarian society worthy of human dignity.

'A genuinely great book'
  – New York Times

281 pages, softcover
UK £7.95
US $13.95
ISBN 1-85168-028-4
225 x 146 (9.5 x 6)

Book Orders

Name _____

Address _____

_____ Date _____

_____ Accents of God . . . . UK £6.95/US $12.95
_____ Achieving Peace by the Year 2000 . . . . UK £4.95/US $7.95
_____ Change and Habit . . . . UK £8.95/US $15.95
_____ Contemplating Life's Greatest Questions . . . . UK £4.50/US $7.95
_____ Creating a Successful Family – SC . . . . UK £6.50/US $11.95
_____ Creating a Successful Family – HC . . . . UK £10.95/US $18.95
_____ The Crisis of Our Age . . . . UK £7.95/US $13.95
_____ Defending the Soul . . . . UK £6.95/US $12.95
_____ Drawings, Verse & Belief. . . . . UK £12.95/US $19.95
_____ Education on Trial. . . . . UK £7.95/US $14.95
_____ Gardeners of God. . . . . UK £6.95/US $12.95
_____ The Inner Limits of Mankind – SC. . . . . UK £4.50/US $7.95
_____ The Inner Limits of Mankind – HC . . . . UK £8.95/US $14.95
_____ Islam & the West. . . . . UK £17.95/US $33.95
_____ The Multicultural Planet. . . . . UK £9.95/US $17.95
_____ Nine Days to Istanbul . . . . UK £4.50/US $7.95
_____ On Being a Teacher. . . . . UK £7.95/US $12.95
_____ One People, One Planet . . . . UK £7.95/US $13.95
_____ Peace With Your Partner. . . . . UK £5.95/US $10.95
_____ Science & Religion . . . . UK £4.50/US $7.50
_____ The Seven Valleys. . . . . UK £4.95/US $8.95
_____ A Theory of Almost Everything . . . . UK £9.95/US $18.95
_____ Transition to a Global Society. . . . . UK £6.95/US $12.95
_____ To Understand & Be Understood. . . . . UK £4.50/US $7.50
_____ Understanding Human Nature . . . . UK £7.95/US $13.95
_____ Way to Inner Freedom. . . . . UK £4.50/US $7.50

	Sub Total	
Please add 15% to cover postage	Postage & Handling	
and handling (min. £1/$2)	Total £ or US$	

Payment by: _____ Check/Money Order
_____ American Express
_____ Mastercard/Access
_____ Diners Club   Exp. Date _____
_____ Visa
Credit
Card No. | | | | | | | | | | | | | | | | | | |

Signature _____

Send all orders to:

Oneworld
Publications
185 Banbury Road
Oxford, OX2 7AR
England
Tel: (0865)–310597
Fax: (0865)–310598